Other McGraw-Hill Books in Mini and Mainframe Computing

ISBN	AUTHOR	TITLE
0-07-056578-3	Sherman	The CD-ROM Handbook
0-07-039006-1	Lusardi	
	(hardcover)	Database Experts' Guide to SQL
0-07-039002-9	Lusardi	
	(softcover)	Database Experts' Guide to SQL
0-07-016609-6	DeVita	
	(hardcover)	Database Experts' Guide to FOCUS
0-07-016604-8	DeVita	
	(softcover)	Database Experts' Guide to FOCUS
0-07-036488-5	Larson	
	(hardcover)	Database Experts' Guide to Database 2
0-07-023267-9	Larson	
	(softcover)	Database Experts' Guide to Database 2
0-07-000474-9	Adrian	The Workstation Data Link
0-07-057336-0	Simpson, Casey	Developing Effective User Documentation
0-07-007248-5	Brathwaite	Analysis, Design, and Implementation of Data Dictionaries
0-07-035119-8	Knightson	Standards for Open Systems Interconnection
0-07-044938-4	McClain	
	(hardcover)	VM and Departmental Computing
0-07-044939-2	McClain	
	(softcover)	VM and Departmental Computing
0-07-046302-6	Nemzow	Keeping the Link
0-07-038006-6	Lipton	User Guide to FOCUS™
0-07-057296-8	Simon	How to Be a Successful Computer Consultant
0-07-016188-7	Dayton	
	(Ranade, Ed.)	Integrating Digital Services
0-07-002673-4	Azevedo	
	(Ranade Series)	ISPF: The Strategic Dialog Manager
0-07-050054-1	Piggott	
	(Ranade Series)	CICS: A Practical Guide to System Fine Tuning
0-07-043152-3	Morgan, McGilton	Introducing UNIX™ System V
0-07-050686-8	Prasad	
	(Ranade Series)	IBM Mainframes
0-07-065087-X	Towner	
	(Ranade Series)	IDMS/R Cookbook
0-07-062879-3	Tare (hardcover)	UNIX™ Utilities
0-07-062884-X	Tare (softcover)	UNIX™ Utilities
0-07-045001-3	McGilton, Morgan	Introducing the UNIX™ System
0-07-062295-7	Su	Database Computers
0-07-041920-5	Milenkovic	Operating Systems Concepts and Design
0-07-010829-3	Ceri/Pelagatti	Distributed Databases

For more information about other McGraw-Hill materials,
call 1-800-2-MCGRAW in the United States. In other
countries, call your nearest McGraw-Hill office.

Using AutoCAD with AutoLISP

John D. Hood, CET
Cambrian College

McGraw-Hill Publishing Company
New York   St. Louis   San Francisco   Auckland   Bogotá
Caracas   Hamburg   Lisbon   London   Madrid   Mexico
Milan   Montreal   New Delhi   Oklahoma City
Paris   San Juan   São Paulo   Singapore
Sydney   Tokyo   Toronto

Library of Congress Cataloging-in-Publication Data

Hood, John D.
  Using AutoCAD with AutoLISP / John D. Hood.
    p. cm.
  ISBN 0-07-029748-7
  1. AutoCAD (Computer program)   2. AutoLISP (Computer program
language) I. Title.
T385.H69 1989
620′.00425′02855369—dc20   89-12367
                                                         CIP

1234567890 DOC/DOC 895432109

ISBN 0-07-029748-7

*The editors for this book were Theron Shreve and Nancy Young, the
designer was Naomi Auerbach, and the production supervisor was
Dianne L. Walber. This book was set in Century Schoolbook. It was
composed by the McGraw-Hill Publishing Company Professional &
Reference Division composition unit.*

Printed and bound by R. R. Donnelley and Sons Company.

AutoCAD and AutoLISP are trademarks of Autodesk, Inc.

*For more information about other McGraw-Hill materials,
call 1-800-2-MCGRAW in the United States. In other
countries, call your nearest McGraw-Hill office.*

For Allan

Good luck in your new career, son!

Contents

Chapter 7. Traverse Program   99

Chapter 8. Adding Text and Locating Entities   125

Introduction

If you want to learn AutoLISP, this book was written for you. My purpose in writing it is to provide a set of tutorial notes that will make it easy for those with little or no programming background to learn how to apply AutoLISP in their professions. This book, however, is not only about AutoLISP. You will also learn drawing and file management procedures, how to access the drawing database, and how to automate your AutoCAD drawing startup process.

What Do I Need?

To accompany *Using AutoCAD with AutoLISP* you will need a micro-computer capable of running AutoCAD, with 640K of memory and a fixed (hard) drive. And, of course, you will need a copy of AutoCAD. All commands used in this book will work with Vers. 2.6 through to Release 10 and should also work on future releases of AutoCAD and AutoLISP. Most commands will work with Ver. 2.18 as well.

To write the programs illustrated in this text you will need a copy of EDLIN (provided free on your DOS disk) or another text editor such as The Norton Editor, WordPerfect, WordStar, etc. You should also be familiar with using AutoCAD beyond the level of a novice.

How Do I Use This Book?

Using AutoCAD with AutoLISP is written for the AutoCAD drafter who wishes to learn how to use AutoLISP. Even those who are already familiar with AutoLISP will find the text useful since it goes beyond illustrating the syntax (structure) of function and shows how to use the functions in real applications.

If you are a novice, you should start at the first chapter and progress sequentially through the text *doing the programs on your computer.* Those familiar with AutoLISP may find it a learning experience to progress through the text sequentially or may want to use the text as a reference when writing AutoLISP functions and programs.

At the end of each program, function, or menu there is a discussion of the program. Read the line-by-line explanation and refer to the program, carefully noting how the line is structured.

When a new function (primitive) is introduced, the syntax of the function is described. Review the syntax and included examples, and read the explanation of how the function is used in the text program. Then refer to the program to observe how the function is applied.

Terminology

The following definitions explain how terms are used in this book:

LISP Evaluator   Execution of code in LISP is called "evaluation," and it is done by the LISP evaluator.

Function   A function is a predefined procedure that tells the Auto-LISP evaluator how to do something. In this text procedures defined *by the programmer* are referred to as "functions," whereas procedures supplied by AutoLISP are referred to as "primitives."

Primitive   A function supplied by AutoLISP. In the *AutoLISP Programmer's Reference* manual they are called "functions." The author is using the LISP term *"primitive"* so it is easier to differentiate between user-defined procedures (functions) and AutoLISP-supplied procedures (primitives). When speaking in general about primitives and functions, the term "function" is used.

Expression   An AutoLISP procedure. It may be a single function or a sequence of functions.

Program   An AutoLISP file containing functions and expressions grouped together to perform a specific procedure. AutoLISP files have the extension LSP.

Argument   Things that a function or primitive works with.

String   Textural data.

Symbols   Variables used by AutoLISP are referred to as "symbols."

Function Notational Convention

The following convention is used for primitives and functions:

$$(\text{funcname} <\text{string}> <\text{number}>\dots)$$

Bracketed items following the function name, "funcname" in the example, indicate the number and type of arguments required.

( )   All LISP functions begin with a left parenthesis and end with a right parenthesis.

< >   Triangular brackets delineate descriptions of arguments that are to be included when the function is invoked.

...   Ellipses indicate that additional arguments (of the type preceding the ellipses) may be supplied to the function.

[ ]   Arguments enclosed in rectangular brackets are optional. Triangular brackets are used within rectangular brackets to delineate arguments.

Other Conventions Used

The AutoLISP evaluator is generally not case sensitive. Where case is important, it is indicated.

The author has written functions and programs in lowercase form; however, when symbol (variable) and function names are referenced in the text body, they are printed in uppercase so they will be more prominent.

Computer prompts are printed in computer-like type. Data you are to type in is in bold computer-like type, and items you are to select from the AutoCAD menu are printed in uppercase in computer-like type. Comments from the author are in text type. For example:

LINE **<return>** From point: **2.2 <return>** To point: Move the cursor to the right of the screen and pick a point.**<return>** To point: **<return>**

<pick> means to press the Enter (or Return) key on the keyboard, mouse, or display. <pick> means to press the Enter Key on the keyboard or, if you are using a mouse or digitizer, the *pick* button on the mouse or digitizer. To exit a command, as illustrated in the preceding, press the Enter key on the keyboard or the *Enter* button on the mouse or digitizer.

Program Listings

Every effort has been made to ensure that program and menu listings in the text are correct; however, with the process required to convert a manuscript into a text, small errors invariably evolve. Since even a small error can be very frustrating to the student, all the major programs and menus in the text are reproduced in the appendixes from computer printouts.

Drawing Management

OBJECTIVE *To develop a standard
procedure for CAD drawing and file
management that can be used as a model for
a drafting office.*

1.1 Introduction

Computer-aided drafting, CAD, is displacing classical drafting in in-
dustry at an overwhelming rate. Many offices, however, are not prepared for all of the repercussions of this new technology. After the
wrapper is removed from the program, the drafters are faced with the
prospect of learning how to use this new tool. My first book, *Easy
AutoCAD,* was written to assist the new user with that problem.

Another problem of equal importance is how to run the drafting office on CAD when it has been geared to produce classical drawings.
Using AutoCAD with AutoLISP is written to address that problem as
well as to provide you with a set of tutorial notes on using AutoLISP.

In this chapter, drawing and file management procedures will be
studied. Later chapters deal with procedures that will improve the
skills of the AutoCAD drafter.

1.2 File Management

Since each drawing created becomes a data file, it is extremely important that the drawing office develop a standard procedure for storing
and naming files. Drawing files can be stored on the microcomputer's
fixed disk or on a floppy disk. Most drafting offices will initially store
the drawings on the fixed disk and later transfer the files onto another
storage medium such as floppy disks or tape for archival storage. In a
classroom setting students will usually store their drawings on a per-
sonal floppy disk. In both cases the AutoCAD program is stored on the

fixed disk. In this text it will be assumed that the AutoCAD program is stored in a directory named ACAD. The procedure for creating the ACAD directory and transferring the AutoCAD program to it is discussed in your *AutoCAD Installation Guide* and also in Appendix D of *Easy AutoCAD*.

1.2.1 Subdirectory files

Drawings should be stored in subdirectories of the ACAD directory. Each project should be in a separate subdirectory of the hard disk with all of the drawings related to that project filed in that subdirectory.

Names of subdirectories should be standardized—possibly following the system currently being used in your office for classical drawings. The subdirectory file name is limited by DOS to a maximum of eight letters and/or numbers. Many firms use a system that includes the job number, year, and other relevant data such as plant identification. A subdirectory file system might be as follows:

jjjppyy

In this system jjj is a three-digit job number, pp is a two-letter plant (or other) identification such as nm for North Mill, and yy is the current year. The subdirectory name for Job No. 101, started in 1987 and located at the North Mill, would then be 101NM87. If further identification is required, DOS also allows a three-digit extension to be used. However, subdirectory file names are usually easier to identify in a directory listing if extensions are not used.

Prior to creating subdirectories, you may wish to set up your DOS prompt to include the current subdirectory. This is done by entering the PROMPT command as follows:

C>PROMPT PG

The $P requests the current directory and the $G requests the > symbol. If you wish to have this prompt installed each time you boot the computer, the request may be included in the AUTOEXEC.BAT file. This is discussed in Section 2.2.1.

As an example of creating subdirectories, it will be assumed that your firm has two projects, one with a job number of 101 at the North Mill and another with a job number of 102 at the South Mill, both started in 1987. The procedure for creating the subdirectories is as follows:

```
C:\>CD \ACAD (Change the directory to the ACAD subdirectory.)
C:\ACAD>MD 101NM87 (Make the first subdirectory.)
C:\ACAD>MD 102SM87 (Make the next subdirectory.)
```

To return to the root directory enter:

```
C:\ACAD>CD \
```

1.2.2 Logging onto a file

Prior to starting AutoCAD, you should log onto the appropriate project subdirectory; however, you will first have to tell DOS where to find the AutoCAD program files. This is done with the PATH command as follows:

```
C:\>PATH \ACAD
```

To log onto the 101NM87 subdirectory the CD (change directory) command is used:

```
C:\>CD\ACAD\101NM87
```

The DOS prompt will now display the path to the current directory as follows:

```
C:\ACAD\101NM87>__
```

To load AutoCAD you now type **acad**. If you are storing your drawings on the fixed disk in the 101NM87 subdirectory, you will not have to precede the drawing name with any path. If the drawings are to be saved on a floppy data disk, the drawing file name will have to be preceded with the drive letter, i.e., B:.

1.2.3 Drawing names

A standardized procedure must also be developed for naming drawings. DOS limits the drawing names to a maximum combination of eight letters and numbers. Most firms have a system in place for naming paper drawings and will use the same system for CAD drawings, often with a letter added to indicate that the drawing was done using CAD. If a system is not already in place, the following might be considered:

```
jjjttnnC
```

Here jjj is the project number, tt is the drawing type, nn is a sequential drawing number, and C indicates that this is a CAD drawing. A standardized drawing-type identification should be adopted such as:

SP—Structural steel plan

EP—Electrical plan

MP—Mechanical plan

SE—Structural steel elevation

FP—Foundation plan

QP—Equipment layout plan

The first structural steel plan drawing for project No. 101 might then have the drawing name 101SP01C.

1.2.4 File tree

In the preceding sections a system was developed with the AutoCAD program stored in a directory named ACAD. Each project started then becomes a subdirectory of ACAD, and all of the drawings related to that project are stored in that subdirectory giving a file tree similar to that illustrated below:

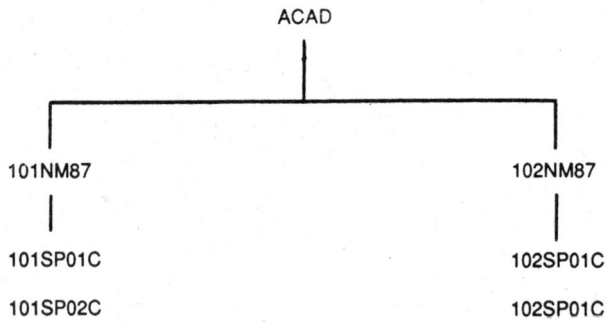

Drawing 101SP01C is the steel plan for the first floor, and 101SP02C is the steel plan for the roof.

1.3 Layer Names, Linetypes, and Colors

As with file names and drawing names, a standard procedure should be developed for naming layers to ensure that all drafters in an office are following the same procedure. This procedure also accommodates the creation of standard prototype drawings, thereby saving considerable time when beginning a new drawing. In Chapter 2 prototype drawings will be created that contain desired drawing parameters and standard layers. The following layers, with associated colors and linetypes, are suggested:

Layer entities	Name	Color	Linetype	Pen
Border and title block	BORDER	green	continuous	6
Structural steel	SS	red	continuous	1
Concrete foundation	CF	white	continuous	4
Electrical	EL	yellow	continuous	2
Mechanical layout	MC	blue	continuous	5
HVAC ducts	HV	blue	continuous	5
Equipment layout	EQ	cyan	continuous	2
Building dimensions	DIM	white	continuous	4
Notes	TXT	white	continuous	4
Construction lines	CON	white	continuous	4
Hatching	HCH	white	continuous	4
Center lines	CL	white	center	4
Hidden lines	HL	white	dashed	4

Combinations of the above may be used. For instance, structural steel plan notes would be placed on a layer named SSTXT to separate them from general notes. Structural steel center lines would be on a layer named SSCL, etc.

Linetypes can also be defined by entities—except for versions of AutoCAD prior to 2.62. If you decide to vary the linetypes for entities without creating new layers, the CL and HL layers may not be required. You should, however, decide on the method to be used, i.e., linetypes by layers or by entities, and you should not mix the two since it can become confusing to new drafters or to someone else who might have to revise the drawing.

Even if you do not have a color monitor, it is important to vary colors for entities or layers. With a multipen plotter each color may be assigned to a pen so that, for instance, entities colored white will always be drawn with pen No. 4, which contains a 0.3-millimeter (mm) pen, and green entities (border and title block) will always be drawn with pen No. 6, which contains a 0.7-mm pen.

1.4 Text Height, Hatch, and LTSCALE Factors

The tables in Appendix A specify the AutoCAD text height (TXT), dimension scale (DIMSCALE), hatch scale (HATCH), and linetype scale

(LTSCALE) factors for various drawing plot scales. Table A.1 lists values in Imperial units with AutoCAD text heights specified to provide 3/32-, 1/8- or 3/16-inch (in) text on the plotted drawing. Table A.2 lists values in SI units with AutoCAD text heights specified to provide 2.5-, 3-, or 4-mm text on the plotted drawing.

The text height, TXT, is calculated using Equation (1.1):

$$TXT = \frac{plot\ text\ height}{plot\ scale} \tag{1.1}$$

For example:

- Drawing is in AutoCAD's architectural units and is to be plotted to a scale of 1/8 in equals 1 ft 0 in. AutoCAD is working internally in inches so the scale is 1/8 in equals 12 in, or 1/96. For a desired plot-text height of 3/16 in the screen-text height, TXT equals 3/16 in divided by 1/96 equals 18 in.

- Drawing is in meters and is to be plotted to a scale of 1:300. For a desired plot-text height of 3 mm, the monitor text height TXT equals 3 mm divided by 1/300 equals 900 mm, or 0.9 meters (m).

- Drawing is in decimal feet and is to be plotted using a scale of 1/8 in equals 1 ft, or 1/96. For a desired plot-text height of 3/16, the screen text TXT equals 3/16 divided by 1/96 equals 18 in = 1.5 feet (ft).

The dimension scale (DIMSCALE) factor is calculated using Equation (1.2), which relates the text height to AutoCAD's default dimension text height of 0.18 units:

$$DIMSCALE = \frac{TXT}{0.18} \tag{1.2}$$

The hatch scale is calculated with Equation (1.3):

$$HATCH = \frac{CONV}{plot\ ratio} \tag{1.3}$$

where CONV = 25.4 for SI units and 1 for Imperial units
     Plot ratio = plot increment/drawing increment

The linetype scale (LTSCALE) is calculated with Equation (1.4):

$$LTSCALE = \frac{0.75 \times CONV}{plot\ ratio} \tag{1.4}$$

1.5   CAD Standards Manual

As you develop a standardized procedure for CAD, it becomes imperative that this procedure be recorded in a CAD Standards Manual so that all drafters are able to follow the standard. The manual should contain the following sections:

General information
   Standards objectives
   Project management
     Project control
     Drawing backups
   Systems description
   Peripheral descriptions
   Interfacing instructions
   File structure
   Interrelated software
Drafting standards
   Log on/off procedure
   Project names
   Drawing names
   Layer names
   Blocks
     Use of
     Descriptions
     Creating new
   Use of linetypes
   Use of colors and pens
   Use of hatch
   Use of text fonts
   Scales—text, dimension, linetype, hatch
   LISP routines
   Macros
   Plotting

Some of the headings in the Standards Manual have already been discussed. Items to be included under standards objectives and project management are discussed in Sections 1.5.1 and 1.5.2, respectively. The procedure for making drawing backups is discussed in Section 1.6.

The sections in the manual covering systems and peripheral descriptions are to contain relevant technical information about the microcomputer and its peripheral equipment such as plotters, printers, digitizing tablets, etc.

The file structure section is to tell the drafter how to create new files, log onto files, etc., as discussed earlier in this chapter. It should also specify the file structure to be used (see Section 1.2.5) and may contain a file tree diagram to illustrate the office standard file structure.

The section on interrelated software will have a number of subheadings, one for each program you have that interfaces with AutoCAD. In this section you should include the following information for each program: what the program is used for, where the program manual is stored, and how to interface the software with AutoCAD.

The drafting standards section explicitly defines the office standards under the headings listed. Most of the material to be included is discussed earlier in this chapter. Blocks, LISP routines, and macros are discussed in Section 1.5.3. Plotting will be discussed in Chapter 2.

1.5.1   Standards objectives

The primary objective of the CAD Standards Manual is to ensure that an efficient, orderly procedure is followed when drawing with the CAD system. If a rigid system is not developed and followed, it could become extremely difficult for drafters in the office to share blocks or to work from the same drawing layout. The result will be that text heights and dimension variables will be of different sizes depending on which drafter drew the block, and standard blocks will be drawn up by each drafter, resulting in a lot of repetition. It could also become very difficult to keep track of drawing revisions, and layering procedures and layer names will vary among drafters.

1.5.2   Project control

Under project control in the CAD Standards Manual, you should specify how the CAD projects are to be managed, such as how revisions to CAD drawings are to be handled and when as-built drawings are to be prepared.

When the CAD drawing is initially issued, a mylar or vellum plot is made. This plot is then stored in the drawing vault and prints are produced from it as required. Minor revisions can often be made in pencil by hand on this drawing; however, all revisions, along with the date they were made, must be noted on the drawing and in a Project Log Book. Major revisions should be done using AutoCAD, and a new mylar or vellum plot should be made. The previous plot should be destroyed by the CAD operator (or another designated person) to ensure that there is only one original drawing. This must also be recorded in the Project Log Book.

When the project is complete, the project leader instructs the CAD operator to do the as-built CAD drawing. A vellum or mylar plot of the as-built drawing is then done, recorded in the Project Log Book, and the previous original is destroyed by a designated person (usually the project leader or the CAD operator). This is also recorded in the Project Log Book.

1.5.3 Blocks, LISP routines, and macros

The section on blocks in the CAD Standards Manual should contain drawings of all the blocks used by your firm and should include the block symbol, name, insertion point, and the file path and disk directory in which the block is stored. (You should store all blocks in a subdirectory of ACAD named BLOCK.) As new blocks are created, they must be immediately added to the manual.

Usually LISP routines will be stored on the hard disk in a subdirectory of ACAD called LISP. All available LISP routines will be listed in the manual along with a description of how to call the routines from the AutoCAD drawing editor. It will also describe each LISP routine, specifying how to use the routines and describing what the routine will do. The LISP routine (program) should also be listed.

Each available macro is also to be described in a manner similar to that used for LISP routines. LISP routines and macros are discussed further in later chapters.

1.6 Drawing-File Backups

It is extremely important to back up all your drawing files on a regular basis. Each drafter should back up his or her files at the end of the day or more often. The drafting office should develop a procedure for making a backup of all files at the end of each week. The weekly backup files should be stored in a safe location, possibly isolated from the CAD room. In both cases, the files may be backed up on a tape drive, a Bernoulli box, a floppy disk, another fixed disk, etc. Since most readers will have a floppy drive on their computer, a procedure for making backups onto a floppy disk will be discussed.

1.6.1 DOS BACKUP command

The DOS BACKUP command may be used to copy one, some, or all files from any directory, subdirectory, subtree of subdirectories, or the

entire fixed disk onto a series of preformatted floppy disks or onto another fixed disk. (DOS versions prior to 3.0 allow only BACKUP to
floppy disks.) It also makes provisions for backups of only those files
that have been modified since the last BACKUP was run or that have
been created after a specified date. The syntax of the BACKUP command is:

```
BACKUP d1:[path] [<filename>] d2:[/A/M/S] [/D:<date>] [path]
```

Optional items are enclosed in rectangular brackets ([]). Angle brackets (< >) indicate that you supply the text for the enclosed item.
    The drive specification d1: indicates the drive containing the files to
be backed up. The optional <filename> contains wildcards like * or ?.
If no file data is specified, all files in the current directory are backed
up. If only the path is given, all files in the specified directory are
backed up.
    In the second set of parameters the drive specification d2: indicates
the drive that contains the disk you will be backing up your files onto.
With DOS versions earlier than 3.0 this must be a floppy drive, A: or
B:. With DOS Ver. 3.0 a hard drive, i.e., C:, may be specified.
    The next parameter contains switches which may be set; they are:

Switch	Purpose
/A	Allows backing up files to a disk which already has backup files. Otherwise all files originally on the disk will be deleted.
/M	Tells BACKUP not to back up files which are unmodified since the previous backup.
/S	Forces BACKUP to look in every subdirectory below the one specified in the first parameter.

The next parameter may be used to back up files that were created
after a specified date, using the format D:date.
    Prior to using the BACKUP command you must format a data disk
to be used as the backup disk. To do this, place a new floppy disk in
drive A, and from the root directory (or the directory in which you
have saved the DOS files), indicated as C> or C:\>, enter:

```
C:\>FORMAT A:
```

You will need to have a sufficient supply of formatted data disks available when creating backups. When a disk is full, the computer will

prompt you to insert another formatted disk. If you do not have one available and have to interrupt the backup to format a disk, you will have to restart the backup from the beginning. It is a good idea to have a supply of formatted data disks available if you intend to back up a number of files on the hard disk.

The first use of the BACKUP command with a newly formatted data disk must not contain the /A switch. Assuming you wish to back up all the files in the 101NM87 subdirectory of the ACAD directory onto a formatted data disk in drive A, and you have not previously backed up files on this disk, the following command should be entered:

`C:\>BACKUP C:\ACAD\101NM87 A:`

The next time you do a backup on the same disk, you may wish to save time by backing up only those files that have been created or modified since the previous backup by including the /M switch in the BACKUP command. Since a backup of the 101NM87 directory has previously been made to this disk, the /A switch will also be included in the BACKUP command. To update the backup of the 101NM87 subdirectory with only modified files and without deleting any other backup files currently on the disk in drive A enter

`C:\>BACKUP C:ACAD\101NM87 A:/A/M`

If you wish to back up only AutoCAD drawing files (which have the DWG extension) and not AutoCAD backup files (which have the BAK extension), you enter

`C:\>BACKUP C:\ACAD\101NM87\*.DWG A:/A/M`

If the 101NM87 subdirectory has other subdirectories, as shown below,

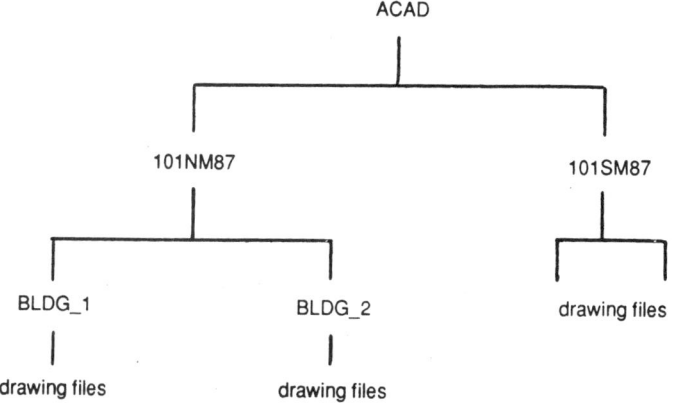

you may back up all drawing files in the subdirectories of 101NM87 by including the /S option in the BACKUP command. To back up all the drawing files in the subdirectories of the 101NM87 subdirectory that were modified since the previous BACKUP enter

```
C:\>BACKUP D:\ACAD\101NM87\*.DWG A:/A/S/M
```

If the total size of the files to be backed up exceeds the capacity of the floppy disk, BACKUP will direct you to insert another formatted disk. Each backup floppy disk must be numbered in sequence, i.e., 01, 02, etc. When the disks are used to restore the files, they must be inserted in the exact same order they were in when the backup was made.

Files created under BACKUP are unusable by AutoCAD unless they have been restored on the fixed disk with the RESTORE command.

1.6.2   Creating a BACKUP batch file

To simplify the backup procedure, especially that done on a daily basis, a batch file may be used. The EDLIN program discussed in Appendix H will be used to create the batch file.

You may wish to place a new batch file at the beginning of each ACAD drawing subdirectory. For example, to create a backup batch file named SAVE.BAT in the 101NM87 drawing subdirectory, load EDLIN.COM using the following (if your DOS files are in a directory other than the root directory, use the change directory command to log onto that directory prior to entering the following command):

```
C:\>EDLIN\ ACAD\101NM87\SAVE.BAT
```

The batch file named SAVE.BAT is created as follows with EDLIN (remember, the numbers and colons are the EDLIN prompt):

```
New file
*I
    1: CD \
    2: BACKUP C:\ACAD\101NM87\*.DWG A:/A/M
    3: ^c (Ctrl-C)
*E
C:\>
```

If you have saved your DOS files in a subdirectory named "system," change line 1 to read

```
1: CD \SYSTEM
```

At the end of each day, you may back up all of the drawings done in the 101NM87 subdirectory by logging onto that subdirectory and running SAVE as follows:

```
C:\>CD\ACAD\101NM87       (Not necessary if you are already in the drawing
                           directory)
C:\ACAD\101NM87>SAVE
```

Remember, the very first use of the BACKUP command cannot contain the /M option since BACKUP must delete all files on the disk when it is first used and creates a special file, BACKUPID.@@@. Therefore, you cannot use the SAVE.BAT program file for your very first use of BACKUP on a new backup disk. Use EDLIN to create the following 1ST-SAVE.BAT batch file:

```
C:\>EDLIN\ACAD\101NM87\1ST-SAVE.BAT
New File
*I
    1: CD\
    2: REM Warning: All existing files on this disk
    3: REM will be erased.
    4: REM To cancel this batch file press Ctrl-C.
    5: PAUSE To continue press any key.
    6: BACKUP C:ACAD\101NM87\*.DWG A:
    7: ^C
*E
C:\>
```

For the very first backup made of the files in the 101NM87 subdirectory, place a formatted floppy disk in drive A and log onto the drawing directory and enter

```
C:\ACAD\101NM87>1ST-SAVE
REM Warning: All existing files on this disk
REM will be erased.
REM To cancel batch file press Ctrl-C.
PAUSE To continue press any key.
```

Press any key to continue the batch file. The REM DOS command allows the inclusion of remarks in a batch file. The PAUSE command suspends execution of the batch file, in this case, until the user presses Ctrl-C to cancel or any other key to continue.

For all other backups of drawings in the 101NM87 subdirectory, use the SAVE.BAT batch file, which will only back up new files created since the last backup or files that have been modified. When backups of modified files are made, the backup command does not delete the previous backup from the disk on which the backups are being made. Because of this, it is possible to quickly fill up a disk with consecutive updates of a file. If you find this to be a problem, use the 1ST-SAVE.BAT file to reback up the entire file, deleting all older versions.

The DOS BACKUP program saves a new version of the file without deleting the previous copy each time BACKUP is used. Consequently the disk is rapidly filled if you make a number of backups. You may find it worthwhile to do a 1ST-SAVE onto a new formatted disk at specific intervals to get a compacted version of the directory. If the backup is successful, the previous backup disks can be reused.

1.7 Restoring Files

The RESTORE command is used to restore files to the hard disk. RE-STORE can be used only to restore files that were put on the floppy disk by the BACKUP command. The syntax of the RESTORE command is as follows:

```
RESTORE d1: [d2:][pathname][/S][/P]
```

The first parameter d1: indicates the floppy disk drive from which the restored files are to be transferred.

The second parameter specifies the fixed disk drive designation on which the files are to be restored. The file name may contain the wildcard characters * and ?. If only d1: is specified, files on the current directory will be restored. If only a path is given, files on the specified directory will be restored.

The /S option tells RESTORE to restore specified files on the current directory plus all of its subdirectories.

The /P option tells RESTORE not to restore any files on the hard disk that have been modified since the last backup, or files that are marked as read only.

If the ACAD\101NM87 files backed up earlier are to be restored to the fixed drive from the floppy disk in drive A, the following would be entered:

```
C:>RESTORE A: C:ACAD\101NM87\*.*
```

If you wish to restore only drawing files in 101NM87 that were not modified since the last backup, enter

```
C:>RESTORE A: C:\ACAD\101NM87\*.DWG/P
```

If subdirectories 101NM87 has subtrees that are to also be restored, enter:

```
C:>RESTORE A: C:\ACAD\101NM87\*.DWG/S/P
```

If more than one disk was used when the backup was created, RE-STORE will prompt you to enter each of the disks. They must be inserted in the correct order, hence the need to properly number the disks during the BACKUP process.

Assignment

1. If you have not already stored your AutoCAD files in a separate directory, create a new directory named ACAD and transfer the files into that directory (use the DOS COPY command). Then make a new subdirectory of ACAD named MISC in which you will store any draw-

ings created while using this text. Next write a SAVE.BAT and 1ST-SAVE.BAT file in the \ACAD\MISC directory to automate the procedure for backing up drawing files. Log onto the directory in which you have saved the DOS files and format a new data disk for use as a backup disk; then use the BACKUP command to do the first backup onto the formatted disk, creating the BACKUP.$$$ file. Label the disk MISC #1 BACKUP.

2. Write a CAD Standards Manual using the headings specified in Section 1.5. As you progress through this book, the manual is to be expanded to include the material covered in each chapter. You should now be able to complete the project management section based on the material covered in this chapter, plus technical information about the microcomputer system you are using, which you can obtain from the manuals or other sources in your firm or school. Some of the sections on drafting standards may be started now but will have to be completed as more material is covered in later chapters.

3. Review Appendix C, "File Management." If you do not have a file management program, prepare one for your computer following the procedure discussed there.

2

Getting Ready

OBJECTIVE *To set up your microcomputer system to run AutoLISP and to improve the efficiency of your microcomputer.*

2.1 Introduction

In this chapter you will learn how to prepare your microcomputer system so that you can run AutoLISP efficiently. The first requirement is that you must have 640K of memory installed and a hard disk drive. With Release 10 of AutoCAD you will also require a math coprocessor. If you do not have sufficient RAM, or if you have sufficient RAM but too much memory is taken up with memory resident programs such as Sidekick, ProKey, and print spoolers, you will see the following displayed when you boot AutoCAD:

```
Insufficient memory — AutoLISP disabled
```

If this happens, you will have to increase the RAM in your system prior to running AutoLISP or remove some, or all, of the memory resident software.

In this chapter, and many of the chapters that follow, you will be writing routines using the EDLIN.COM program that is on your DOS disk. If you are unfamiliar with using EDLIN, you should review the appendix or Section 11.6 in my previous text, *Easy AutoCAD*. It is assumed here that you are familiar with EDLIN.

2.2 Automatic DOS Command Execution

When the microcomputer is booted, DOS looks for files named AUTOEXEC.BAT and CONFIG.SYS. If the files are present, DOS executes the commands in those files. Both AUTOEXEC.BAT and CONFIG.SYS must be located in the DOS root directory if they are to be executed during the boot-up sequence.

2.2.1   Improved DOS prompt

In Section 1.2 you were shown how to set the DOS prompt to include the current subdirectory. If that command is put in the AUTOEXEC.BAT file, it will be invoked when the microcomputer is booted up.

If you are not logged onto the root directory, use the CD command to move there now. For instance, if you are in the ACAD directory enter

```
C:\ACAD>CD \
C:\>_
```

List the directory to see if you already have an AUTOEXEC.BAT file:

```
C:\>DIR/W
```

If you have an AUTOEXEC.BAT file, enter the following command to make a copy of the current file. (It is always a good practice to make a copy of any resident file before making any changes to it. This way you can always recover the initial file.) To make a safety copy enter

```
C:\>COPY AUTOEXEC.BAT AUTOEXEC.SAV
```

If you have an AUTOEXEC.BAT file, use the TYPE command to list the file. The file may appear as follows:

```
C:\>TYPE AUTOEXEC.BAT
ECHO OFF
CLS
DATE
TIME
```

If you do not have an AUTOEXEC.BAT, the next command entered will create one.

To add the prompt command to the AUTOEXEC.BAT file, or create a new one, the EDLIN program is called as follows (if your EDLIN file is not in your root directory go on to the next paragraph):

```
C:\>EDLIN AUTOEXEC.BAT
```

If your EDLIN file is in a directory other than the root directory, precede the EDLIN file name with the path. For instance, if EDLIN is in a subdirectory named SYSTEM enter

```
C:\>SYSTEM\EDLIN AUTOEXEC.BAT
```

If you do not have an AUTOEXEC.BAT file, EDLIN will indicate that this is a new file. You begin entering commands by using the Insert command as follows:

```
New file
*I
   1:*
```

If you have an AUTOEXEC.BAT file the response will be

```
End of input file
*
```

Prior to entering data into an existing AUTOEXEC.BAT file, list the file. It may appear as follows:

```
*L
   1: ECHO OFF
   2: CLS
   3: DATE
   4: TIME
*
```

To add to an existing file (listed above) at line 5 use the Insert command as follows (depending on your file listing, you may have to use a different line number; with a new file you will be starting at line 1, already displayed):

```
*5I
   5:*
```

Now the commands to be entered will be the same whether you are adding to an existing file or creating a new one. The only difference will be the line number at which you are starting. Assuming you are adding to an existing file starting at line 5, the entry is as follows:

```
   5:*PROMPT $P$G
```

Do not exit EDLIN. Additional commands discussed in Section 2.3 are to be added to the current file.

2.3 AutoLISP Memory Space

AutoLISP maintains two areas of memory for itself, called the "stack" and the "heap." The stack area is where AutoLISP stores function arguments and intermediate calculations, and the heap is where it stores all functions and variables (do not worry about these terms as they will be discussed in later chapters). With Release 10 of AutoCAD the default sizes are 40,000 bytes for the heap and 3000 bytes for the stack. (To use Release 10's Extended AutoLISP, refer to Chapter 6 in your *AutoLISP Programmer's Reference* for more information.) The limitation on their size is that the total of the two areas cannot exceed 45,000 bytes. If you run out of space when running AutoLISP, the function being run will be terminated and the following message will be displayed:

```
Insufficient node space.
```

The following lines are to be included in the AUTOEXEC.BAT file to SET the LISPHEAP to 40000 and the LISPSTACK to 5000 when DOS is booted:

```
6: SET LISPHEAP=40000
7: SET LISPSTACK=5000
8: SET ACADFREERAM=24
9: PATH C:\;C:SYSTEM C:ACAD
10: ^C     (Ctrl-C)
*E        (Exit EDLIN.)
C:\>
```

Do not precede or follow the equal signs with a space.

The ACADFREERAM setting in line 8 reserves 24 kB of memory for a working storage area. These commands will affect only memory reserved for AutoCAD. You will not lose any memory while running other programs.

The PATH command in line 9 tells DOS where to look for files. Reboot your microcomputer. The display should be

```
C:\>
```

2.4   DOS Buffers and Files

The CONFIG.SYS file is used to define operating characteristics of DOS. Certain application programs and accessory devices require that commands be placed in CONFIG.SYS. You can increase the processing speed of your system by as much as 20 percent if you increase the working area in memory that DOS uses when reading and writing to and from a hard disk.

Use the CD command to return to the root directory, and then list the directory to see if you have a CONFIG.SYS file. (See Section 2.2.1 if you do not remember the procedure.)

If you have a CONFIG.SYS file, use the COPY command to make a copy of it with a new name CONFIG.SAV as was done for the AUTOEXEC.BAT file in Section 2.2.1. Now load EDLIN to edit the current CONFIG.SYS, or write a new one with the following command:

```
C:>EDLIN CONFIG.SYS
```

If you already have a CONFIG.SYS file, use the L (List) command to list the file. If there are three lines in the file, enter 4I to begin insertion at line 4.

If you do not have a CONFIG.SYS file, enter I to begin inserting commands into the file. The commands to enter into the CONFIG.SYS file are as follows (the line numbers will be different if you are adding to an existing file):

```
1: FILES=22
```

```
   2: BUFFERS=32
   3: ^C     (Ctrl-C)
*E         (Exit EDLIN)
C:\>
```

The FILES command tells DOS how many files it can use at one time. Unless otherwise directed, this number is eight.

The BUFFER command defines the number of work areas in memory that DOS opens for reading from, and writing to, a disk. Unless otherwise instructed, DOS uses two buffers.

The numbers 22 and 32 for files and buffers, respectively, are values generally recommended for improved hard disk performance. You may find by experimentation that better results can be obtained for your system with slightly different numbers.

2.5   EDLIN and AutoCAD

EDLIN will be used throughout this text. You can write files with EDLIN when AutoCAD is loaded by exiting AutoCAD and loading EDLIN from DOS, using AutoCAD's SHELL command to call EDLIN from within AutoCAD, or defining EDLIN in the ACAD.PGP, which also allows you to access EDLIN from within AutoCAD. The latter procedure is much more efficient providing there is sufficient free memory (SHELL puts an even greater demand on memory).

The ACAD.PGP file contains information about utility programs that are called from within AutoCAD. Log onto the ACAD subdirectory and display the contents of the ACAD.PGP file using the TYPE command:

```
C:\>CD\ACAD
C:ACAD>TYPE ACAD.PGP
```

The file may appear as follows:

```
CATALOG,DIR /W,30000,*Files: ,0
DEL,DEL,30000,File to delete: ,0
DIR,DIR,30000,File specification: 0
EDIT,EDLIN,42000,File to edit: ,0
SH,,30000,*DOS Command: ,0
SHELL,,127000,*DOS Command: ,0
TYPE,TYPE,30000,File to list: ,0
```

Notice that there is an EDLIN command in the listing.

If your ACAD.PGP file does not contain an EDLIN command, you will have to add a line to the file describing EDLIN to AutoCAD. If there is an EDLIN command in your file similar to that illustrated in line 4 of the preceding listing of an ACAD.PGP file, you will not have to add a line describing EDLIN; however, if the line describing EDLIN in your listing starts off with EDIT, you may wish to change the file as described below. You must also specify the path to EDLIN.

Prior to adding a line or modifying the ACAD.PGP file, make a copy of the existing file:

```
C:\ACAD>PATH\
C:\ACAD>COPY ACAD.PGP ACAD.SAV
C:\ACAD>
```

Now load EDLIN and list the ACAD.PGP file:

```
C:\ACAD>EDLIN ACAD.PGP
End of input file
*L
```

If in your listing the line with EDLIN begins with EDIT, EDIT is the command name that is used to call EDLIN. The author prefers to use EDLIN. You must also specify the path to EDLIN. Assuming the EDLIN command is on line 4, begin editing as follows:

```
*4
  4: EDIT,EDLIN,42000,File to edit: ,0
  4:
```

To edit the line, move the cursor to the I in EDIT and type **LI**:

```
  4: EDLI (Do not press ENTER yet.)
```

Now press the Ins (Insert) key and type **N**:

```
  4: EDLIN (Do not press ENTER yet.)
```

Now move the cursor to the E in the second EDLIN, press the Ins (Insert) key, and enter the following (if necessary, replace SYSTEM with the directory in which you have saved EDLIN):

```
  4: EDLIN, C:\SYSTEM\
```

Move the cursor to the end of the line and press the Enter key. The new line entered should appear as follows:

```
  4: EDLIN,C:\SYSTEM\EDLIN,42000,File to edit: ,0
*E    (Exit EDLIN)
```

There are five fields (separated by commas) in the line informing AutoCAD about EDLIN (see line 4 above). Each field gives the following information:

Field	Text	Information
First	EDLIN	Command name to use when calling this command with SHELL
Second	C:\SYSTEM\ EDLIN	Name and path of file, EDLIN, to be loaded from DOS

Field	Text	Information
Third	42000	Amount of memory to be released by AutoCAD for use by EDLIN
Fourth	File specification	Prompt to be displayed to the user—in this case the name of the file to be operated on with EDLIN
Fifth	Return flag	Return code controlling options when returning to the screen; zero (0) to return to the text screen, 1 to return to the graphics screen

The shell command may be used to execute any DOS command such as DIR, TYPE, etc. It can also be used to access other programs such as database and word processing programs. Occasionally the SHELL command will cause the drawing to appear disorganized when you return to it. This may be rectified by issuing the REDRAW command.

To load programs defined in the PGP file from within AutoCAD, enter the "command name" you specified for the program in the PGP file, i.e.,

Command: `edlin` (or edit)

AutoCAD responds with the prompt specified in the PGP file, i.e.,

`File to edit:`

You may now enter the appropriate command (in this case, the name of the file to be edited by EDLIN). When you exit from the file, you will be returned to the drawing editor.

You may add other programs to the PGP file, providing the size of the program does not exceed 50 kB in size. To determine the amount of memory to allocate, list the file from DOS using the DIR command and note the size of the file. The amount of memory to be specified in the PGP file is the program size plus 17,000 bytes for DOS functions plus 30,000 to 40,000 for file buffer.

3

Automating Drawing
Start-Ups

OBJECTIVE *To develop an automated
start-up procedure for beginning a new
drawing with AutoCAD using a prototype
drawing and custom menu to create a set of
border drawings.*

3.1 Introduction

Computer-aided drafting is supposed to simplify the drawing process. Unfortunately, because of the need to draw borders and title blocks and set screen limits, linetype scales, dimension variables, text heights, etc., the start-up procedure is in many ways more complex with CAD than with classical drafting—hence the need for an automated start-up procedure.

3.2 Prototype Drawings

When you begin a drawing, there are a number of default sizes, limits, and modes that become part of the initial environment. The values may be the standard default values supplied by AutoCAD in the ACAD.DWG file, or they may be defined by the user in a "prototype drawing." The standard prototype drawing, ACAD.DWG, values are listed in Appendix A of your *AutoCAD Reference Manual*. This chapter lists typical values in the ACAD.DWG prototype drawing.

When configuring AutoCAD, one of the "Configure operating parameters" options is the "Initial drawing setup." If this option is selected, you will be asked to "Enter name of default prototype file for new drawings." If you enter the name of a drawing file, that file will define the environment for all subsequent new drawings. The environment may include a predrawn border, title block, preinitialized layer names, or any other convention you wish to use. You can adjust the defaults set by the prototype drawing for subsequent drawings by editing the prototype drawing.

A prototype drawing other than the default one may be called when beginning a new drawing by entering the name of the new drawing using the following format:

```
New-drawing-name = Prototype-drawing-name
```

The "New-drawing-name" is any legitimate drawing file name. The "Prototype-drawing-name" is the name of a drawing file you wish to use to set the environment for your new drawing. Both names may be preceded by appropriate file paths.

The default prototype drawing file supplied by AutoCAD is ACAD.DWG. Unless you specify another prototype drawing during the configuration process, or when starting a new drawing, ACAD.DWG is the file that defines the environment for all new drawings. If another file is specified as a prototype drawing, everything in that file is appended to the new drawing. Whatever is drawn in the prototype drawing file is included (it may of course be edited out). Consequently, prototype drawings should include only those items you wish to become part of the new drawing environment.

To create a prototype drawing you begin a new drawing with the name to be specified when calling the prototype drawing. When the drawing editor is loaded, set the desired parameters, such as limits and layers, and draw anything you wish to include in drawings using this prototype, such as borders, title blocks, etc. When the file contains all of the parameters you wish to include, the drawing is saved. The drawing file may then be specified as a prototype drawing.

3.3   Drawing Parameters

Table 3.1 lists a typical initial drawing environment established by the ACAD.DWG file. Although the ACAD.DWG prototype drawing can be edited to set whatever initial condition you desire, you should create a new prototype drawing and then reconfigure AutoCAD to load the new prototype. This way you can always go back to the initial ACAD.DWG environment by reconfiguring AutoCAD again. Our prototype drawing will be called PROTO1.

3.4   PROTO1 Drawing Environment

The modes to be changed for our prototype drawing, PROTO1, for DIM variables are as listed after Table 3.1.

TABLE 3.1   ACAD.DWG Initial Environment

Item	Setting			
APERTURE	10 pixels			
Attributes	Controlled individually using prompts			
AXIS	Off, spacing (0.0, 0.0)			
BASE	Insertion base point (0.0, 0.0, 0.0)			
BLIPMODE	On			
CHAMFER	Distance 0.0			
COLOR	Entity color BYLAYER			
Coordinate display	Updated on point entry			
DIM variables	DIMALT	Off	DIMSAH	Off
	DIMALTD	2	DIMSCALE	1.00
	DIMALTF	25.40	DIMSE1	Off
	DIMAPOST	nil	DIMSE2	Off
	DIMASO	On	DIMSHO	Off
	DIMASZ	0.18	DIMSOXD	Off
	DIMBLK	nil	DIMTAD	Off
	DIMBLK1	nil	DIMTIH	On
	DIMBLK2	nil	DIMTIX	Off
	DIMCEN	0.09	DIMTM	0.00
	DIMDLE	0.00	DIMOFL	Off
	DIMDLI	0.38	DIMTOH	On
	DIMEXE	0.18	DIMTOL	Off
	DIMEXO	0.0625	DIMTP	0.00
	DIMFLAC	1.00	DIMTSZ	0.00
	DIMLIM	Off	DIMTVP	0.00
	DIMPOST	nil	DIMTXT	0.18
	DIMRND	0.00	DIMZIN	0
DRAGMODE	Auto			
ELEV	Elevation 0.0, thickness 0.0			
FILL	On			
FILLET	Radius 0.0			
FLATLAND	0 (full 3-D enabled)			
GRID	Off, spacing (0.0, 0.0)			
HANDLES	Off			
Highlighting	Enabled			
ISOPLANE	Left			
LAYER	Current/only layer 0, On, with color 7 (white) and linetype CONTINUOUS			
LIMITS	Off, drawing limits (0.0, 0.0) to (12.0, 9.0)			
LINETYPE	Entity linetype BYLAYER, only loaded linetype is CONTINUOUS			
LTSCALE	1.0			
MENU	acad			

TABLE 3.1   ACAD.DWG Initial Environment (*Continued*)

Item	Setting
MIRROR	Text mirrored same as other entities
Object selection	Pick box size 3 pixels
ORTHO	Off
OSNAP	None
PLINE	Line width 0.0
POINT	Display mode 0, size 0.00
QTEXT	Off
REGENAUTO	On
SKETCH	Record increment 0.10, producing lines
SNAP	Off, spacing (1.0, 1.0)
SNAP/GRID	Standard style, base point (0.0, 0.0), rotation 0.0 degrees
Spline curves	Frame off, segments 8, cubic spline
STYLE	Only defined text style: STANDARD, using font file txt, with variable height, width factor 1.0, horizontal orientation, and no special modes
Surfaces	6 tabulations in M & N direction, 6 segments for smoothing in U & V directions, smooth surface type: cubic B-spline
TABLET	Off
TEXT	Style STANDARD, height 0.20, rotation 0.0 degrees
TIME	User elapsed timer on
TRACE	Width 0.05
UCS	Current UCS same as WCS, origin at
WCS	(0,0,0), auto plan view off, coordinate system icon on (at origin)
UCSICON	On
UNITS (linear)	Decimal, 4 decimal places
UNITS (angular)	Decimal degrees, 0 decimal places, angle 0 direction is to the right, angles increase counterclockwise
Viewing modes	One active viewport, plan view, perspective off, target point (0,0,0), front & back clipping off, lengths length 50 mm, twist angle 0.0, fast zoom on, circle zoom 100 percent, WORLDVIEW 0
ZOOM	To drawing limits

DIMSCALE is an overall scale factor applied to all dimensioning variables. It will be set by a macro in the menu to suit the drawing scale selected from the menu.

DIMTAD off breaks the dimension line and centers the dimension text along the dimension line. DIMTAD will be set on to place the text above an unbroken dimension line.

DIMTIH on places all text falling inside dimension extension lines horizontally. DIMTIH will be set off so as to align the text with the dimension line.

DIMTOH on places all text falling outside dimension extension lines horizontally. DIMTOH will be set off to align the text with the dimension line.

DIMZIN set at 0 (off for Ver. 2.5) does not print 0 in for even feet distances. DIMZIN will be set at 3 (on for Ver 2.5) to print 0 in.

Depending on your drafting discipline you may wish to set other dimension variables such as DIMTOL (tolerances), etc., in your prototype drawing. The modes for other variables are as follows:

LAYER	The layers specified in Section 1.3 will be set. Linetypes and colors will be set by layer in our prototype drawing.
LIMITS	LIMITS will be set in the menu to suit the drawing scale and plot-drawing sheet size selected.
LTSCALE	LTSCALE will be set in the menu to suit the drawing scale selected.
MENU	The menu attached to the prototype drawing will be called PROTO1. The PROTO1 menu will allow selection of the scale and drawing size.
UCSICON	Release 10 User Coordinate System icon will be set off to disable the icon, which is distracting in 2-D drawings. If you do a lot of 3-D drawings, leave it on.
UNITS	Linear units will be selected in the menu by the drafter.

There may be other modes you wish to change in your prototype drawing, such as setting a specific GRID and SNAPing a specialized drawing type. The environment defined above is for general drafting.

3.5   Creating the Prototype Drawing— PROTO1

Prior to beginning the drawing, a subdirectory of ACAD called PROTO must be created. The prototype drawing, PROTO1.DWG; menu file, PROTO1.MNU; script file, PROTO1.SCR; and related border drawings are to be filed in this subdirectory:

```
C:\>CD ACAD
C:\ACAD>MD PROTO
```

Now log onto the PROTO subdirectory, boot AutoCAD, and begin a new drawing named PROTO1. When the drawing editor is loaded, set the units to decimal with two digits to the right of the decimal. Next, use the LAYER command to create the new layers specified in Section 1.3, using the two- or three-letter names specified for each layer. Assign the appropriate linetype and color to each layer.

After you have completed the LAYER settings, set the following DIMVARS:

DIMTAD—on, DIMTIH—off, DIMTOH—off, and DIMZIN—3 (on for Ver. 2.5).

Make any other settings you wish to have as part of your prototype drawing. For instance, you may wish to set associative dimensioning, DIMASO, off.

Use the END command to save the drawing and exit from the AutoCAD editor.

From the AutoCAD Main menu select Task 5, Configure AutoCAD. The current configuration will be displayed. Press Enter to display the Configuration menu and then select Task 8, Configure operating parameters. Make the following selections and entries:

```
Operating parameters menu
    0. Exit configuration menu
    1. Alarm on error
    2. Initial drawing setup
    3. Default plot file name
    4. Plot spooler directory
    5. Placement of temporary files
    6. Network node name
    7. AutoLISP feature
Enter selection: 2 <return>
Enter name of default prototype file for new drawings or . for none
<acad>: proto\proto1
```

Select Task 0 to exit the configuration process and save the new configuration.

3.6 Menu Files

An AutoCAD menu file is a text file with the extension .MNU. The customized text file may be created with any text editor or word processor that does not place extra coding characters in the text. In this text EDLIN will be used.

The menu file may contain any sequence of individual AutoCAD commands or macros made up of a string of commands. The menu may also call submenus and request input from the user. It is assumed you have some familiarity with writing menu files. If not, read Chapter 11 of *Easy AutoCAD*.

The following summary lists menu items and procedures with which you should be familiar:

Process	Procedure
Macro	String together standard AutoCAD commands separated by a single space or a semicolon.
Command titles	Only the first eight characters of a menu can appear on the monitor. To place a command or macro title at the beginning of the macro or command, enclose the title in square brackets ([ ]).
Submenus	To indicate a submenu, precede the submenu name with two asterisks (**).
Call a submenu	To call a screen submenu use: $S=submenu-name
Last submenu	To call the previous submenu use: $S=
Screen menu	When submenus are used, the main menu is indicated with the heading: ***SCREEN
User input	To allow keyboard (user) input, place a backslash (\) in the menu at the location where input is required. Do not follow the backslash with a space or semicolon.
Enter key	The Enter key is embedded in the menu by placing a space or semicolon (;) at the location at which the Enter key is required.
Line extension	If a macro line in the menu is to extend to the next line of text, place a plus (+) at the end of the line to be continued.
File path	File paths are indicated with a forward slash (/) rather than a backslash (\), which is reserved for user input.

Menus may also contain AutoLISP expressions, which will be used in this menu but discussed in the next chapter.

3.7 PROTO1 Menu

PROTO1.MNU is a custom menu to be loaded by the prototype drawing whenever a new drawing is started. It will allow you to select the plot-sheet size and the desired scale for the final plot.

PROTO1 highlights

When starting a new drawing, load the prototype drawing with the custom PROTO1 *menu*. You begin by selecting the drawing plot-sheet size from the PROTO1 menu. Your selection invokes a macro that sets the screen limits to suit the plot-sheet size, draws an appropriate border, and inserts a title block into the drawing. It then saves the drawing of the border and title block as a block named B2.

Next, a submenu is displayed with drawing plot-scale options. You select the desired scale from the menu and a scale factor is calculated based on the scale selected. The menu loads an AutoCAD "script" file that resets the drawing limits using the original plot-sheet size multiplied by the scale factor and INSERTS the border and title-block block B2 using the scale factor as the x and y insertion factor.

The drawing is now done full size within the scaled border dimensions.

The text height and the hatch, linetype, and dimension scales are also set automatically by the script file when the drawing scale is selected. The script file will be written in the next chapter.

There is some use of AutoLISP in the menu file macros. Copy the menu exactly as illustrated. Places where you may make changes are indicated. The AutoLISP items will be discussed in detail in the next chapter.

PROTO subdirectory. Log onto the root directory, or wherever EDLIN is stored, and load EDLIN to begin a file named PROTO1.MNU, which is to be stored in the PROTO subdirectory of ACAD:

```
C:\>EDLIN\ ACAD\PROTO\PROTO1.MNU
New file
*I      (Insert text)
     1:*
```

The number and colon at the beginning of each line are part of the EDLIN prompt and are not to be keyed in. Also remember that EDLIN includes an asterisk as part of its prompt. Be careful to not count that asterisk as one of those required at the heading of the SCREEN and submenu listings.

In the menu the screen limits are set to the drawing frame sizes illustrated in Tables 3.2 and 3.3. For the A and A4 sheets a larger binding margin is allowed for on the long side of the sheet (top of screen). For the B and A3 sheets a binding margin is allowed for on the short (left) side of the sheet. You may wish to change the border line dimensions to suit your office practice or your plotter limitations. The menu lines affected are lines 4 through 21. The menu illustrated in Section 3.7.4 is limited to A- (A4) and B- (A3) size drawings with the long side horizontal. If you are plotting on larger sheets or using the long side vertical, you will have to extend the menu. For instance, if you are

TABLE 3.2   Imperial Drawing Frame Sizes (inches)

Sheet size	Sheet dimension	Binding boarder	Other boarders	Frame dimension
A	8.5 × 11	¾	½	7.25 × 10
B	11 × 17	¾	½	10 × 15.75
C	17 × 22	¾	½	16 × 20.75
D	22 × 34	1	½	21 × 32.5

TABLE 3.3   SI Drawing Frame Sizes (Millimeters)

Sheet size	Sheet dimension	Binding boarder	Other boarders	Frame dimension
A4	210 × 297	20	10	180 × 277
A3	297 × 420	20	10	277 × 390
A2	420 × 594	20	10	400 × 564
A1	594 × 841	26	14	566 × 801

drawing in SI and using Imperial-size paper, you will have to change the frame dimensions.

3.7.1   SCREEN menu

```
1: ***SCREEN
2: [-PLOT-]
3: [-SHEET-]
4: [A4-HOR]^Clayer;make;border;color;green;border;;limits;+
5: 0,0;277,180;zoom;all;line;0,0;277,0;280,180;0,180;c;+
6: insert;/acad/proto/title;277,0;;;;\\\\\\\\\\block;+
7: b2;0,0;w;-1,-1;278,181;;(setqw 277 h 181);$s=si
8: [A3-HOR]^Clayer;make;border;color;green;border;;limits;+
9: 0,0;390,277;zoom;all;line;0,0;390,0;390,277;0,277;c;+
10: insert;/acad/proto/title;390,0;;;;\\\\\\\\\\block;+
11: b2;0,0;w;-1,-1;391,278;;(setqw 390 h 277);$s=si
12: [A-HOR]^Clayer;make;border;color;green;border;;limits;+
13: 0,0;10,7.25;zoom;all;line;0,0;10,0;10,7.25;+
14: 0,7.25;c;insert;/acad/proto/title;10,0;.039;;;+
15: \\\\\\\\\\block;b2;0,0;w;-.1,-.1;10.1,7.3;;+
16: (setqw 10.0 h 7.25);$s=i
17: [B-HOR]^Clayer;make;border;color;green;border;;limits;+
18: 0,0;15.75,10;zoom;all;line;0,0;15.75,0;+
19: 15.75,10;0,10;c;insert;/acad/proto/title;+
20: 15,75;0;.039;;;\\\\\\\\\\block;b2;0,0;+
21: w;-.1,-.1;15.8,10.1;;(setqw 15.75 h 10.0);$s=i
22:
23: [ACADMNU]menu;acad;
24:
25: quit
26: end
27: save
28:
29:
30:
31:
32:
33:
34:
```

Discussion of SCREEN menu. The Proto1 SCREEN menu begins at line 1 and extends to line 34, encompassing a total of *20 menu lines* (including blanks). When counting menu lines, some lines are a continuation of the previous line (i.e., lines 5, 6, and 7 are a continuation of line 4) and are not counted as screen lines in the menu (even though

EDLIN places a line number in front of the line). A plus (+) at the end of a line indicates that it continues on the next line. Line 4 is analyzed as follows:

^C (Ctrl-C) cancels any current command. The LAYER command is initiated and the MAKE option is selected to create a new layer called Border and set it as the current layer. The Enter key is embedded after each command by a semicolon (;). Next the COLOR option is entered and green is specified for the Border layer. The second semicolon (Enter) after the layer name causes an exit from the LAYER command.

The LIMIT command is then invoked and the limits are set at 0,0 and 277,180 to match the drawing frame dimensions for an A4 sheet in Table 3.3.

The ZOOM-All command sets the screen to the limits.

The LINE command is called and a border line is drawn around the frame. Note the use of C to close the line on the start point.

Next the INSERT command is invoked to insert a block named Title (your title block, to be drawn later) with a file path of /acad/proto/. (Note the use of the forward slash (/) for the file path rather than the DOS backslash, which is used to embed keyboard input in an AutoCAD menu.) The insertion point is the lower-right corner of the border frame, coordinate 277,0. The second, third, and fourth semicolons following the insertion point select the default x- and y-insertion scale factors of 1 and the default rotation angle of 0.

The block being inserted has six attributes used to tag user input information (name, date, etc.) to the block. The Attribute Verify mode is set on so each attribute entered is to be verified. Consequently 12 user inputs (twice 6) are required via 12 backslashes.

A block named B2 is created next with an insertion point of 0,0. It is selected using a window slightly larger than the drawing frame (-1,-1 and 278,181) to include the entire drawing. A second semicolon is required to exit the BLOCK command.

The data within the parentheses, (), is AutoLISP. It is used to store the border frame size in memory for later use. The exact meaning will be discussed in the next chapter.

Finally, a submenu named si is called.

Lines 8, 12, and 17 are similar to line 4.

3.7.2 Submenu si

The si submenu is displayed by the macro in line 4 of the Screen menu. It provides the drafter with two drawing options, meters or millimeters:

```
35: **si
36: [-DWG-]
37: [-UNITS-]
38: [meters](setq txt 2.5 conv 25.4);$s=m
39: [ mm ](setq txt 2.5 conv 25.4);$s=mm
40:
41: [ROOTMENU]$s=SCREEN
42:
43:
44:
45:
46:
47:
48:
49:
50:
51:
52:
53:
54:
```

Discussion of si submenu. The command $s=si at the end of line 4 of the PROTO1 menu displays a screen submenu with the name **si (line 35). The submenu contains 20 lines (including its label) to completely blank out the prior SCREEN menu on the monitor. The user selects the drawing units, meters or millimeters, from the submenu thereby displaying another submenu named m or mm.

The data within parentheses is AutoLISP. It will be discussed in detail in the next chapter; it simply assigns the text height, 2.5 mm, and a conversion factor, 25.4, to convert millimeters to inches, which is required when calculating the LTSCALE factor.

3.7.3 Submenus m and mm

The mm and m submenus display a set of metric plot scales for the drafter to select from:

```
55: **m
56: [-SCALE-]
57: [1:10](setq f 0.01);script;/acad/proto/proto1;
58: [1:20](setq f 0.02);script;/acad/proto/proto1;
59: [1:50](setq f 0.05);script;/acad/proto/proto1;
60: [1:100](setq f 0.1);script;/acad/proto/proto1;
61: [1:200](setq f 0.2);script;/acad/proto/proto1;
62: [1:250](setq f 0.25);script;/acad/proto/proto1;
63: [1:300](setq f 0.3);script;/acad/proto/proto1;
64: [1:400](setq f 0.4);script;/acad/proto/proto1;
```

```
65: [1:500](setq f 0.5);script;/acad/proto/protol;
66: [1:1000](setq f 1);script;/acad/proto/protol;
67: [1:2000](setq f 2);script;/acad/proto/protol;
68:
69:
70:
71:
72: [-LAST-]$s=si
73: [ROOT MENU]$s=SCREEN
74:
75: **mm
76: [-SCALE-]
77: [1:1](setq f 1);script;/acad/proto/protol;
78: [1:2](setq f 2);script;/acad/proto/protol;
79: [1:5](setq f 5);script;/acad/proto/protol;
80: [1:10](setq f 10);script;/acad/proto/protol;
81: [1:20](setq f 20);script;/acad/proto/protol;
82: [1:50](setq f 50);script;/acad/proto/protol;
83: [1:100](setq f 100);script;/acad/proto/protol;
84: [1:200](setq f 200);script;/acad/proto/protol;
85: [1:250](setq f 250);script;/acad/proto/protol;
86: [1:300](setq f 300);script;/acad/proto/protol;
87: [1:400](setq f 400);script;/acad/proto/protol;
88: [1:500](setq f 500);script;/acad/proto/protol;
89: [1:1000](setq f 1000);script;/acad/proto/protol;
90: [1:2000](setq f 2000);script;/acad/proto/protol;
91:
92:
93: [-LAST-]$s=
94: [ROOTMENU]$s=SCREEN
```

Discussion of m and mm submenus. Submenus m and mm are called from line 38 or 39, respectively, of the si submenu, which allows the user to select the drawing plot scale desired.

The data within the parentheses is AutoLISP, which will be discussed in the next chapter. It saves an insertion factor, f, to be used in an AutoCAD script to reinsert the border into the drawing, bringing it up to the scale selected. For instance, if the border to be inserted was drawn using millimeters and the drawing was done in meters, you would select [meters] in the si submenu (line 38). The macro in line 38 then displays the m submenu which has scale options. If the scale selected from that menu is 1:10 (line 57), which means 1 mm = 10 mm, the scale factor, which equals the drawing increment divided by the plot increment, is 0.01-m drawing increment divided by 1-mm plot increment, resulting in an insertion factor of 0.01 (Section 4.3.1).

The macro then invokes the SCRIPT command and loads a script with the file path /acad/proto/proto1—yet to be created. The script will use the scale factor to set the screen limits and insert block B2 (the border and title block) using the appropriate scale factor. It will be discussed in detail in the next chapter.

3.7.4 Submenu i

The i submenu is called when the drafter selects [A4-HOR] or [A3-HOR] in the SCREEN menu. In this menu the user may select [arch/eng] to use AutoCAD's architectural or engineering units, [civ-eng] to use civil engineering units (i.e., 1 in = 30 ft), or [mech-eng] to use mechanical engineering units (i.e., 1:10). In each case the data enclosed in parentheses is AutoLISP and is discussed in the next chapter. Depending on the selection, submenus a, c, or mm are then displayed to allow the user to select a plot scale.

```
 95: **i
 96: [ -DWG- ]
 97: [-UNITS-]
 98:
 99: [arch/eng](setq txt (/ 3.0 32) conv 1);$s=a
100:
101: [civ-eng](setq txt (/ 3.0 32) conv 1);$s=c
102:
103: [mech-eng](setq txt (/ 3.0 32) conv 1);$s=mm
104:
105: [ROOTMENU]$s=SCREEN
106:
107:
108:
109:
110:
111:
112:
113:
114:
```

3.7.5 Submenus a and c

Submenus a and c provide Imperial unit plot scales for the drafter to select from:

```
115: **a
116: [-SCALE-]
117: [3/32'' = 1'](setq f 128);script;/acad/proto/proto1;
118: [1/8''  = 1'](setq f 96);script;/acad/proto/proto1;
119: [3/16'' = 1'](setq f 64);script;/acad/proto/proto1;
120: [1/4''  = 1'](setq f 48);script;/acad/proto/proto1;
121: [3/8''  = 1'](setq f 32);script;/acad/proto/proto1;
122: [1/2''  = 1'](setq f 24);script;/acad/proto/proto1;
123: [3/4''  = 1'](setq f 16);script;/acad/proto/proto1;
124: [1'' = 1'](setq f 12);script;/acad/proto/proto1;
125: [1¹/₂'' = 1'](setq f 8);script;/acad/proto/proto1;
126: [3'' = 1'](setq f 4);script;/acad/proto/proto1;
127: [6'' = 1'](setq f 2);script;/acad/proto/proto1;
128: [Fullsize](setq f 1);script;/acad/proto/proto1;
129:
130:
131:
```

```
132: [-LAST-]$s=
133:
134: [ROOTMENU]$s=SCREEN
135: **c
136: [-SCALE-]
137: [1'' =  1'](setq f 1);script;/acad/proto/proto1;
138: [1'' =  5'](setq f 5);script;/acad/proto/proto1;
139: [1'' = 10'](setq f 10);script;/acad/proto/proto1;
140: [1'' = 15'](setq f 15);script;/acad/proto/proto1;
141: [1'' = 20'](setq f 20);script;/acad/proto/proto1;
142: [1'' = 30'](setq f 30);script;/acad/proto/proto1;
143: [1'' = 50'](setq f 50);script;/acad/proto/proto1;
144: [1'' = 100'](setq f 100);script;/acad/proto/proto1;
145: [1'' = 200'](setq f 200);script;/acad/proto/proto1;
146: [1'' = 300'](setq f 300);script;/acad/proto/proto1;
147: [1'' = 400'](setq f 400);script;/acad/proto/proto1;
148: [1'' = 500'](setq f 500);script;/acad/proto/proto1;
149:
150:
151:
152: [-LAST-]$s=
153:
154: [ROOTMENU]$s=SCREEN
155: ^c    (Ctrl-C)
*
```

Discussion of submenus a and c. In submenu a, AutoCAD's architectural units are used, and although you appear to be working in feet when drawing, AutoCAD is working internally in inches. For a scale of ³⁄₃₂ in = 1 ft, the drawing increment is 12 in and the plot increment is ³⁄₃₂ in. The scale factor f = drawing increment / the plot increment so that

$$f = \frac{12}{3/32} = 128$$

Next, as in the previous scale selection submenu, the SCRIPT command is invoked and a script file named Proto1 is loaded. In line 139 the drawing units are feet and the plot scale is 1 ft = 10 ft. Since the plot increment is inches, the scale factor f = 10 / 1 = 10.

Review the entire PROTO1 *menu* and ensure that you understand its workings. Write the entire menu using EDLIN. When through, use EDLIN's LIST command to list your file in sections and carefully compare your menu with the text menu to ensure it matches. To list the file from lines 20 to 40, enter **20,40 L.** When you are satisfied that your menu is accurate, exit EDLIN as follows:

```
*e
c:\>
```

Adding PROTO1.MNU to your PROTO1.DWG. Boot up AutoCAD and edit your prototype drawing named ACAD\PROTO\PROTO1. When the drawing is loaded, use the menu command to load the PROTO1 menu as follows:

```
MENU <return>
Menu file name or . for none <acad>: proto\proto1
```

Since the menu is new, AutoCAD will compile it and create a PROTO1.MNX file. Compiled files have the file extension .MNX and have a more compact internal format than .MNU files. In the next chapter you will be expanding the PROTO1.MNU file. When AutoCAD loads a file and the file is not new, it compares the date of the MNU file with that of the MNX file. If the corresponding MNU file is newer, AutoCAD recompiles the file creating an updated MNX file. If you are revising a menu file, it is very important that you enter the date when booting your computer so that the MNU file has the new date attached to it. If the file date of the MNU file is not updated, AutoCAD will not reconfigure the file to create an updated .MNX file and the menu in the drawing will not be the updated menu. **Note:** Do *not* test the menu since it calls a block named Title and a script file which have not been prepared yet. Use the END command to exit and save the PROTO1 prototype drawing.

3.8   Title-Block Drawing

The PROTO1 menu inserts a drawing of a standard title block into the border drawing. To draw the title block, boot AutoCAD and begin a new drawing named

`\acad\proto\title`

The title block is drawn in millimeters and is illustrated in Figure 3.1. You may wish to draw a different title block than that illustrated. If you do not use millimeter units, you will have to change the insertion scale factor in the PROTO1 menu (if you have reservations about changing the menu, draw the border in millimeter units).

Set the screen limits to suit the size of title block you will be draw-

Figure 3.1   Title block.

ing and set the drawing units to decimal with zero digits to the right of the decimal.

Now use the LAYER and MAKE commands to establish a layer named Border and make it the current layer. Change the color of the layer to green and exit the layer command.

Draw the title block as illustrated in Figure 3.1 (or another if you wish). Prior to adding the headings to the title block, Make another layer called Btext0 (border text zero) and set the color to white. Since the headings are on the Btext0 layer rather than on the text layer, you can plot your drawing on a preprinted sheet simply by turning the Border and Btext0 layers off (and freezing them). Now, using a text height of 4 mm, add the headings illustrated in Figure 3.1.

Variable attributes will be used to tag information input by the user to the title block. Prior to adding the attributes, Make and set the current layer to Btext1 with a color of white. Enter the first attribute as follows:

```
ATTDEF <return>
Attribute modes —
Invisible:N Constant:N Verify:N Preset:N
Enter (ICVP) to change, RETURN when done: v <return>
Attribute modes —
Invisible:N Constant:N Verify:Y Preset:N
Enter (ICVP) to change, RETURN when done: <return>
Attribute tag: project <return>
Attribute prompt: Proj. name (21 letters max.) <return>
Default Attribute value: <return>
Starting point (or ACRS): Digitize the text start point.
Height : 3 <return>
Rotation angle :<return>
```

The attribute tag will appear on the screen in the location of the text. Complete the remaining attributes—for the scale you may wish to use NTS (not to scale) as a default value.

If you use more or less than six attributes, you will have to increase or decrease the backslashes in the PROTO1 menu, which allow user input of the data (refer to the discussion of the SCREEN menu). Since Verify was set on, the number of backslashes required is twice the number of attributes used.

Save the drawing as a WBLOCK file as follows:

```
WBLOCK <return>File name (or ?): \proto\title <return>
Block name: <return>Insertion base point: (Enter the lower right corner
coordinate of your title block.) <return>Select objects:
Window <return> (Place a window around the title block)
```

Use the Quit command to exit the drawing without saving it.

You cannot test your PROTO1 menu until your script file, which is to be created in the next chapter, is completed.

AutoLISP and Menu and Script Files

OBJECTIVE *Introduction to AutoLISP.*
Use AutoLISP expressions in a menu and
script file.

4.1 Introduction to AutoLISP

LISP is a programming language that was developed in 1959 by John McCarthy at MIT for use in programming artificial intelligence. There are numerous dialects of LISP—AutoLISP is one of them.

LISP is an acronym for LISt Processing, which indicates that LISP works with lists. If you keep that in mind as you progress through the AutoLISP sections in this text, the advantages of LISP as a language for programming in AutoCAD will eventually become quite clear. Also, if you keep in mind that LISP is often referred to as an acronym for "Lost In Stupid Parentheses," you will have fewer problems when writing LISP routines.

AutoCAD is written in the C language, which is quite different from LISP. AutoLISP is a language embedded in AutoCAD's ADE-3 package. It allows users to do immediate mode mathematics from the Editor mode (while doing a drawing) and to write programs that do calculations and manipulate AutoCAD commands. The programs may be part of macros within menus, LISP expressions, or user-defined functions that are called by the menu or script file or directly by the drafter. The use of AutoLISP for immediate mode calculations and in the PROTO1.MNU and PROTO1.SCR files written in Chapter 3 will be discussed in this chapter. In Chapter 6 the use of AutoLISP in user-defined functions is introduced.

4.2 Mathematical Primitives

The evaluation technique used by LISP is Hsilop (reverse Polish). Those of you using calculators that work in reverse Polish notation will quickly understand the technique. The remainder of us find it a little strange to get used to at first. All LISP instructions are evaluated as mathematical functions: They take some values, operate on them, and return a value. The function is stated first, then the values to be operated on are stated. The function and its values must be enclosed in parentheses so that they are recognized by the LISP evaluator. The addition of 5 plus 3 looks like this: (+ 5 3). The + is an arithmetic function, and the values to be operated on are 5 and 3. In this text functions predefined by AutoLISP are called "primitives" so they stand out from user-defined functions.

4.2.1 Arithmetic primitives

Some AutoLISP arithmetic primitives (functions) are listed in Table 4.1. Numbers used in arithmetic primitives may be integers or real. Integers are whole numbers such as 2, −35, −32768, and 32767. Integers do *not* contain a decimal point. Real numbers are floating point numbers such as 2.1, −35.0, 0.5167, and −25.67. Real numbers *must* contain a decimal point, and a zero must precede the decimal point of numbers less than 1 (i.e., 0.23) or follow the decimal point for real numbers with no fractional part (i.e., 17.0). In most cases, if one of the numbers in an arithmetic expression is a real number, the value returned by the primitive will be a real number; otherwise an integer will be returned. The exception to this in the primitives listed in Table 4.1 is SQRT, which always returns a real number. Up to Release 9, AutoCAD returned real numbers truncated to seven digits of accuracy and with six digits to the right of the decimal (inserting zeros if necessary). Release 10 returns real numbers rounded with up to six digits.

In order to try some immediate mode arithmetic expressions, boot

TABLE 4.1 Arithmetic Primitives

Primitive	Arithmetic operation
+	Addition
-	Subtraction
*	Multiplication
/	Division
ABS	Returns the absolute value of a number
EXPT	Returns base number raised to the specified power
SQRT	Returns the square root of a number

up AutoCAD and begin a new drawing named x. When the command line appears, enter the following expressions, pressing Enter at the end of each line:

You enter	AutoCAD returns	Release 10 returns
(+ 3 2)	5	5
(+ 3.256 2)	5.256000	5.256
(- 30 20)	10	10
(- -30 20)	-50	-50
(+ 40 20 5.2)	65.200000	65.2
(- 40 20 5.2)	14.800000	14.8
(* 2 3)	6	6
(* 2 3.0 4)	24.00000	24.0
(/ 6 3)	2	2
(/ 24.0 6 2)	2.000000	2.0
(abs 99)	99	99
(abs -99)	99	99
(abs -99.15)	99.150000	99.15
(expt 2 3)	8	8
(expt 2 -3)	0	0
(expt 16 0.5)	4.000000	4.0
(sqrt 16)	4.000000	4.0
(+ 3.0 5 8 12.12	1>	1>

Notice that the result returned for the last expression is 1—providing you typed in the expression exactly as illustrated in the text, leaving out the usual closing parenthesis. The AutoLISP interpreter is informing you that one right parenthesis is required to close the expression. Type in a right parenthesis,), and the result of the expression will be returned as 28.12.

Enter the following expressions (the mathematical representation of the expression is listed also):

You enter	Mathematical equivalent
(* (+ 32 28 12) 4)	$4 * (32 + 28 + 12)$
(/ 560 (* 5 3 2))	$560 / (5 * 3 * 2)$
(/ 560.0 (* 5 3 2))	$560. / (5 * 3 * 2)$
(sqrt (/ (* 72 4) 2))	$((72 * 4) / 2)^{(1/2)}$
(expt 9 (/ 1.0 3))	$9^{(1/3)}$

Note that the results for the first two expressions are integers since each of the data is an integer. In the third expression the decimal point followed by a zero makes the number 560.0 a real number and forces AutoLISP to return a real number. In the last expression, 1.0 is a real number; therefore a real number is returned by AutoLISP.

4.3 AutoLISP Expressions

You have already been working with LISP expressions to solve immediate mode arithmetic problems. It is unlikely, however, that you will do much LISP work in immediate mode. It was included here to introduce you to LISP and illustrate that you do not have to reach for your calculator if you need to solve a mathematical problem when working with AutoCAD. Usually you will use AutoLISP expressions in your menu files, script files, and user-defined functions.

Every LISP expression returns an answer. In some cases the answer will be "nil" or the original data, but in all cases an answer of some form is returned.

4.3.1 SETQ primitive

Data is bound (assigned) to a symbol (variable) by the SETQ primitive (function), which stands for "set quote." (LISP is a very old computer language, and some of the cryptic commands will seem strange. They originally represented a computerese word or phrase which often is now obscure.) SETQ is easier to understand if you think of it as "set equal." The syntax is as follows:

```
(setq a b)
```

The primitive is interpreted as taking the result of B and binding it to the symbol A (or set equal to A the value B). The purpose of this command is to assign data to a symbol for later retrieval. Consider the two AutoLISP expressions:

```
(setq a 5)
(setq b 6)
```

In the first expression the integer 5 is bound to the symbol A. In the second expression the integer 6 is bound to the symbol B. The following expression retrieves the bindings of A and B and returns the integer 11:

```
(+ a b)
```

Scale factor. In your PROTO1 menu written in Chapter 3 you initially select a plot-sheet size. The menu macro draws a border, inserts a title block, saves the drawing as a block, and activates a submenu from which you select the drawing units. That selection activates another submenu from which you may select a plot scale.

Line 57 of the PROTO1 menu in Chapter 3 is as follows:

```
57:[1:10](setq f 0.01);script;/acad/proto/proto1;
```

The LISP expression (setq f 0.01) binds the value of 0.01 to the symbol F. The value bound to F is a scale factor and is calculated using Equation (4.1):

$$f = \frac{\text{drawing increment}}{\text{plot increment}} \tag{4.1}$$

The plot increment is in inches or millimeters, and the drawing increment is in the drawing units.

For the scale of 1:10 in line 57 of the menu, the following applies:

1. Drawing units are meters (this submenu is "called" at line 38 of the menu where the drafter has selected [meters]).

2. The ratio of 1:10 means that a 1-mm increment on the plot is to contain 10-mm increments of the drawing.

3. Since the drawing units are meters, the drawing increment of 10 mm is converted to meters giving 10 / 1000 = 0.01 meters (1000 mm = 1 m).

Using Equation (4.1), the scale factor is

$$f = \frac{\text{drawing increment}}{\text{plot increment}}$$
$$= \frac{0.01}{1}$$
$$= 0.01$$

Continuing the macro in line 57, the AutoCAD SCRIPT command is invoked to load a script with the path /ACAD/PROTO/PROTO1. The PROTO1 *script* is discussed in detail in Section 4.4.

Multiple symbol binding.   In line 7 (which is a continuation of line 4) of the PROTO1 *menu* the LISP SETQ function is used to bind the drawing border width and height to the symbols W and H, respectively. The assignment function appears as follows:

```
(setq w 277 h 181)
```

In this expression the SETQ command is used once to bind values to two symbols. As usual, the entire LISP function is enclosed within parentheses. A similar function is used in lines 11, 16, and 21.

Text height and metric conversion factor.   Line 38 in the menu is as follows:

```
38: [meters](setq txt 2.5 conv 25.4);$s=m
```

The LISP expression binds the desired text height of 2.5 mm to the symbol TXT and binds the metric conversion factor 25.4 to the symbol CONV. The conversion factor is required when calculating the LTSCALE (linetype scale) setting [see Equation (1.4)] later in the PROTO1 script file.

Nesting LISP expressions. LISP expressions may also be nested (one expression placed inside another). This is illustrated in line 99 of the PROTO1 menu, where the symbol TXT is assigned the value of 3/32 (for a text height of 3/32 in). The division expression is nested within the SETQ expression. This is also a multiple expression since the integer 1 is bound to the symbol CONV in the same expression:

```
99: [arch/eng](setq txt (/ 3.0 32) conv 1);$s=a
```

The expression (/ 3.0 32) is nested inside the (setq txt value...) expression. Notice that each expression is enclosed in parentheses. Since you want to have a real number returned from the division, one of the values is entered as a real number, i.e., 3.0. The LISP evaluator returns the result for the calculation of 3/32 as 0.093750. If both numbers in the expression were integers, the value returned by the LISP evaluator would be 0. The value bound to CONV is 1 as specified in Section 1.4.

In line 101, civil engineering units are selected. The text height of 3/32 in is bound to the symbol TXT and the value 1 is bound to CONV as specified for Imperial units in Section 1.4. The macro calls a subroutine named c where the units are based on the format 1 in = n ft (i.e., 1 in = 20 ft):

```
101: [civ-eng](setq txt (/ 3.0 32) conv 1);$s=c
```

4.3.2   Variable names (symbols)

In the preceding LISP expressions, the symbols (variable names) TXT, F, W, H, and CONV are used. A symbol can be any set of alphanumeric characters providing the first character is alphabetic. (AutoLISP's built-in functions should not be used as symbols. These are discussed in other chapters.)

The symbol PI is preset to the value 3.1415926 and may be used in your expressions just like variables you have assigned yourself. Two other symbols that are preset are T (true) and NIL. They should not be assigned other values.

4.3.3   User input primitives

There are a series of primitives that may be used to get input from the user. Each primitive begins with the word GET, followed by the type of variable to get, and an optional prompt. In AutoLISP, there are four basic variable types: integer numbers, real numbers, text strings, and points.

The syntax of four basic GETxxx primitives is as follows:

Variable type	Input syntax
Real number	(getreal [prompt])
Integer number	(getint [prompt])
Text string	(getstring [T] [prompt])
2-D or 3-D point	(getpoint [prompt])

The [prompt] is an optional string (text) displayed to prompt the user to input the data. GETSTRING also has an optional flag [T]. If T is included, the input string may include spaces. An example of a GETSTRING primitive is

```
(getstring T ''What is your name? '')
```

If you wish to save the data entered in response to the GETxxx expression, it is nested into a SETQ expression as follows:

```
(setq name (getstring T ''What is your name? ''))
```

The GETSTRING primitive requests the user's name, which is then bound to the symbol NAME by the SETQ primitive. Since the optional flag T is included, the user may use the space bar to place a space between the first and last name. The string must be entered by pressing the Return key.

AutoLISP includes a number of other GETxxx input primitives which are used to input items such as distances, angles, system variables, etc. They are listed in your *AutoLISP Programmer's Reference Manual*.

In line 69 of the PROTO1 *menu* an expression is to be included to allow the user to input a scale other than those included in the options. The line is as follows:

```
69: [1:n ](setq f1 (getreal ''Scale Factor 1: ''));\+
70: (setq f (/ f1 1000));script;/acad/proto/proto1;
```

Line 70 is an extension of line 69. It is an extra line added to the menu and is not counted as one of the 20 menu lines in the submenu. The LISP expression (setq f1 (getreal "Scale factor n: ")) assigns to the symbol F1 the real number input by the user in response to the GETREAL command. The message "Scale Factor 1: " is displayed to prompt the user to input a specific piece of data. The semicolon following the closing parenthesis of the first expression enters the function and is important, and, unfortunately, easy to forget. The backslash (\) following the semicolon causes AutoCAD to pause and accept input of the data requested by the GET primitive. The backslash is required only when a GETxxx primitive is used in a *menu*. It is not required when a GETxxx primitive is used in a *script* file or a user-defined function.

The + at the end of line 69 indicates to AutoCAD that the macro continues on the next line. The LISP expression (setq f (/ f1 1000)) binds to the symbol F the result of the value assigned to F1 divided by 1000.

Equation (4.1) is used to determine the scale factor F. The number entered by the user in response to GETREAL is bound to the symbol F1 and represents a scale ratio of 1:F1. The ratio 1:F1 means that 1 mm of the plot contains F1 mm of the drawing. Since the drawing is done in meters, the drawing increment must be in meters; consequently F1 is to be divided by 1000. The scale factor, F, is

$$F = \frac{\text{drawing increment}}{\text{plot increment}}$$

$$= \frac{(F1/1000)}{1}$$

$$= \frac{F1}{1000}$$

Note the use of parentheses around each of the expressions in lines 69 and 70. You must have exactly the same number of closing and opening parentheses.

Write the macro for line 92 (this was line 91 prior to the extension of line 69 onto line 70) of your PROTO1 menu to allow the user to enter the scale factor. The menu title is [1:n]. Your new macro for line 92 will extend onto a new line 93. The drawing units are millimeters, and the border is drawn in millimeters; hence the scale factor F is equal to the value n, input by the user. The correct macro is illustrated at the end of this section.

In line 132 in your menu (this was line 130 prior to the insertion of lines 70 and 93), the drawing units are AutoCAD's architectural or engineering units. Although you can enter data into the drawing using feet units, i.e., 3', AutoCAD uses the data internally in inches. To illustrate the determination of a scale factor F by Equation (4.1), a scale of ¼ in = 1 ft is used:

Plot increment = ¼ in = 0.125

Drawing increment = 1 × 12   (drawing units are in inches)

$$F = \frac{\text{drawing increment}}{\text{plot increment}}$$

$$= \frac{12}{0.125}$$

$$= 48$$

Line 132 is as follows (note that it extends onto a new line, 133):

```
132: [n'' = 1'](setq fl (getreal ''Decimal scale factor n: ''));\+
133: (setq f (/ 12 fl));script;/acad/proto/proto1;
```

Write the macro for line 153 of your menu (this was line 150 prior to the insertion of lines 70, 93, and 133). In this line the scale factor Fl is equal to the value entered by the user, so you do not need to use the symbol F1.

If you have not already done so, load EDLIN and add the lines listed below to your \ACAD\PROTO\PROTO1.MNU file. Before doing so, remember you should have entered the current date when booting your system so that DOS will update the date attached to the PROTO1.MNU file. If the date attached to the file is not updated, AutoCAD will not recompile the menu when you next load it. If the file is not recompiled, AutoCAD will load the old version into the drawing editor. The lines are:

```
69: [1:n ](setq fl (getreal ''Scale Factor 1: ''));\+
70: (setq f (/ fl 1000));script;/acad/proto/proto1;
93: [1:n ](setq f (getreal ''Scale Factor 1: ''));\+
94: script;/acad/proto/proto1;
132: [n'' = 1'](setq fl (getreal ''Decimal scale Factor n = ''));\+
133: (setq f (/ 12 fl));script;/acad/proto/proto1;
153: [1'' = n'](setq f (getreal ''Scale Factor n = ''));\+
154: script;/acad/proto/proto1;
```

4.4 PROTO1 Script File

A script file is a text file with the extension .SCR. It contains a list of AutoCAD commands incorporating a sequence of drawing operations and/or AutoLISP expressions that are executed sequentially by AutoCAD.

The script file may be written using EDLIN. The syntax for writing script files is different in many ways from that used in menu files. In both, a space invokes the Enter key; however, the semicolon does *not* invoke the Enter key in a script file. Other menu file commands such as \ (user input) and + also do not apply to script files. Unlike menu files, script files can be read by AutoCAD *both* within the drawing editor and after control has returned to the Main menu. Hence the script file can issue commands to exit the drawing editor, start a new drawing, set plotting parameters, and plot a drawing (see Appendix G). It can also be used to invoke other programs with the AutoCAD SHELL command. A script file cannot invoke a macro, but it can call LISP functions (to be discussed in later chapters).

The PROTO1.MNU *menu* file calls a PROTO1.SCR *script* file to issue a series of AutoCAD commands. The script file is being used as a subroutine called by a number of different macros in the menu file rather than including the series of commands in each macro. After completion of the sequence of commands in the script file, control returns to the macro in the menu that called the script. Since there are no further operations in the macro calling our script file, control is subsequently returned to the user.

Review of the PROTO1 menu process

Lines 4 to 7, inclusive, of the PROTO1 menu file, contain commands to draw a border to suit the paper size selected. The title-block drawing named Title is inserted into the border drawing, and the entire drawing is saved as a block named B2. Finally, a LISP function is used to assign the border width and height dimensions to the variables W and H, respectively, and a submenu is called.

The submenu displays drawing-unit options. The user selects the drawing units, and another submenu with drawing scale options is activated. When a drawing scale is selected, a scale factor is bound to the symbol F using an AutoLISP SETQ expression. The PROTO1 script file, PROTO1.SCR, is then loaded.

The script file is developed in stages. The complete file listing is at the end of this chapter.

4.4.1 Atoms and lists

LISP was developed to manipulate lists. An atom is the fundamental data element that lists are composed of, and it is simply a computer word that may be used to represent a character or a number. A *list* is composed of a group of atoms and may even contain other lists.

Previously you were dealing with real numbers and integer numbers. Those data are atoms. If you wish to define a 2-D point on the screen, you will have to specify its X and Y coordinates. The point is composed of two atoms (two real numbers) and is a *list*.

4.4.2 LIST primitive

Macros in the PROTO1 *menu* have bound the drawing border width, height, and scale factor to the symbols W, H, and F, respectively, and the desired plot text height has been bound to the symbol TXT. Each of these bindings is to be recalled in the PROTO1 *script* file.

The lower left screen limit is defined by a 2-D coordinate pair of real numbers 0.0,0.0. The upper right corner of the screen may be defined by the coordinate point X,Y, where X is equal to the border width W times the scale factor F and Y is equal to the border height H times F. After X and Y have been calculated, they are grouped together to form a list (or point) using the LIST primitive. The format of LIST is as follows:

```
(list a b)
```

The first segment of the PROTO1 script is to set the screen limits as follows:

```
1: (setq x (* f w) y (* f h))
2: (setq p (list x y))
3: limits 0,0 !p zoom all
```

The multiple, nested SETQ expression in line 1 binds to the symbol X the product of the scale factor F times the border width W and binds to the symbol Y the scale factor F times the border height H. In line 2 the LIST command is used to produce a list composed of the two atoms X and Y defining the upper right corner for the scaled screen limits. The resulting point is bound to the symbol P.

In line 3, the LIMITS command is invoked. The lower left corner is set as point 0,0, and the upper right corner is set as the coordinate list bound to the symbol P. Notice that an exclamation mark (!) is placed in front of the symbol P (see Section 4.4.3). The ZOOM-All commands are then used to zoom the monitor to the scaled screen limits.

4.4.3   Variable recall and !

Whenever a variable is called (referenced) outside of an expression, it must be preceded by an exclamation mark. In line 1 of the PROTO1 script listing, the symbol F is referenced within an expression and is not preceded with an exclamation mark. In line 3, however, the symbol P is referenced outside of a LISP expression—in response to an AutoCAD command—and must be preceded by an exclamation mark.

In the next line of the script the block B2 containing the border and title block is to be inserted into the drawing. The insertion point is 0,0, and the block insertion x- and y-scale factors equal the scale factor bound to the symbol F. Since the symbol is being referenced outside of a LISP expression, it must be preceded with !. The rotation angle is 0 degrees. You are to write line 4. The complete script file is listed in Appendix D.

4.4.4   System variables

AutoCAD system variables are the various modes, limit values, and unit values currently active in the drawing editor. A listing of

AutoCAD's system variables is illustrated in Appendix B of this text and Appendix A of your *AutoCAD Reference Manual.*

System variables can be set directly from the drawing editor (while drawing) or from a script or menu file using the SETVAR command. The format of AutoCAD's SETVAR command is

```
SETVAR <return>
Variable name or ?:
```

If you reply with ?, AutoCAD flips to the text screen and displays the names and current values of all system variables. Some of the system variables are "read only" and cannot be changed. If you enter the name of a system variable that is not read only, AutoCAD will respond with

```
New value for variable name <current value>:
```

You may enter a new value for the system variable selected. If the system variable selected is read only, AutoCAD will display its current value and you will not be asked for a new value.

In lines 38, 39, 99, 101, and 103 of the PROTO1 *menu* file, the symbol TXT is assigned a value equal to the text height desired in the final plot. Equation 4.2 may be used to set the *screen* text height:

$$STXT = F \times TXT \tag{4.2}$$

STXT = screen text height
   F = scale factor
TXT = plot-text height

The system variable TEXTSIZE is a real number that specifies the drawing default text height and is set using the SETVAR command as illustrated in line 5 of the PROTO1 *script* file:

```
5: (setq stxt (* f txt)) setvar textsize !stxt
```

The symbols F and TXT are referenced within a LISP expression and are not preceded with an exclamation mark. The symbol STXT is referenced outside of an expression to set the system variable TEXTSIZE and is preceded by an exclamation mark.

Equation (1.4) is used to determine the linetype scale factor:

$$LTSCALE = 0.75 \times Conv/Plot \text{ ratio}$$

LTSCALE = linetype scale factor
    Conv = 1 for Imperial units and 25.4 for SI units
Plot ratio = inverse of scale factor F
        = $\frac{1}{f}$ (also see Section 1.4)

The system variable LTSCALE defines the default linetype scale setting.

System variables may also be set using AutoLISP's SETVAR function. The syntax is as follows:

```
(setvar <varname> <value>)
```

The LTSCALE system variable is set in the PROTO1 *script* file as follows:

```
6: (setvar ''ltscale'' (* 0.75 conv f))
```

Note that when the SETVAR command is used in an AutoLISP expression, the variable name must be enclosed in quotation marks.

You are to write a LISP expression for line 7 of the script to set the DIMSCALE system variable (Release 9 and 10 only) using Equation (1.2).

In Ver. 2.6 of AutoCAD DIMSCALE is not a system variable and must be set using AutoCAD commands in the *script* file. If you are using Ver. 2.6, calculate the DIMSCALE value using Equation (1.2) and bind it to the symbol DIMS. Then, in the next line of the *script* file write commands to invoke the DIM command and set DIMSCALE equal to the value bound to the symbol DIMS. After DIMSCALE is set, the DIM command will have to be exited. This is be done by adding the AutoCAD command EXIT to the end of the line.

Complete the script file by adding lines to set the current layer to 0. The LAYER command is exited by following it with a blank line, which invokes Enter. Control characters such as ^C, which may be used in a menu, cannot be used in a script file, which only accepts valid AutoCAD commands. The last line of the script calls the standard ACAD menu. The listing should be similar to that listed below:

```
 1: (setq x (* f w) y (* f h))
 2: (setq p (list x y))
 3: limits 0,0 !p zoom all
 4: insert b2 0,0 !f !f 0
 5: (setq stxt (* f txt)) setvar textsize !stxt
 6: (setvar ''ltscale'' (* 0.75 conv f))
 7: (setvar ''dimscale'' (/ stxt 0.18))
 8: layer set 0
 9:
10: menu acad
```

The following changes are to be made if you are using Ver. 2.6 of AutoCAD:

```
 7: (setq dims (/ stxt 0.18))
 8: dim dimscale !dims exit
 9: layer set 0
10:
11: menu acad
```

In Ver. 2.62, although the system variable TEXTSIZE can be assigned values, AutoCAD does not seem to read the value assigned. Check this with your version. If it does not work, you can use the AutoCAD TEXT command to set the text height by modifying the script as follows:

```
11: text 1,1 !stxt 0
12: erase L
13:
14: menu acad
```

In line 11 the TEXT command is invoked with a start point of 1,1, a text height equal to the value bound to STXT, and a rotation angle of 0. The text height bound to STXT is now the default text height. In line 12 the ERASE-LAST commands are invoked. The blank line, 13, is required to exit the ERASE command.

4.4.5   Add PROTO1.MNU to the prototype drawing

When you have completed the PROTO1 script file, boot AutoCAD and edit the PROTO1 drawing which you created in Section 3.5. Use the MENU command to change the menu from the ACAD menu to the new PROTO1 menu you created, and then END the drawing. Your PROTO1 prototype drawing is now complete. (Until we find other items to add later.)

Test the PROTO1 *menu* and *script* files thoroughly in test drawings by using the various drawing sizes and scales.

Assignment. AutoCAD has two system variables that can be used to set the drawing units mode and decimal places:

LUNITS   linear   units   mode   (1 = scientific,   2 = decimal, 3 = engineering, 4 = architectural, 5 = fractional)

LUPREC   linear units decimal places or denominator

These variables may be set using the SETVAR command discussed in Section 4.4.4.

1. Edit the PROTO1 *script* file and use the SETVAR command to set the drawing units and precision by inserting a new line 10 (line 14 with Ver. 2.6). Assume the variable UNTS contains the LUNITS integer and the variable PRECISE contains the LUPREC integer (these variables will be assigned their values in the PROTO1 *menu* in assignment 3).

2. The cursor coordinate display may be activated by the system variable COORDS. If COORDS is 0, the coordinate display is updated on point picks only. If it is 1, the display is continuously updated, and if it is 2, distance and angle from last point are displayed when a dis-

tance or angle is requested. Continue line 10 (line 14 with Ver. 2.6) in the PROTO1 *script* file using the SETVAR command to set the COORDS system variable to continuously update the coordinate display.

3. Edit the PROTO1 *menu* file to bind data to the symbols UNTS and PRECISE, which are used in the script file in assignment 1:

   a. In the SI drawing units submenu, if the drafter selects meters, the symbol UNTS is to be assigned the integer 2 (for decimal units) and PRECISE is to be assigned the integer 2 (for two digits to the right of the decimal). If the drafter selects millimeters, UNTS and PRECISE are to be set for decimal units with zero digits to the right of the decimal. Modify the LISP expressions in lines 38 and 39 of the PROTO1 *menu* file using the existing SETQ primitive to also assign the specified integers to UNTS and PRECISE.

   b. In the Imperial units submenu, if the drafter selects [civ-eng] or [mech-eng], the units are to be decimal, i.e., UNTS is assigned the integer 2. The number of digits to the right of the decimal point is to be requested from the user by a GETINT primitive and assigned to the symbol PRECISE. Add the UNTS and PRE-CISE expressions to the macros.

   c. If the drafter selects [arch/eng], another submenu named **ae is to be activated instead of the **a submenu. The **ae submenu is to present two options, [Architec] and [Engineer], for AutoCAD's architectural units (for example, 1'-3 ½") or engineering units (1'-3.50").

If the drafter selects [Engineer], the symbol UNTS is to be assigned the integer 3, and the SETQ and GETINT primitives are to be used to get from the drafter the number of digits to the right of the decimal and to assign the input to the symbol PRECISE. At the end of the macro the **a submenu, which lists the architectural and engineering units scale options, is to be called.. If the drafter selects [Architec], the symbol UNTS is to be assigned the integer 4; however, the fraction of inches to be bound to the symbol PRECISE cannot be entered directly. A conversion is necessary since the LUPREC system variable stores the fraction as a power of 2 (because of the digital system used by computers). The integers assigned to LUPREC for the desired fraction are listed in Table 4.2. To accommodate the conversion, extend the [Architec] macro to call a submenu labeled **arch. The arch submenu is to list the fraction option titles, such as:

```
[none ]
[1/2'']
[1/4'']
```

Each option is to invoke an AutoLISP expression which binds the

TABLE 4.2   LUPREC Values for Arch/Eng Units

Denominator	Fraction	Number in LUPREC	Logic
1	0	0	$2^0 = 1$
2	½	1	$2^{1^1} = 2$
4	¼	2	$2^{2^2} = 4$
8	⅛	3	$2^{3^3} = 8$
16	1/16	4	$2^{4^4} = 16$
32	1/32	5	$2^{5^5} = 32$
64	1/64	6	$2^{6^6} = 64$

LUPREC number indicated in Table 4.2 to the symbol PRECISE. After the assignment, the submenu name **a is to be activated.

4. When assignments 1 to 3 are complete, test the prototype menu again. When beginning a test drawing, remember that you may give the drawing any name except PROTO1 since that is the name of our prototype drawing. The complete listing of both the PROTO1 menu and PROTO1 script files for this chapter are listed in Appendix D.

4.4.6 Plotting

When plotting drawings, if you specify the plot-sheet size equal to the frame dimensions used in the PROTO1 menu, you can use the FIT option for the scale, and the drawing will be plotted exactly to scale. For instance, if you selected [A-HOR] in the PROTO1.MNU, you should specify the plot-sheet size as 10.0,7.25 (see Table 3.2) when entering the plot specifications. Then enter the FIT option for the plot scale. To fit the border on the sheet you may have to specify a plot origin other than 0,0. This can be determined from a trial plot. Consider using a plot script file in a similar manner to that discussed in Appendix G.

AutoLISP Functions

OBJECTIVE   *Construct AutoLISP
procedures using DEFUN; create an
AutoLISP "screen-print" utility and a
"yes-no" response utility routine for
application in programs; use the following
new primitives: GETDIST, FOREACH,
PRINC, STRCASE, IF, WHILE, NOT,
MEMBER, PROMPT, GETKWORD, and
INITGET; and control characters.*

5.1 Defined Functions

One of the primary advantages of LISP is that it allows hierarchical
program layering. The programmer does this by developing procedures to perform primary functions. Those procedures may then be
embedded into higher-level procedures, and so on, thereby developing
a complex process from a combination of lower-level procedures.
AutoCAD also has built-in procedures, called primitives, that can be
incorporated into the program. If you are writing a program to draw a
rectangle at a given angle you might:

Create procedure A to convert a given angle from degrees to radians
(AutoCAD works internally with radians).

Create procedure B to accept input of the corners of the rectangle
and the angle of a side. This procedure would call procedure A to
change the given angle from degrees to radians.

Create a final procedure, C, that invokes B and uses AutoCAD's
built-in procedure to draw the desired rectangle.

If you are to plot a survey traverse, a similar process might be used
to input the data, make survey corrections, and draw the traverse (see
Chapter 8).

In LISP, procedures are established by the DEFUN (DEFine FUNction) primitive. The syntax of DEFUN is as follows:

```
(defun <symbol> <argument list> <expression>...)
```

DEFUN defines a function with the name <symbol>. It has an
<argument list>, which may be void or contain global variables
and/or local variables. The <expression> is the procedure that is to be
processed when the function is called. The function begins with a left
parenthesis and ends with a right parenthesis.

A function name is not case sensitive and may be any set of alphanumeric characters providing the first character is alphabetic. Never
use the name of an AutoLISP primitive (built-in function) since this
will make the primitive inaccessible.

5.1.1 Function argument list

The function's <argument list> may contain a list of arguments and/or
local symbols enclosed within a set of parentheses. If local symbols are to
be defined, they must follow any argument symbols and be preceded by a
slash. If no arguments or local symbols are to be defined, an empty set of
parentheses must be supplied after the function name. For example:

```
(defun myfunc (a b)...)        Takes two arguments A and B
(defun myfunc (a b / c)...)    Takes two arguments A and B and one
                                  local symbol, C
(defun myfunc (/ c)...)        Takes one local symbol C
(defun myfunc ()...)           Has no arguments or local symbols
```

Function arguments and argument symbols.   Arguments are data that is
to be transferred to the function when it is invoked. Argument symbols are the symbols in the <argument list> to which the arguments
transferred to the function are bound. The arguments are used in the
function expression (procedure that is to be processed by the function).
For example, the following function takes two arguments A and B:

```
(defun adder (a b)
   (+ a b)
)
```

Since ADDER takes two arguments, you must provide values for those
arguments when invoking the function. To invoke the ADDER function and bind the integer 5 to the symbol A and the integer 3 to the
symbol B you enter:

```
(adder 5 3)
```

The expression is evaluated as follows and returns the integer 8:

```
(+  5 3)
```

The arguments can also be transferred to the function as variables. For instance: ((setq x 5 y 3) (adder x y)) binds the integer 5 to X and the integer 3 to Y. When the ADDER function is invoked, the current binding of X is bound to A and the current binding of Y is bound to B. The expression returns the integer 8.

Variables defined in the functions argument list are "bound variables" and even though their value may be changed in the expression, their initial value is restored on exit from the procedure. Variables not defined in the argument list are "free variables" (or global variables) and if assigned a new value by the expression, they retain that value after the function is exited. For example, in the following function the variables A, B, and X are bound whereas C is free:

```
(defun test (a b x)
   (setq c (+ a x)
   (setq a (+ a b)
   (setq b (+ c a)
   (setq x (* b x)
)
```

It is not necessary to place each expression on a new line and to tab, as illustrated in this example. The indentation and line breaks, however, serve to make the structure of the program clearer and more readable and is called "pretty printing."

Prior to invoking the function, the following bindings are to be made using AutoLISP's SETQ primitive:

```
(setq a 1.5 b 2.0 c 3.0)
```

The TEST function takes three arguments when it is invoked. If you wish to bind the current outside binding of A to the symbol A (in the function), the current outside binding of B to the symbol B, and the real number 3.0 to the symbol X, invoke the function as follows:

```
(test a b 3.0)
```

AutoLISP returns 24.0 (or 24.000000 depending on your version). The evaluation of the TEST function is as follows (remember, initially A = 1.5, B = 2.0, and X = 3.0). The bold text is the internal binding:

```
(setq c (+  1.5 3.0))    c = 4.5
(setq a (+  1.5 2.0))    a = 3.5
(setq b (+  4.5 3.5))    b = 8.0
(setq x (*  8.0 3.0))    x = 24.0
```

AutoLISP returns the result of the last expression evaluated, 24.0, which is the current binding of X. If the variables are recalled, the following values are returned (to recall an AutoLISP variable outside an expression, the symbol is preceded by !):

!c   Returns 4.5, the value bound to C in the expression since C is a free variable.

!a   Returns 1.5, the initial value bound to A, since A is a bound variable.

!b   Returns 2.0 since B is a bound variable.

!x   Returns nil since X is a bound variable and its initial value was nil. The real number 3.0 was assigned to X when the function was invoked and 24.0 was assigned to it during evaluation. When the expression is completed, X is reassigned its outer level binding.

Local symbols.   Local symbols are listed in the function argument list *preceded* by a slash. Unlike function arguments, local symbols are not assigned values when invoking a function. They are used as temporary assignments within the function and, when the function is exited, are reassigned their outer level binding. The following DRW-LINE function has two local symbols, PT1 and PT2:

```
(defun drw-line (/ pt1 pt2)
    (setq pt1 (getpoint ''Select start of line: \n''))
    (setq pt2 (getpoint ''Select end of line: \n''))
    (command ''line'' pt1 pt2 '''') )
```

The local symbols may have data bound to them prior to the DWR-LINE function being invoked. That binding is referred to as their outer binding. If they do not have a value bound to them, their outer binding is nil. When the function is invoked, they take on a new binding—in this case, the start and end points of a line. When the function is exited, the local symbols are reassigned their outer binding. Do not worry about the details of the DRW-LINE function now. The other commands used in the function will be discussed later in this chapter.

Many programmers do not define local symbols when they are not used elsewhere in the program. It is, however, a worthwhile effort to do so, because upon exiting the procedure, the symbols are then reassigned their outer level binding of nil and hence do not take up memory space.

5.2   LOAD Primitive

The LOAD primitive is used to load a file of AutoLISP expressions and evaluate those expressions. The syntax is as follows:

```
(load <filename>[<onfailure>])
```

The <filename> may include the file path. As will be seen later in this text, the backslash (\) indicates a control character to AutoLISP, so to indicate a directory path a forward slash (/) is used. To load a LISP file named TEST.LSP from a subdirectory of the ACAD directory named LISP, the DOS path is \ACAD\LISP\TEST. The file is loaded using:

```
(load ''/acad/lisp/test'')
```

Note that you do not include the .LSP extension in the file name, and the file name is enclosed in quotation marks.

If the LOAD operation fails, it normally causes an AutoLISP error. If the optional Release 10 <onfailure> argument is supplied, LOAD returns the value of this argument on failure instead of failing.

5.3 AutoLISP Files

An AutoLISP file is a text file with the extension .LSP. It may be created using EDLIN or any text editor or word processor that does not place extra coding in the text. For example, an AutoLISP function named HYPOT is to be written to calculate the hypotenuse of a right-angle triangle using the pythagorean theorem: $c = \sqrt{(a^2 + b^2)}$. It will be written to a file named PYTHAG.LSP, which will have the path \ACAD\LISP\PYTHAG.LSP.

Prior to beginning this example, boot DOS and use the MD (Make Directory) command to create a subdirectory of ACAD named LISP as follows:

```
C:\>cd\acad
C:\ACAD>md lisp
```

Now log onto the directory where EDLIN is located and load EDLIN to write to a file named PYTHAG.LSP. If EDLIN is in the root directory, enter the following:

```
C:\ACAD>cd\
C:>edlin\acad\lisp\pythag.lsp
New file
*i
    1: (defun hypot (/ a b)
    2: (setq a (getdist ''Base length: ''))
    3: (setq b (getdist ''Rise: ''))
    4: (setq c (sqrt (+ (* a a)(* b b))))
    5: )
    6: ^c (Ctrl-C)
*e
```

The HYPOT function has no arguments since the expression will request sides A and B of the triangle from the drafter using AutoLISP's GETDIST function. Both A and B are declared as local symbols because their value is not required after the procedure is exited, at which time they will be assigned their previous binding of nil. The hypotenuse is calculated and assigned to the symbol C. It is not declared as a local symbol so that its value can be used after the function is exited.

5.3.1 GETDIST primitive

The HYPOT function uses the AutoLISP GETDIST primitive. The syntax of the GETDIST primitive is:

```
(getdist [<pt>] [<prompt>])
```

When invoked, this expression pauses for input of a distance which may be entered from the keyboard, or AutoLISP may be shown the distance by pointing to two locations on the graphics screen. The <pt> is an optional base point, the drafter has only to point to the second location on the graphics screen, and <prompt> is an optional string to be displayed as a prompt.

To continue the example, boot AutoCAD and begin a new drawing named TEST. Load the PYTHAG.LSP file from the drawing editor as follows:

```
(load ''/acad/lisp/pythag'')
```

AutoLISP loads the file and evaluates the expression, returning the value of the last expression evaluated, which in this case is the HYPOT function. When a function is evaluated, the name of the function is returned by AutoLISP:

```
HYPOT
```

If an error is indicated, AutoLISP returns the name of the file, and you will have to either exit AutoCAD and reload EDLIN from DOS or, if you completed the tasks outlined in Section 2.3, you can load EDLIN from within AutoCAD as follows (you could have written the PYTHAG.LSP file from within AutoCAD this way also):

```
EDLIN    (or EDIT)
File to edit: \acad\lisp\pythag.lsp
End of input file
*
```

Correct the file as required. If you loaded EDLIN from within AutoCAD, you will be returned to the AutoCAD drawing editor when EDLIN is exited. If not, reboot AutoCAD and return to the drawing named TEST.

5.3.2 Invoking a function

If you made corrections to the PYTHAG.LSP file, reload it prior to invoking HYPOT. To invoke the HYPOT function enter:

```
(hypot)
```

AutoLISP evaluates the HYPOT function, pausing for user input at the GETDIST primitives, and returns the last assignment (the real number bound to C—which is the hypotenuse):

```
Base length:4
Rise:3
5.0    (or 5.000000)
```

Even though integers were entered for the base length and rise, a real number is returned by AutoLISP since both the GETDIST and SQRT primitives always return a real number. Try the function again. This time specify the distances by pointing on the screen. Note the syntax of the command line when doing so.

You have completed your first AutoLISP program. That wasn't so hard, was it?

Assignment. Reload EDLIN from within AutoCAD or by exiting AutoCAD, and add another function to the PYTHAG.LSP file to solve for one side of a right-angle triangle given the other side and the hypotenuse. The equation is: $a = \sqrt{(c^2 - b^2)}$. The function is to be added to the file in the line immediately below the HYPOT function. When the file is complete, reload the PYTHAG.LSP file, which now contains two functions. Either function may be invoked by entering its name surrounded by parenthesis.

Although an AutoLISP file may contain a number of different functions, you should not put all of your LISP functions in one large file. To load one function you would have to load the entire file and may be using up a lot of memory space.

5.4   PRINLIST Utility Function

The following function is useful in numerous AutoLISP programs. Such functions are referred to as utility functions. The HYPOT function would be improved with a descriptive output. A print function is created to display a list of items on the screen. Using EDLIN, write the following PRINLIST function to the file \ACAD\LISP\ UTILITY.LSP:

```
; PRINLIST prints a LIST of items to the monitor
; Syntax: (prinlist (list <exp> ...))
(defun prinlist (args / a)
   (foreach a args
      (princ a)) ()
)
```

The first two lines in the program are comment lines. Any text following a semicolon is ignored by the LISP evaluator. It is good housekeeping to incorporate comments throughout a program to improve its readability. The PRINLIST function is discussed in detail in the following sections.

This function takes one argument, ARGS, and has one local symbol, A. When the function is invoked, an argument has to be passed to it and is bound to the symbol ARGS. For instance, the function could be invoked as follows: (prinlist "hello"). The string argument "hello" is bound to the symbol ARGS, and the function prints hello. If the desired output of the HYPOT function is Hypotenuse: 5.0, where 5.0 is a real number calculated by the HYPOT function, the expression to be added to the HYPOT function to invoke your PRINLIST function is

```
(prinlist (list ''\nHypotenuse: '' c ''\n''))
```

The HYPOT function listing is now

```
(defun hypot (/ a b)
   (setq a (getdist ''Base length: ''))
   (setq b (getdist ''Rise: ''))
   (setq c (sqrt ( +  (* a a)(* b b))))
   (prinlist (list ''\nHypotenuse: '' c ''\n''))
)
```

In this new line the result of the expression (list "\nHypotenuse: " c "\n") becomes the argument that is passed to the PRINLIST function and bound to the symbol ARGS. You now have a function, HYPOT, that invokes another function, PRINLIST.

5.4.1 LIST primitive

The LIST primitive takes any number of expressions and strings them together. The syntax is

```
(list <expression> ... )
```

The LIST primitive is used in the HYPOT function to string together a list of expressions as elements of a new list which is transferred to the PRINLIST function as an argument to be bound to the symbol ARGS. For instance, if the real number 5.0 is bound to the symbol C, (list "\nHypotenuse: " c "\n") returns ("\nHypotenuse: " 5.0 "\n") as a list composed of three elements.

5.4.2 Control characters

Characters enclosed by double quotes (" ") are interpreted as a literal string. A character preceded by a backslash in a literal string is interpreted as a control character code. Some codes currently recognized are

\\	means the character "\"
\e	means escape
\n	means newline

\r   means return and

\t   means tab

Note: Do not *use* control characters in LISP expressions that are used in AutoCAD *menu* files. In a menu file the backslash is reserved for user input and is not recognized as a symbol for a control character code.

5.4.3 FOREACH and PRINC primitives

The AutoLISP primitive FOREACH is used in our PRINLIST function. The syntax of FOREACH is

```
(foreach <name> <list> <expression> . . . .)
```

The primitive steps through <list>, assigning each element to <name>, and evaluates each <expression> for every element in the list.

In the HYPOT function, the PRINLIST function is invoked using (prinlist (list "\nHypotenuse: " c "\n")). Assuming the HYPOT function has bound 5.0 to the symbol C, (list "\nHypotenuse: " c "\n") becomes (list "\nHypotenuse: " 5.0 "\n"). The LIST primitive returns ("\nHypotenuse: " 5.0 "\n"), which is passed to the PRINLIST function and bound to the symbol ARGS.

In the expression (foreach a args (princ a)) the symbol A is sequentially assigned each element of the list bound to ARGS and the expression (princ a) is invoked. This is equivalent to

```
(princ ''\nHypotenuse: '')
(princ 5.0)
(princ ''\n'')
```

The output process is as follows:

The PRINC primitive edits the "\n" as a control character and prints to a new line, following which "Hypotenuse: " is edited as a literal string and printed.

The real number 5.0 is printed.

"\n" causes another line feed.

The syntax of the PRINC primitive is

```
(princ <expression> [<file pointer>])
```

PRINC prints the <expression> on the screen interpreting control characters, such as new line, in the expression and returns <expression>. If <file pointer> is present, the <expression> is written to the appropriate disk file—this will be discussed in a later chapter.

When PRINC is invoked, it prints the <expression>and returns the <expression>. If PRINC is the last expression in a function, this results in two printouts of <expression>to the monitor. This is an idiosyncrasy of LISP you have to learn to adapt to and is the reason for the left and right parentheses at the end of the PRINLIST function. The () is a null expression and, since AutoLISP always returns the last expression, nil is printed on the screen. The "\n" invokes a line feed so that the final printout caused by PRINTLST is

```
Hypotenuse: 5.0
nil
```

If the final parentheses are removed from the program, AutoLISP returns the last expression processed, 5.0; therefore, the printout is

```
Hypotenuse: 5.0
5.0
```

5.5   Function Loading

The HYPOT function uses your PRINLIST utility function to print the hypotenuse to the monitor. With Release 10 an AutoLISP routine can be written to check to see if the PRINLIST function is available and, if it is not, to LOAD the UTILITY1.LSP file. Unfortunately with earlier releases the LOAD primitive cannot be invoked from within another LISP function. It must be entered either directly from the keyboard or from a menu or script file. However, each time you boot AutoCAD, it loads the file ACAD.LSP (if it exists); consequently, if you place your commonly used utility files in the ACAD.LSP file, they will be loaded automatically. Remember though, if you do so with too many files, it will use up memory space. Often it is better to simply put the primary function plus all the functions it uses in the same LISP file so that they are all loaded at once.

Assignment.   Add the PRINLIST function to the end of the PYTHAG.LSP file and also modify the function you wrote to calculate the side of a right-angle triangle so that it provides a descriptive output.

5.6   YESNO Utility Routine

Often it is necessary in a function to elicit a yes or no response from the person using it. The following YESNO utility function can be used when a Y or N response is required, or it can be modified to request other responses:

```
; YESNO waits for a Y, y, N, or n response
; Returns Y or N
; Syntax: (yesno <arg>)
; Example: (yesno ''Do another? (Y)es or (N)o: '')
(defun YESNO (arg)
   ; Wait for Y, y, N or n response
   (while (not (member ans '(''Y'' ''N'')))
      (setq ans
         (strcase
            (getstring arg))))
)
```

The YESNO function can be used with any version of AutoCAD from 2.1 on. Add the YESNO function to your UTILITY1.LSP file. The function takes one argument, which is bound to the symbol ARG, and uses one global variable. Since ANS is not defined as a local variable, it retains its binding (in this case "Y" or "N") after evaluation of the function is complete. It is referred to as a "global variable."

The function uses the GETSTRING primitive to display ARG and pauses for user input. The WHILE and NOT primitives are used to wait for the specified response.

The YESNO function is evaluated from the inside out. The GETSTRING primitive displays the expression bound to the symbol ARG; for example, if ("Do another? (Y)es or (N)o: ") is bound to ARGS, GETSTRING displays the following prompt and waits for a response:

```
Do another? (Y)es or (N)o:
```

5.6.1 STRCASE primitive

The STRCASE primitive converts the value returned by the GETSTRING primitive to uppercase text; therefore, if the user responds with n or y, STRCASE returns N or Y. The syntax of STRCASE is

```
(strcase <string> [ <which> ])
```

STRCASE takes the <string> argument and returns a copy with all alphabetic characters converted to upper- or lowercase. If [<which>] is provided and is not nil, the characters returned will be lowercase. In our program [<which>] is not provided; hence STRCASE returns uppercase text. Next, the response, Y or N, is bound to the symbol ANS.

A number of primitives are used in the next expression:

```
(while (not (member ans '(''Y'' ''N'')))
```

This expression, simply stated, determines if a "Y" or "N" is bound to ANS. If they are not, the <expression> of the WHILE function is evaluated, i.e., the prompt and GETSTRING. If a "Y" or "N" is bound to ANS, the evaluator exits the WHILE function.

5.6.2   MEMBER primitive

The syntax of the MEMBER primitive is

```
(member <expression> <list>)
```

This primitive searches the <list>for an occurrence of the <expression> and returns the remainder of the list starting with the first occurrence of <expression>. If there is no occurrence of <expression> in <list>, MEMBER returns nil.

In the expression (member ans '("Y" "N")), MEMBER searches the list ("Y" "N") for the first occurrence of the argument bound to the symbol ANS. If "Y" is bound to ANS, MEMBER returns (Y N). If "N" is bound to ANS, MEMBER returns (N). If neither "Y" nor "N" is bound to ARGS, MEMBER returns nil. The apostrophe preceding the is explained in Section 5.6.5.

5.6.3   NOT primitive

The NOT primitive returns T if the expression is nil and nil otherwise. If the MEMBER primitive in your YESNO function returns nil, NOT returns T. If MEMBER returns (Y N) or (N), NOT returns nil. The syntax of the NOT function is

```
(not <expression>)
```

5.6.4   WHILE primitive

The WHILE primitive evaluates a test expression, which in your YESNO function will be either T or nil because of the NOT primitive. If it is not nil, i.e., T, it evaluates its expression—the prompt and GETSTRING primitive. If it is nil, WHILE returns the most recent value of its expression, which is the argument bound to ANS, either "Y" or "N".

The syntax of WHILE is

```
(while <test expression> <expression> ...)
```

This primitive evaluates <test expression> and, if not nil, evaluates the other <expression>s and then evaluates <test expression> again.

This continues until <test expression> is nil. WHILE then returns the most recent value of the last <expression>.

5.6.5 Inhibiting evaluation

When the LISP evaluator is given a list to evaluate, it looks at the first character in the list and assumes it to be either a user-defined procedure or a primitive (internal function). You can specify that the evaluator is to stop evaluation by supplying an evaluator-inhibiting signal in the form of a single-quote character (').

In our use of the MEMBER primitive, if we do not precede (Y N) with a single-quote character, the evaluator will "wade in" and assume Y to be the name of a procedure. We want Y to be an element of a list. Note the difference in the following (where Y is bound to the symbol ANS):

```
(member 'y '(w x y z)) returns (Y Z)
(member ans '(Y N) returns (Y N)
```

In the first case we want the interpreter to take Y as an expression to search for in the list; hence it is preceded by the evaluator-inhibiting quote. In the second case we want the interpreter to evaluate ANS prior to it using ANS as an expression. Since Y is bound to ANS, Y is returned when ANS is evaluated, and Y becomes the expression to be searched for in the list rather than ANS.

5.7 GETKWORD Primitive

Version 2.6 and later versions of AutoCAD have a GETKWORD primitive that may be used to simplify the YESNO function created above. The GETKWORD primitive requests a keyword from the user. The list of valid keywords is set prior to the GETKWORD call by the INITGET primitive. AutoCAD retries if the input does not match the keyword. The syntax of GETKWORD is

```
(getkword [<prompt>])
```

The syntax of the INITGET primitive is

```
(initget [<bits>] [<strings>])
```

If the optional <bit> argument is the integer 1, a null response is not accepted by GETKWORD. If it is not included, GETKWORD returns nil if a null entry is made. An example of the use of these functions is

```
(initget 1 ''Yes No'')
(setq x (getkword ''Do another? (Yes No) ''))
```

The YESNO function (using GETKWORD) is

```
;YESNO waits for a Y, y, N or n response
; Returns Y or N
;Syntax: (YESNO )
;Example (yesno ''Do another? (Y)es or (N)o: '')
(defun YESNO (args)
   (initget 1 ''Y y N n'')
   (setq ans (strcase (getkword arg)))
)
```

In this version of YESNO, the INITGET primitive establishes the option for the next GETxxx primitive, which is GETKWORD, as Y, y, N, or n. Since the optional <bit> is 1, a null response is not accepted.

GETKWORD uses the argument bound to ARG as its prompt and waits for a Y, y, N, or n response and then returns that response. The STRCASE primitive takes the response from GETKWORD and returns a copy in uppercase. The response is then bound to the symbol ANS.

5.8   IF Primitive

The AutoLISP IF primitive has the basic format IF-THEN-ELSE. It conditionally evaluates a test expression <test expr.> and, if it is not nil, it evaluates a then expression <then expr.> and returns the result. Otherwise it evaluates an else expression <else expr.>, which is optional. If <test expr.> is nil and <else expr.> is missing, IF returns nil. The syntax of IF is

```
(if <test expr.> <then expr.>[<else expr.>])
```

(= a b)	Tests if a is *equal* to b.
(> a b)	Tests if a is *greater than* b.
(< a b)	Tests if a is *less than* b.
(/= a b)	Tests if a is *not equal* to b.
(>= a b)	Tests if a is *greater than or equal* to b.
(<= a b)	Tests if a is *less than or equal* to b.

Use EDLIN to write the following function using the file path \ACAD\LISP\TESTX.LSP (refer to Section 5.3):

```
(defun x (a b)
   (if (= a b) (princ ''a = b\n''))
   (if (> a b) (princ ''a>b\n''))
   (if (< a b) (princ ''a<b\n''))
   (if (/= a b) (princ ''a /= b\n''))
   (if (>= a b) (princ ''a>= b\n''))
   (if (<= a b) (princ ''a<= b\n''))
   (princ ''Try another!\n'') ()
```

Begin a new drawing and load the TESTX LISP file from the AutoCAD command line by entering (**load "/acad/lisp/testx"**). When the file is loaded, run the X function by entering (**x 3 7**). Try it again by entering some other values, i.e., (**x 4 4**).

The IF primitive can be used with the YESNO user function as follows (also, note the new PROMPT primitive):

```
; Test of yesno function
(defun test1 ()
    (prompt ''Testing yesno.'') (
    if (= (yesno ''\nAnother? (Y)es or (N)o: '') ''Y'')
       (princ ''\nYes!\n'') (princ ''\nNo!\n'')) () )
```

This function uses the YESNO function to display on a new line, "Another? (Y)es or (N)o: ". If the user responds y or Y, the YESNO function returns Y, and "Yes!" is printed on a new line on the monitor, followed by a line feed; otherwise, if the user responds with n or N, the YESNO function returns N, and "No!" is printed on a new line on the monitor, followed by a line feed. The null expression, (), at the end returns nil.

Using EDLIN, write the TEST1 function using the file path \CAD\LISP\TEST1.LSP. Then boot AutoCAD and begin a new drawing named ABC. Use the AutoLISP LOAD primitive to load UTILITY1.LSP. This is necessary since the TEST1 function calls the YESNO function that is stored in the UTILITY1.LSP file. Also LOAD the TEST1.LSP file. Now invoke the TEST1.LSP function (see Section 5.3.1) and try a y response. Run it again trying a N response. If there is an error in your function, AutoLISP will stop and print the line containing the error and, often, the lines following it.

5.9   Using Functions in a Menu File

In the PROTO1 menu file created in Chapters 4 and 5, the [mech-eng] option in the file (line 107 in Appendix D.1) allows the user to select a scale based on a ratio, i.e., 1:2, by activating the **mm submenu. In the mm submenu the scale factor F is calculated assuming that the plot units and drawing units are the same; hence for a 1:2 scale the symbol F is assigned the value 2.

The [mech-eng] menu command is in the **i submenu, which is activated when the user selects an Imperial-size drawing (see PROTO1.MNU macro's lines 12 and 17). The drawing units might be in feet and the plot units in inches, or both might be in inches. The [mech-eng] macro is to be modified to allow the drafter those options. Line 107 currently is as follows:

```
107: [mech-eng](setq txt (/ 3 32) conv 1 unts 2 +
108: precise (getint ''Number of digits to right of decimal: ''));\+
109: $s=mm
```

The current macro in line 107 is to be removed and will later be included in a user-defined function named MENG filed in MENG.LSP. Modify lines 107 and 108 as follows, and delete line 109:

```
107: [mech-eng](if (not meng) (load ''/acad/lisp/meng''));+
108: (meng);\\$s=mm
```

In the preceding, an IF expression using the test expression (not meng) is used to check to see if the function MENG is loaded. If MENG is not available, a null response is returned and the *then* expression (load "/acad/lisp/meng") is invoked to load the MENG file. Note the use of directory paths with a forward slash. Next the macro invokes the MENG function in line 108. The two backslashes are included in the macro since the MENG function (see below) uses two GETxxx primitives. If the backslashes are not included, the macro and function will still work; however, the mm submenu will be displayed prior to the macro halting for input from the user in the GETxxx functions. After the user enters responses to the GETxxx functions, the mm submenu is displayed.

The MENG.LSP file loaded in line 107 has the file path \ACAD\LISP\MENG.LSP. Write the function using EDLIN:

```
; MENG function—mechanical engineering units.
  (defun meng ()
    (setq txt (/ 3.0 32) conv 1 unts 2)
    (while (not (member ans '(''F'' ''I'')))
      (setq ans (strcase
        (getstring ''Screen units Inches or Feet? I/F: '')))
    )
    (setq precise
      (getint ''Number of digits to right of decimal: ''))
) ; End of function.
```

The MENG function takes no arguments and has the following global variables: TXT, CONV, UNTS, and ANS. Since those variables are not defined as local variables, their assignments remain after the function is exited.

The fourth to seventh lines follow the format of our YESNO function. Working from the inside out, the GETSTRING primitive returns a string which is converted to uppercase by the STRCASE primitive and bound to the symbol ANS. The MEMBER primitive searches the list ("F" "I") for the first occurrence of the string bound to ANS. If neither is bound to ANS, it returns nil. If "F" is bound to ANS, it returns ("F" "I"), and if "I" is bound to ANS, it returns ("I"). The NOT primitive returns T if its expression is nil and nil otherwise; hence if ("F" "I") or ("I") is returned by MEMBER, NOT returns nil, otherwise it returns T. The WHILE primitive evaluates the test expression, and if it is not nil (meaning ANS is not assigned "F" or "I"), it evaluates the test expression again. If the test expression returns nil, ANS has been assigned "I" or "F" and evaluation is terminated. The GETINT primitive gets the precision desired for the units, which is then bound to the symbol PRECISE.

When evaluation of the MENG is complete, the evaluator returns to the line of the menu file following the one at which the function was loaded (line 108) and processes the command $s = mm, displaying the mm submenu. The drafter selects the scale from the menu and a scale factor is assigned to the symbol F (i.e., selecting [1:2] assigns 2 to F, see App. D1, line 79). The PROTO1 *script* file is then invoked (see line 79).

The scale factor assigned to the symbol F is correct if drawing units are inches. If drawing units are feet, the value bound to F is to be multiplied by $1/12$. An IF function is inserted as line 1 of the PROTO1 *script* file to perform this operation as follows:

```
C:\> edlin \acad\proto\protol.scr
End of input file
*1i
    1: (if (= ans ''F'') (setq f (/ f 12.0)))
    2: ^c (Ctrl-C)
*e
```

This new line 1 inserted into the PROTO1 *script* file uses the IF function to test to see if the string "F" has been bound to the symbol ANS. If the test expression is not nil, i.e., "F" is bound to ANS, the SETQ function multiplies the current binding of F by $1/12$.

Assignment.

1. Write a LISP program to convert Celsius degrees to Fahrenheit. The equation is: F = 9/5 * C + 32. Output is to be as follows (tabbed):

```
Degrees Fahrenheit xx Degrees Celsius xx
```

Pseudocode for the program is as follows:

Start function
    Set ANS = Y
    WHILE ANS equals Y, loop
        Request degrees Celsius to be converted
        Do calculation
        Print result using your PRINLIST function
        Another conversion? YESNO function
    Close WHILE loop
Exit

2. In the PROTO1 *script* file you have written, the text size is fixed as 2.5 mm for SI units and $3/32$ in for Imperial units. Write a function

named TXTHT.LSP that will assign three alternate text heights to the symbols SMALL, MEDIUM, and LARGE. The plot text height is bound to the symbol TXT. The pseudocode for the function is as follows:

Function name: TXTHT
IF TXT <2.5, the drawing units are Imperial
  Then small = f * 3⁄32
       medium = f * 1⁄8
       large = f * 3⁄16
Else the drawing units are SI, and
      small = f * 2.5
      medium = f * 3.0
      large = f * 4.0

The *then* and *else* in an IF function can be only one expression, so a multiple SETQ assignment must be used in both the then and else expressions in order to assign three text heights to symbols.. Save the TXTHT function using the file path \ACAD\LISP\TXTHT.LSP. Insert a line 11 (12 for Ver. 2.6) in your PROTO1 *script* file to check to see if TXTHT is loaded. If it is not, the script is to load the file. A new line 12 (13 for Ver. 2.6) is also to be created to invoke the TXTHT *script* file.

When drawing with AutoCAD, you may set the text height to small, medium, or large by entering the TEXT command and responding with !SMALL, !MEDIUM, or !LARGE in response to the request for the text height.

3. Review the menu in Appendix D, noting the use of examples in lines 102, 107, 111, 167, and 171. The "^P" is a menu echo toggle. Try the menu without the ^P's to see why they are necessary.

The final listings of the PROTO1.MNU, TXTHT.SCR, and PROTO1.SCR files are in Appendix E.

6

Multiscale Drawings and AutoLISP Files

OBJECTIVE *Use AutoLISP to OPEN data files for reading, writing, and appending; write a PROTO2 menu for drawing multiscale drawings; use AutoLISP's error-handling function; apply the following functions: OPEN, CLOSE, PRINC, PRIN1, PRINT, WRITE-LINE, READ-LINE, FOREACH, GETVAR, STRCAT, RTOS, ITOA, ATOF, ATOI, NULL, and EVAL.*

6.1 MultiScale Drawings

The PROTO1 menu and script files created in Chapters 4 and 5 are adequate for single-scale drawings but cannot be used for multiscale drawings.

AutoCAD does not allow the entry of varying scale factors for units (distance between points) in a drawing. In order to draw a multiscale drawing you must separately draw each component that has a different scale and later insert the components into a composite drawing using their appropriate scales. The limits of the composite drawing are set equal to the size of the sheet on which the drawing is to be plotted, and the plot is done using a 1:1 scale.

When composing a multiscale drawing, you will require information about the drawings being inserted into the composite drawing. For instance in Chapter 4 a scale factor F was calculated to bring the border drawing up to the plot scale selected. When a drawing is inserted into a composite plot drawing, which has its limits set to the size of the plot sheet, it must be scaled down using a factor equal to the inverse of the scale-up factor 1/F. Data can be transferred across drawings using

AutoLISP to write the data to a data file in one drawing and read it in the other.

6.2   AutoLISP Data-File Commands

To open a data file in AutoLISP, the OPEN primitive is used within a SETQ primitive that binds the "file pointer" (created by AutoLISP when the file is opened) to a symbol. The format of OPEN is

```
(setq a (open <filename> <mode>))
```

<filename> is a string enclosed in quotation marks specifying the name and extension of the file to be opened. A file path may be included. Valid <mode> letters are listed in Table 6.1. **Note:** Although AutoLISP is generally not case sensitive, the <mode> must be a lowercase letter.

TABLE 6.1   Valid Open-File Modes

Mode	Description
"r"	Open for reading. If <filename> does not exist, nil is returned.
"w"	Open for writing. If <filename> does not exist, a new file is created and opened. If <filename> exists, it is opened. Any new data will be written over the existing data, with the resulting loss of the old data.
"a"	Open for appending. If <filename> does not exist, a new file is created and opened. If <filename> exists, it is opened. Any new data will be appended to the end of the existing data.

6.2.1   Opening a new data file for writing

Boot AutoCAD and begin a new drawing named X. Open a file named TEST1.TST for writing to as follows:

```
Command: (setq file1 (open ''test1.tst'' ''w''))
```

AutoCAD opens the file for writing and returns the file pointer in the form <File #nnn>. You do not need to worry about the file pointer since it has been bound to the symbol FILE1. If any problems are encountered when opening the file, AutoCAD returns nil instead of the file pointer.

Now, to write to FILE1 use the PRINC command that was introduced in Section 5.4.3. For example, enter

```
Command: (princ ''Hello eh!\n'' file1)
```

Notice when a <file pointer>, i.e., FILE1, is used with the PRINC command, the data is written to the file rather than the screen. The data written to the file is "Hello eh!" (Canadian greeting). A carriage return "\n" has been included with the data to mark the end of the record.

6.2.2 Closing a data file

You should close files as soon as you are through with them; otherwise AutoCAD may have too many files open at one time. You may change the number of open files by modifying the "FILES = nn" command in the DOS CONFIG.SYS file as discussed in Section 2.2.3. The syntax of the CLOSE primitive is:

```
(close <file pointer>)
```

To close FILE1, enter

```
Command: (close file1)
```

6.2.3 Reading a data file

To open TEST1.TST file for reading, enter

```
Command: (setq file2 (open ''test1.tst'' ''r''))
```

To read data from an open file the READ-LINE primitive may be used. The syntax is as follows:

```
(read-line [<file pointer>])
```

READ-LINE reads a string from the keyboard or from the opened file described by <file pointer>. The string read is defined by a series of bytes terminated by a carriage return ("\n"), a line feed, or the end of file. If the end of file is encountered, READ-LINE returns nil; otherwise it returns the string that was read. The data is read as *string* (text) data. If the data is to represent a real or integer number, it must be converted by the ATOF or ATOI primitive (see Section 6.3.2).

To read the data in FILE2 that is open for reading, enter

```
Command: (read-line file2)
```

AutoLISP reads the bytes in the file up to the carriage return "\n" and returns:

```
Hello eh!
```

Read the file again. The response should be nil, indicating that the end of file was encountered. Note that the file is read sequentially. Close the file prior to continuing (see Section 6.2.2).

6.3   PRINC, PRIN1, PRINT, and WRITE-LINE Primitives

There are three print primitives that may be used to write data to the screen or to an open file: PRINC, PRIN1, and PRINT. The WRITE-LINE primitive is used to write string data to the screen or to an open file.

The syntax of PRINx (PRINC, PRIN1, PRINT) is

```
(PRINx <expression>[<file pointer>])
```

The <expression> is printed on the screen in the format outlined below for each of the PRINx primitives. If <file pointer>is present, the <expression> is written to the file described by the file pointer exactly as it would appear on the screen.

PRINC prints the <expression> interpreting control characters, such as new line, "\n" (carriage return), and tab, "\t", and returns the expression. The output is not quoted (enclosed in quotation marks). PRINC is generally used to produce output that can be read by people; for example:

```
(princ ''\tProgramming AutoCAD'') returns
Programming AutoCAD'\tProgramming AutoCAD''
```

The tab is interpreted, and the output is tabbed as illustrated. The <expression> is returned following the output.

PRIN1 prints the results without interpreting any of the control characters, and it returns <expression>. The output is quoted. PRIN1 produces output that is suitable to be fed back into LISP since control characters are intact; for example:

```
(prin1 "\tProgramming AutoCAD") returns
''\tProgramming AutoCAD''''\tProgramming AutoCAD''
```

The tab is not interpreted, and the output is quoted. The expression is returned following the output.

PRINT outputs the expression and adds a new-line character (carriage return) preceding the expression and a space character following it and returns <expression>. Control characters within the results are not interpreted, and the output is quoted; for example:

```
(print ''\tProgramming AutoCAD'') returns
```

''\tProgramming AutoCAD'' ''\tProgramming AutoCAD''

The output is quoted, preceded by a leading new (blank) line and followed by a trailing space. The expression is returned following the output.

WRITE-LINE writes a <string> to the screen or to an open file described by <file-pointer>. The output is not quoted and control characters are interpreted. WRITE-LINE forces a Return and returns <string>. String data is nonnumeric text data. Numbers represented as string data cannot be used mathematically.

The syntax for the WRITE-LINE primitive is

```
(write-line <string>[<file pointer>])
```

For example:

```
(write-line ''\tProgramming AutoCAD'') returns
        Programming AutoCAD
''\tProgramming AutoCAD''
```

The following functions illustrate the PRINx and WRITE-LINE primitives. Load EDLIN from DOS or from within AutoCAD and enter the following AutoLISP program. The EDLIN COPY command is introduced in the example to reduce the required typing. The functions are explained at the end of the listing.

```
Command:EDLIN
File to edit:lisp\file0.lsp
*i
    1: ; FILE1—Test of PRINC function
    2: (defun file1 (/ a b c d e n)
    3:    (setq a 2.34 b 5.67 c ''Hello eh!'' d ''G'Day\n'' e 8)
    4:    (setq file1 (open ''lisp/file1.tst'' ''w''))
    5:    (foreach n '(a b c d e) (princ (eval n) file1))
    6:    (close file1)
    7: )
    8: ^c    (Ctrl-C)
*1,7,8c
```

The last EDLIN command entered copies lines 1 through 7 to lines starting at line 8. List the file and observe that lines 8 through 14 now contain a copy of lines 1 through 7. Edit lines 8 to 14 to match the following (modified data is underlined);

```
    8: ; FILE2—Test of PRIN1 function
    9: (defun file2 (/ a b c d e n)
   10:    (setq a 2.34 b 5.67 c ''Hello eh!'' ''G'Day\n'' e 8)
   11:    (setq file2 (open ''lisp/file2.tst'' ''w''))
   12:    (foreach n '(a b c d e) (prin1 (eval n) file2))
   13:    (close file2)
   14: )
```

Now, use the EDLIN COPY command to copy lines 1 through 7 to 15. Edit the lines to use file FILE3 and the PRINT command. Next, use the EDLIN Copy command to copy lines 1 through 7 to 22. Modify the lines as follows:

```
22: ;    FILE4—Test of WRITE-LINE function
23: (defun file4 (/ a b c d e n)
24:   (setq a (rtos 2.34 2 2) b (rtos 5.67 2 2)
25:     c ''hello eh!'' ''G'day\n'' e (itoa 8))
26:   (setq file4 (open ''lisp/file4.tst'' ''w''))
27:   (foreach n '(a b c d e) (write-line (eval n) file4))
28:   (close file4)
29: )
```

6.3.1 FOREACH and EVAL primitives

In line 4 of the FILE1 function, a file named FILE1 in the LISP subdirectory of ACAD is opened. Its file pointer is bound to the symbol FILE1. In line 5 the AutoLISP FOREACH primitive is used. The syntax of FOREACH is as follows (also see Section 5.4.3):

```
(foreach <name> <list> <expression> ... )
```

FOREACH steps through <list>, assigning each element to <name>, and evaluates each <expression> for every element in the list. The result of the last <expression> is returned. For example:

```
(foreach n '(a b) (princ n)
```

is equivalent to:

```
(princ a)
(princ b)
```

In the preceding, the PRINC function would print ab and return b, so the output is abb.

The FOREACH primitive in line 5 steps through the list '(a b c d e), assigning each element sequentially to N, and evaluates the (PRINC (eval n)) primitives. The FOREACH primitive is repeated for each element in the list. Notice that the <list> is preceded by a single-quote character (') so that the LISP evaluator does not wade into the list, attempting to evaluate the first character as a procedure (see Section 5.6.5).

Without the EVAL primitive, the FOREACH primitive in line 5 would be: (foreach n '(a b c d e) (princ n file1)). As its first step, the FOREACH primitive assigns a to N, and the expression is equivalent to (princ a), which would print a to the file described by the file pointer FILE1.

In the FILE1 function, A is a symbol that has the value 2.34 bound to it (line 3). The data to be printed to the file is the value bound to A, not the symbol a. In order to extract the value 2.34 from the symbol A, another round of evaluation is required. The EVAL primitive is used to force evaluation of A. The syntax of EVAL is

```
(eval <expression>)
```

EVAL returns the result of the evaluation. The file is closed in line 6. The other functions are similar to the FILE1 function.

6.3.2 RTOS, ITOA, ATOF, and ATOI primitives

The WRITE-LINE primitive writes string (text) data to the screen or an open file. In the FILE4 function some of the data is numeric and must be converted to string data prior to using the WRITE-LINE primitive to write it to file.

The RTOS primitive returns a string (text) that is the representation of a real <number> according to the settings of <mode> and <precision> and the AutoCAD DIMZIN dimensioning variable. The syntax is

```
(rtos <number> [<mode>] [<precision>])
```

<mode> is an integer as outlined in Table 6.2. In line 24 of the FILE4 function, the real number 2.34 is a decimal number with two digits following the decimal point. It is converted to a string (text) using (rtos 2.34 2 2).

TABLE 6.2   RTOS Modes

RTOS mode	Editing format
1	Scientific
2	Decimal
3	Engineering (e.g., 3'-5.50")
4	Architectural (e.g., 3'-5 1/2")
5	Arbitrary fractional units (e.g., 41 1/2)

The ITOA primitive returns the conversion of an integer into a string (text). The syntax is

```
(itoa <int>)
```

In line 25 of the FILE4 function, the integer 8 is converted to a string using (itoa 8).

The ATOF primitive returns the conversion of a string into a real number. The syntax is

```
(atof <string>)
```

For example, if the string "2.34" is bound to a,

(atof a) returns 2.34 or 2.340000
(atof ''5.67'') returns 5.67 or 5.670000

The ATOI primitive returns the conversion of a string into an integer. The syntax is

```
(atoi <string>)
```

For example, if the string "8" is bound to d,

(atoi d) returns 8
(atoi ''12'') returns 12

6.3.3 Reading the FILEx.DAT files

Functions will now be added to the LISP\FILE0.LSP file to read the files created by the FILEx functions and to print the data to the monitor. The functions begin at line 30 in the file and are as follows:

```
30: ;   READ1—read FILE1.TST
31: (defun read1 (/ x)
32:   (setq file1 (open ''lisp/file1.tst'' ''r''))
33:   (setq x 1) (princ ''File1—PRINC function\n'')
34:   (while x (setq x (read-line file1))
35:     (princ x) (princ ''\n'')
36:   ) (close file1)
37: )
```

Use the EDLIN Copy command to copy lines 30 through 37 to lines starting at 38. Edit the lines as follows:

```
38: ;   READ2—Read FILE2.TST
39: (defun read2 (/ x)
40:   (setq file2 (open ''lisp/file2.tst'' ''r''))
41:   (setq x 1) (princ ''FILE2—PRIN1 Function\n'')
42:   (while x (setq x (read-line file2))
43:     (princ x) (princ ''\n'')
44:   ) (close file2)
45: )
```

Copy lines 30 through 37 to lines starting at 46. Edit the lines to read *FILE3*, which uses the *PRINT* primitive.

Copy lines 30 through 37 to lines starting at the end of the READ3 function, and edit the lines to read *FILE4,* which uses the *WRITE-LINE* primitive.

In line 40 of the READ2 function, FILE2.TST is opened for reading, and its file pointer is bound to the symbol FILE2. In each of these functions the PRINC primitive is used to print a heading (see line 41) to the monitor. If the PRIN1 or PRINT primitives were used, the heading would be printed with the quotation marks and control characters intact.

In line 41 the integer 1 is bound to the symbol X, which is used as <test-expression> for the WHILE primitive in line 42. While X is not nil, the READ-LINE function reads a line from the file and binds it to the symbol X. The PRINC primitive is used to print the line to the monitor. The WHILE primitive retests X and, if not nil, the next line in the file is read and printed. When the end of the file is encountered, nil is returned and assigned to X. When WHILE retests X and returns nil, evaluation is passed to the line following the end of the WHILE, which is the CLOSE primitive in line 44, and the file is closed.

Exit EDLIN and load the file LISP/FILE0 from within the AutoCAD drawing editor and run each of the functions as follows (data returned by AutoLISP is printed in boldface):

```
Command:(load ''lisp/file0'')
(READ4)
Command:(file1)
nil
Command:(file2)
nil
Command:(file3)
nil
Command:(FILE4)
```

All of the print functions have now been executed and files FILE1.TST, FILE2.TST, FILE3.TST, and FILE4.TST have been written to. Prior to using the READx functions, shell to DOS and use the TYPE command to see the data stored. The FILE1.DAT file is listed as follows:

```
Command:edlin (or edit—see Section 2.5)
File to edit:lisp\file1.tst
```

List each file. The data appears in the files as listed below. For FILE1.DAT—PRINC function it is:

```
2.345.67Hello eh!G'Day
8
```

ForFILE2.DAT—PRIN1 function:

```
2.345.67''Hello eh!''''G'Day\n''8
```

For FILE3.DAT—PRINT function:

```
2.34
5.67
''Hello eh!''
```

```
''G'Day\n''
8
```

For FILE4.DAT—WRITE-LINE function:

```
2.34
5.67
Hello eh!
G'Day

8
```

In FILE1, the PRINC primitive has interpreted the new-line control character in the string "G'Day\n", which is bound to the symbol D, and printed the integer 8, which is bound to the symbol E, on a new line.

In FILE2, the PRIN1 primitive has quoted the string data and has not interpreted the new-line character.

In FILE3, the PRINT primitive adds a leading new line and a trailing space to each data written to the file; consequently the file begins with a blank line. Strings are quoted and the new-line control character is not interpreted.

In FILE4, the WRITE-LINE primitive forces a return at the end of each string written and interprets control characters. The embedded control character in the string "G'Day\n" has forced an additional new line before the next character is written. Strings are not quoted.

The "read" functions are now executed:

```
Command: (read1)
FILE1—PRINC function
2.345.67Hello eh!G'Day
8
nil
nil
```

Review the PRINT1 function and the output listed above. In the first loop of the WHILE primitive, the first line in the file is bound to the symbol X and printed with the PRINC primitive. In the next loop, the second line is read and the integer 8 is bound to X and printed. In the next loop, the end of file marker "nil" is bound to X, terminating the WHILE primitive. The most recent value bound to X, nil, is printed. When the file is closed, AutoLISP returns nil.

Review the output from the READ2, READ3, and READ4 functions printed below.

```
Command: (read2)
FILE2—PRIN1 function
2.345.67''Hello eh!''''G'Day\n''8
nil
nil
```

```
Command: (read3)

FILE3—PRINT function
2.34
```

```
5.67
''Hello eh!''
''G'Day\n''
8
nil
nil

Command:(read4)
FILE4-WRITE-LINE function
2.34
5.67
Hello eh!
G'Day

8
nil
nil
```

6.4 Writing PROTO1 Drawing Data to a File

When producing a multiscale drawing, the following information is required from each drawing inserted into it:

Item	Symbol	Where available
Drawing name	DWGNAME	System variable
Insertion scale	F	Proto1.scr

The drawing name is available as a system variable and can be accessed from the drawing database by the PROTO1 *script* file.

An AutoLISP function named DWGDATA is to be written to open a data file and write the PROTO1 data to it. The function will be stored in a file named DWGDATA.LSP with the file path \ACAD\LISP\ DWGDATA.LSP. The PROTO1 *script* file is to invoke the DWGDATA function. **Note:** Insert the following lines into your PROTO1.SCR script file (lines 18 and 19 with Ver. 2.62):

```
14: (if (not dwgdata) (load ''/acad/lisp/dwgdata''))
15: (dwgdata)
```

In line 14 the NOT primitive returns T if the DWGDATA function is not nil (i.e., not loaded). The NOT primitive acts as the test expression for the IF primitive. If a T is returned, the IF primitive evaluates its expression and loads the DWGDATA.LSP file. The function is invoked in line 15.

6.4.1 User-defined function—DWGDATA

The function named DWGDATA is used to open a data file and write the PROTO1 data (drawing name and scale factor) to it. The name of the data file is the drawing name plus the extension .DAT. Using

EDLIN, write the following function using the file path
\ACAD\LISP\DWGDATA.LSP:

```
 1: ; *** DWGDATA Function ***
 2: ; Writes PROTO1 drawing data to a file
 3: ; File-name is: <drawing name>.dat
 4: ; File path is: same as drawing.
 5: ;
 6: (defun dwgdata (/ n name filename file)
 7:    ;  Get the drawing name.
 8:    (setq name (getvar ''dwgname''))
 9:    ;   Open PROTO1 data file for writing.
10:    (setq filename (strcat name ''.dat''))
11:    (setq file (open filename ''w''))
12:    ;   Write data to file.
13:    (foreach n '(name ''\n'' f)
14:       (princ (eval n) file))
15:    (close file)
16: );  End of function.
```

Comment lines (preceded by ;) are used throughout the function to improve its readability. The DWGDATA function and the new AutoLISP
primitives introduced—GETVAR, STRCAT, and EVAL—are discussed in following sections.

6.4.2   GETVAR primitive

In line 8 of the DWGDATA function AutoLISP's GETVAR primitive is
used to read the system variable DWGNAME, which is used by
AutoCAD to save the drawing name. The SETQ primitive assigns the
drawing name to the symbol NAME.

The syntax of GETVAR is as follows:

```
(getvar <varname>)
```

The system variable, <varname>, must be enclosed in double quotes.
GETVAR returns the current value in the system variable.

6.4.3   STRCAT primitive

The PROTO1 data is stored in a file having the same file path and
name as the drawing and the extension ".DAT" (for data). The
STRCAT primitive is used in line 10 to concatenate (string together)
the drawing name (bound to the symbol NAME) and the extension
.DAT. The result is bound to the symbol FILENAME and is the file
path and name for the PROTO1 data file. The syntax of STRCAT is

```
(strcat <string1> <string2> ...)
```

STRCAT returns the concatenated string. For instance, if you are
working on a drawing named 101SP01C and the current directory

is the same as that in which the drawing resides, the data bound to the symbol NAME in line 8 of the DWGDATA function is 101SP01C. In line 11 the STRCAT primitive concatenates the data bound to NAME with .DAT. The SETQ primitive binds the result, 101SP01C.DAT, to the symbol FILENAME.

In line 11 the OPEN primitive is used to open a file for writing, using the file name that is bound to the symbol FILENAME. The file pointer is bound to the symbol FILE.

The FOREACH primitive is used in line 13 of the DWGDATA function to sequentially assign elements in a list to the symbol N for evaluation in the expression. Notice that the list is preceded by a single quote mark to stop the LISP evaluator from wading into the expression (see Section 5.6.5). The data in the list is separated with a newline character ("\n") to print each item on a new line in the file. This is done to facilitate reading of the file using AutoLISP's READ-LINE primitive.

The FOREACH primitive assigns each element to the symbol N and evaluates the (princ (eval n) file) expression. The PRINC primitive is used to print each value assigned to N to a file with the name that is bound to the symbol FILE. The PRINC primitive is used because it does not enclose string data in quotation marks.

The elements in the FOREACH primitives list in line 13 are variables. When FOREACH assigns each to N, another round of evaluation is required to get the value bound to the symbol. The EVAL primitive (see Section 6.3.1) is used in the PRINC expression (line 14) to invoke a second round of evaluation.

The last line in the function closes the file, which has its pointer bound to the symbol FILE.

6.5 Multiscale Drawing Menu

The PROTO1 drawing menu and file are used for drawing single-scale drawings. You are able to begin a new drawing in a scaled sheet with a border and title block. All of the settings are done automatically and you may use *!small, !medium,* or *!large* text. The PROTO1 script file invokes an AutoLISP function that writes the PROTO1 drawing name and scale factor to a data file for retrieval when inserting the drawing into a multiscale drawing.

The next step is to create a menu for a multiscale drawing. This file will be named PROTO2.MNU. It is loaded from a selection, [MULTISCL], which is to be added to the SCREEN menu of the PROTO1 *menu* file.

6.5.1 PROTO2 menu

The PROTO2 *menu* file does the following:

- Provide a selection of plot-sheet sizes
- Draw a border
- Insert a title block with attributes
- Request a drawing name for insertion
- Read the PROTO1 factors from the data file for the drawing being inserted
- Get INSERT options
- Insert the specified drawing to scale
- Allow insertion of other drawings
- Create a summary data file

Using EDLIN, write the PROTO2.MNU file, SCREEN menu, listed below; the file path \ACAD\PROTO\PROTO2.MNU:

```
 1: ***SCREEN
 2: [-PLOT-]
 3: [-SHEET-]
 4: [A4-HOR]^C^Clayer;make;border1;color;green;border1;new;border,+
 5: btext0,btext1;freeze;border,btext0,btext1;;limits;0,0;277,180;+
 6: zoom;all;line;0,0;277,0;277,180;0,180;c;insert;+
 7: /acad/proto/title1;280,0;;;;\\\\\\\\\\+
 8: (setvar ''textsize'' 2.5);layer;set;0;;$s=insrt
 9: [A3-HOR]CClayer;make;border1;color;green;border1;new;border,+
10: btext0,btext1;freeze;border,btext0,btext1;;limits;0,0;390,277;+
11: zoom;all;line;0,0;390,0;390,277;0,277;c;insert;+
12: /acad/proto/title1;390,0;;;;\\\\\\\\\\+
13: (setvar ''textsize'' 2.5);layer;set;0;;$s=insrt
14: [A-HOR]^C^Clayer;make;border1;color;green;border1;new;border,+
15: btext0,btext1;freeze;border,btext0,btext1;;limits;0,0;+
16: 10,7.25;zoom;all;line;0,0;10,0;10,7.25;0,7.25;c;+
17: insert;/acad/proto/title1;10,0;.039;;;\\\\\\\\\\+
18: (setvar ''textsize'' (/ 3.0 32));layer;set;0;;$s=insrt
19: [B-HOR]^C^Clayer;make;border1;color;green;border1;new;border,+
20: btext0,btext1;freeze;border,btext0,btext1;;limits;0,0;+
21: 15.75,10;zoom;all;line;0,0;15.75,0;15.75,10;0,10;+
22: c;insert;/acad/proto/title1;15.75,0;.039;;;\\\\\\\\\\+
23: (setvar ''textsize'' (/ 3.0 32));layer;set;0;;$s=insrt
24:
25: [-INSRT-]$s=insrt
26:
27: [DataList] You will complete this macro later.
28:
29: [ACADMNU]menu;acad
30:
31: quit
32: end
33: save
34:
35: [next]$s=insrt
36:
```

Discussion of SCREEN menu. The PROTO2 SCREEN menu is similar to the PROTO1 SCREEN menu with some minor changes. You should note that in line 4 the current layer is *BORDER1*, not BORDER. The

BORDER layer is created, but the FREEZE command is used to turn it and BTEXT0 and BTEXT1 off. This is necessary since each drawing inserted has a border and title block on those layers, and you do not want those borders and title blocks displayed.

A title block name TITLE1 is inserted into the drawings. It is a copy of TITLE block used in the PROTO1 menu with the layer names changed. The TITLE1 block will be drawn later.

AutoLISP is used to bind the text height of 2.5 mm or ³⁄₃₂ inch to the system variable TEXTSIZE, depending on the drawing sheet selected (lines 8, 13, 18, and 23).

INSRT submenu. The SCREEN menu calls the following INSRT submenu to provide for insertion of drawings:

```
37: **insrt
38: [INSERT](if (not dwgin) (load ''/acad/lisp/dwgin''));+
39: (dwgin)
40:
41: MOVE
42: ERASE
43: FILES
44: [ -TEXT- ]
45: [ small ](if (< (getvar ''textsize'') 1) (setq tq tex (/ 3.0 32))+
46: (setq tex 2.5));text;\!tex;\\
47: [ medium](if (< (getvar ''textsize'') 1) (setq tex (/ 1.0 8))+
48: (setq (tex 3.0));text;\!tex;\\
49: [ large ](if (< (getvar ''textsize'') 1) (setq tex (/ 3.0 16))+
50: (setq tex 4.0));text;\!tex;\\
51:
52: [LTSCALE](if (< (getvar ''textsize'') 1)+
53: (setvar ''ltscale'' (/ 3.0 4))+
54: (setvar ''ltscale'' (* 25.4 (/ 3.0 4))))
55: [DIMSCALE](setq dims (/ (getvar ''textsize'') 0.18));+
56: dim dimscale !dims exit
57:
58: [DataList] You will complete this macro later.
59: [ROOTMENU]$s=SCREEN
60: [ACADMNU]menu;acad;
61: quit
62: end
63: save
```

Discussion of INSRT submenu. The drafter selects the [INSERT] command in line 38 to insert a drawing into the multiscale drawing. The IF primitive is used in the macro in line 38 to determine if the DWGIN function has been loaded. If not, the PROTO2.LSP file containing the function is loaded. The DWGIN function is invoked in line 39 and is listed in Section 6.5.2. A function may be loaded from a menu—as in line 38—but a function *cannot* be loaded from inside another function with AutoCAD releases prior to Release 10.

The AutoCAD FILES command is included in the menu so the user can list drawing files should the name of the drawing to be inserted is forgotten.

Lines 45, 47, and 49 provide the user with text-size options when adding text to the multiscale drawing. If the value bound to the system variable TEXTSIZE is less than 1, the drawing is in Imperial units; otherwise it is SI units. The system variable TEXTSIZE is assigned in lines 8, 13, 18, and 23 of the SCREEN menu.

The drafter sets the linetype scale by selecting [LTSCALE] from the menu. The system variable TEXTSIZE is checked to determine if the drawing is in Imperial units or SI units. Equation 1.4 is used to determine LTSCALE (the plot scale is 1:1 for this drawing).

If it is necessary to add dimensions to the multiscale drawing (generally, it should not be), the drafter may set DIMSCALE prior to beginning dimensioning by selecting [DIMSCALE] from the menu. Equation 1.2 is used to calculate DIMSCALE. The drafter would next select [ACADMENU] to load the standard ACAD menu for dimensioning.

6.5.2 DWGIN user-defined function

The DWGIN function is invoked in line 39 of the PROTO2 menu. This function inserts drawings into the multiscale drawing. The pseudocode for the DWGIN function is as follows:

> Request name of drawing to be inserted
> Check to see if the drawing file exists
> Error: The file does not exist, then
> > Request a new drawing name
> > And/or file path, or
> > Exit
> Read the inserted drawing PROTO1 data file
> Request the insertion point
> Request the insertion scale factor, using 1/f as the default value
> Request the rotation angle
> INSERT the drawing
> Append the inserted drawing data to a data file

Using EDLIN, write the following function using the file path \ACAD\LISP\DWGIN.LSP:

```
1: ; *** DWGIN function ***
2: (defun dwgin (/ indwg      ; name of drawing to insert
3:                 datafile ; file path to <indwg>.dat
4:                 file     ; <indwg> file pointer
5:                 f        ; <indwg> scale factor read
6:                 name     ; <indwg> name read
7:                 pr prmpt a ; prompt strings
8:                 pt scl ang ; insert variables
9:                 thisdwg) ; name of current drawing
10: ;   Get name of drawing to insert.
```

```
11: (setq indwg (getstring ''\nInsert dwg.? [ex. misc/test]: ''))
12: ;   Open drawing PROTO1 data file for reading.
13: (setq datafile (strcat indwg ''.dat''))
14: (setq file (open datafile ''r''))
15: ;   Read file, bind data to symbols & close file.
16: (setq name (read-line file) f (read-line file))
17: (close file)
18: (setq f (atof f)); Convert string ''f'' to real.
19: ;   Create insert scale prompt.
20: (setq pr (rtos (/ 1.0 f) 2 4)); convert 1/f to string.
21: (setq prmpt (strcat ''\nInsertion scale <'' pr ''>:''))
22: ;   Get insertion point, scale & rotation angle.
23: (if (null (setq pt (getpoint ''\nInsertion point <0,0>'')))
24:    (setq pt (list 0 0)))
25: (if (null (setq scl (getreal prmpt)))
26:    (setq scl (/ 1.0 f)))
27: (if (null (setq ang (getangle ''\nRotation angle <0>: '')))
28:    (setq ang 0))
29: ;   Invoke INSERT command.
30: (command ''insert'' indwg pt scl scl ang)
31: ;   Is inserted drawing data to be filed?
32: (setq a (strcat ''\nFile '' indwg '' data? <Y/N>: ''))
33: (if (= (yesno a) ''Y'')
34:    (progn ; If yes read current drawing name.
35:          (setq thisdwg (getvar ''dwgname''))
36:          ; Open drawing PROTO2 data file for appending.
37:          (setq datafile (strcat thisdwg ''.dat''))
38:          (setq file (open datafile ''a''))
39:          ; Write drawing PROTO2 data to file.
40:          (foreach n '(name ''\n'' f ''\n'') (princ (eval n) file))
41:          (close file)); Close file and Exit from PROGN.
42:    );   Exit from IF.
43: );   End of function.
44: ;
45: ; *** ERROR function ***
46: (defun *error* (msg)
47:    (if (= msg ''file not open'')
48:       (progn
49:       (prompt ''\nFile not found. '')
50:       (prompt ''Select [FILES] to view file names.\n''))
51:       (prompt (strcat ''Error: '' msg ''\n'')))
52: ); End of ERROR function.
53: Add your YESNO function here.
```

Discussion of DWGIN function. In line 11 of the function the GETSTRING primitive is used to get from the drafter the name of the drawing to be inserted into the multiscale drawing. Notice the new-line character ("\n") used so that the prompt appears on a new line. The name of the drawing to be inserted is bound to the symbol INDWG.

In line 13 the STRCAT primitive is used to concatenate the string bound to INDWG and the file extension .DAT. For instance, if the drafter enters the drawing name as 101SP01, the file name becomes 101SP01.DAT. The file name is bound to the symbol DATAFILE. In Section 6.4 the PROTO1 *script* file was modified to call a function named DWGDATA (Section 6.4.1), which writes the drawing name and scale factor to the data file. For example, drawing 101SP01 is written to the file 101SP01.DAT.

The file is opened for reading in line 14, and the READ-LINE primitive is used in line 16 to read the name and scale factor of the drawing to be inserted. The name that is read is bound to the symbol NAME, and the scale factor is bound to the symbol F. The file is then closed.

The READ-LINE function always returns data as a string. The scale factor bound to F is to be used mathematically later in the program, so it must be converted to a real number. This conversion is done in line 18 with the ATOF primitive.

If the file name is incorrect or not found, processing is halted and a "File not found" error message is returned. The ERROR function at the end of the program is used to print the error message. The ERROR program is discussed in Section 6.5.8.

6.5.3 GETPOINT primitive. AutoLISP's GETPOINT primitive is used in line 23 to get the insertion point for the drawing being inserted. The syntax of GETPOINT is

```
(getpoint [<pt>] [<prompt>])
```

GETPOINT pauses for input of a point. <pt> is an optional 2-D or 3-D base point from which AutoCAD draws a rubber-band line to the cursor position. The point can be entered by typing in a coordinate or by pointing on the monitor. The <prompt> is an optional string (see Section 6.5.4).

In lines 23 and 24, if a null point (see Section 6.5.4) is entered (by pressing Enter) for the GETPOINT primitive, the list 0,0 is bound to the symbol PT. If a point (non-null) is entered via the keyboard or by pointing with the mouse, the coordinate entered is bound to the symbol PT.

6.5.4 Default input data and NULL primitive. A prompt requesting the insert scale factor is prepared in line 21. The prompt is to include as its default, the insertion scale factor which is calculated as the inverse of the scale factor, F, read from the PROTO1 data file for the drawing to be inserted. The scale factor is converted from a string to a real number using the ATOF primitive in line 18.

The STRCAT primitive used to "string together" the prompt in line 21 requires the insertion scale factor 1/F to be string data. The RTOS primitive is used in line 20 to convert the real number, 1/F, to a string with a decimal mode and four digits to the right of the decimal (see Section 6.3.2). For example, if the scale factor F is 10, the string bound to the symbol PR in line 20 is ("0.1000"), and the string bound to PRMPT in line 21 is ("\nInsertion scale <0.1000>: ").

In lines 25 and 26 the insertion scale is to be entered:

```
25: (if (null (setq scl (getreal prmpt)))
26:     (setq scl (/ 1.0 f)))
```

The GETREAL primitive displays the string assigned to PRMPT. The drafter may input a real number or a null value by pressing Enter without keying in a number. If a real number is entered, it is bound to the symbol SCL by the SETQ primitive in line 25, which returns the real number assigned to it, thereby causing the NULL primitive to return "nil" (see the syntax that follows). Consequently the IF primitive does not evaluate its <then expression> (line 26) since its <test expression> is nil. In this case the value bound to SCL is the real number entered by the drafter.

If the drafter presses Enter without entering a real number, the value bound to SCL is nil. The NULL primitive returns T, and the IF primitive evaluates line 26 where the insertion scale is calculated as 1/F (the default value) and is bound to the symbol SCL.

The syntax of the NULL primitive is

```
(null <argument>)
```

NULL checks to see if its <argument> is an empty list, or nil. If it is, NULL returns T; otherwise it returns nil. For example, if 3 is bound to the symbol A and nil to the symbol B,

```
(null a)    returns nil
(null b)    returns T
(null '( )) returns T
```

6.5.5   GETANGLE primitive

A similar (but simpler) procedure to that discussed in Section 6.5.3 is used in lines 27 and 28 to request the insertion angle with a default value of 0. The GETANGLE primitive is used to request the angle. The syntax of GETANGLE is

```
(getangle [<pt>] [<prompt.])
```

GETANGLE returns, in radians, the angle entered. The angle may be entered as a number in the current angle units format or by pointing to two 2-D locations on the monitor. If <pt> is included, it is assumed byAutoCAD to be the first of these two points. This primitive is used in more applications in Chapter 7.

6.5.6 COMMAND primitive

The AutoCAD INSERT command is invoked using the COMMAND primitive in line 30 to insert the desired drawing. The syntax of the COMMAND primitive is

```
(command <arguments> ...)
```

The <arguments> are AutoCAD commands followed by their subcommands. Each command is issued as a string and hence is enclosed with double quote characters. Invoking (command "") is equivalent to pressing Ctrl-C.

GETxxx primitives cannot be used inside the COMMAND primitive. Since the drafter is to specify insert data, that data must be requested prior to invoking the INSERT command in line 30.

The INSERT command options—insertion point, x- and y- insertion scales, and rotation angle—are obtained using GETxx primitives and bound to symbols in lines 21 to 28. They are referenced in line 30 as follows:

```
30: (command ''insert'' indwg pt scl scl ang)
```

The following data is bound to the symbols referenced as command options:

INDWG   Name of drawing being inserted.

PT   Insertion point

SCL   X and Y insertion scale

ANG   Insertion angle

6.5.7 PROTO2 data file

The PROTO2 data file is to contain a list of names and scale factors for each drawing inserted into the multiscale drawing. In line 32 of the DWGIN function, the STRCAT primitive is used to concatenate a prompt which is used as an argument in the user-defined YESNO utility function (see Section 5.6) in line 33. If the name of the inserted drawing is 101SP01C, the prompt bound to the symbol A is (\nFile 101SP01C data? <Y/N>:). The YESNO user-defined function is used to ask if the drafter wishes to file the drawing name and scale factor; hence, it will have to be included in the same LISP file as the DWGIN function so that it is loaded at the same time.

The YESNO function is combined with AutoLISP's IF primitive in line 33. If the user enters Y, a number of expressions are to be executed, where only one is expected by the IF primitive. The PROGN primitive is necessary in line 34 to invoke a sequence of expressions, where only one is expected by AutoLISP.

In line 35 AutoLISP's GETVAR primitive is used to retrieve the name of the current drawing from AutoCAD's system variable DWGNAME. The drawing name and the file extension .DAT are concatenated to form the name of the PROTO2 data file. The file is opened for appending and the name and scale factor of the inserted drawing are appended to the file, and the file is closed.

6.5.8   Error handling

When the AutoLISP evaluator detects an error during evaluation of a function or expression, processing is halted, an error message is displayed, and the current stack contents are dumped. The *ERROR* symbol is a special symbol recognized by AutoLISP that may be used in a user-defined function to stop the stack dump and provide a more elegant ending. The syntax of *ERROR* is

```
(*error* <string>)
```

The <string> passed to the function is an error message (see Appendix B of your *AUTOLISP Programmer's Reference* manual.)

The following function prints Error:, followed by the standard AutoLISP error message without the stack dump:

```
(defun *error* (msg)
    (prompt (strcat ''Error: '' msg ''\n'')))
```

In the DWGIN function a more elaborate procedure is used. In line 47 a specific error message, "file not open," is checked for and, if encountered, specific instructions are printed:

```
File not found. Select [FILES] to view file names.
```

If any other error message is passed to the function, it is printed out verbatim. For a list of AutoLISP error messages refer to Appendix B in your *AutoLISP Programmer's Reference* manual.

Assignment. **Note:** Some of these assignments *must* be completed for the PROTO2 menu to work.

In Section 6.4 you modified your PROTO1 *script* file to load a function named DWGDATA. DWGDATA has the file path ACAD\LISP\ DWGDATA.LSP and writes the current drawing name and scale factor to a file with the same name as the current drawing, plus the extension .DAT.

In Section 6.5 you wrote a PROTO2 menu with the file path \ACAD\PROTO\PROTO2.MNU for the drafting of a multiscale drawing. The PROTO2 menu allows for the selection of a drawing sheet, draws a border, inserts a title block, and provides for the insertion of a drawing into the multiscale drawing. The menu loads a DWGIN function (see Section 6.5.2) to insert drawings. The file path for the DWGIN function is \ACAD\LISP\DWGIN.LSP.

1. In your PROTO2 menu a block named TITLE1 is inserted into the border. This block is the same as your TITLE block loaded by PROTO1; however, the layers must be changed. This block is to be created as follows:

a. Use the DOS COPY command to copy the file named TITLE.DWG to a file named TITLE1.DWG.

b. Boot up AutoCAD and edit TITLE1. Use the AutoCAD RENAME command as follows (or use the Modify Layer dialogue box):

```
UTILITY <return> RENAME <return>
Block/LAyer/LType/Style/UCS/View/VPort: Layer <return>
Old layer name: border <return>
New layer name: border1<return>
```

Also change the layer name for layer BTEXT0 to BTEXT and BTEXT1 to TEXT.

If you are plotting onto preprinted sheets, you have to turn layers BORDER1 (the border) and BTEXT (the title block heading) off prior to plotting so they do not plot.

2. The PROTO2 *menu* file is to be loaded from the PROTO1 *menu* file. Edit your PROTO1 *menu* file and add to the SCREEN menu the option [MULTISCL], along with a macro that loads the *PROTO2.MNU* file if this option is selected.

When you wish to create a multiscale drawing, you begin a new drawing with an appropriate name. The Author recommends that the drawing name follow the suggestion in Section 1.2.3 with a P (plot) instead of C at the end of the name. For instance, the multiscale structural steel drawing named 101SP01C would have the name 101SP01P.

3. In lines 25 and 58 of your PROTO2 *menu* the selection [DataList] is provided to let the drafter view the names and scale factors for inserted drawings. Write the following expressions that are to be invoked when DATALIST is selected from the menu:

a. An AutoLISP expression that checks to see if a function named DATALIST is loaded, loads the function if necessary, and then invokes the function.

b. A function named DATALIST invoked by the preceding expression. The pseudocode is as follows:

Flip to the text screen using the COMMAND primitive to execute AutoCAD's TEXTSCR command

Read the current drawing name from the System Variable library

Use the STRCAT function to a add the extension .DAT to the drawing name and then assign to a symbol

Set up a WHILE loop, using the NOT and NIL expressions to check to see if a data file with the drawing name plus extension .DAT exists

If the file exists, open it for reading and read the names and scale factors of drawings inserted

Print each name and scale factor on a new line of the monitor as follows:

> name: xxxxxxxx scale:xxxxxxxx

Prompt the user to press any key to continue (use GETSTRING to halt execution and wait for a key to be pressed)

Invoke AutoCAD's GRAPHSCR command to switch from the text screen to the graphics screen End the function

4. Variables (and user-defined functions) are stored in RAM and not with the drawing file. As a result, any AutoLISP variables required when a drawing is reloaded for editing must be saved in a data file and retrieved as required. Insert the following lines in your PROTO1.SCR file (lines 20 and 21 for Ver. 2.62):

```
16: (if (not dwgdata1) (load ''/acad/lisp/dwgdata1''))
17: (dwgdata1)
```

a. Write the user-defined function named DWGDATA1.LSP that opens a file for writing and writes the data bound to the following symbols to the file: CONV, F, STXT, SMALL, MEDIUM, and LARGE. The file code will be similar to that used for the DWGDATA function in Section 6.4.1. The name of the file to be opened is the same as the current drawing name and has the extension .PR1.

b. Write a user-defined function named DWGIN1.LSP that reads the data that was written to the file by DWGDATA1. This function will be similar to DWGIN.LSP function in Section 6.5.2 (but the insert facilities after line 19 are not required).

c. Edit the ACAD.MNU file and add a selection [PROTO-ED], which when selected invokes an expression to load and invoke the DWGIN1 function. When a drawing is to be edited, this command is selected to load in variables stored by the DWGDATA1 function.

Traverse Program

OBJECTIVE   *To study the process of writing a complex AutoLISP program by developing a program that inputs the interior angles and line distances of a closed-loop traverse, adjusts the angles and lines for closure, sets the screen limits, and draws the traverse.*

7.1   What Is a Traverse?

A closed-loop traverse consists of a series of straight lines connecting survey points along the route of a survey, closing on the first point of the traverse. The purpose of a traverse is to provide horizontal control for surveys to locate or establish property boundaries, topographical maps, and construction layouts for highways, railways, etc.

For an interior-angle closed-loop traverse, the surveyor sets up on a first point and measures the angle between a known, or assumed, northerly line and a line connecting the first and second point of the traverse. This angle is known as the "azimuth" of the first line of the traverse (see Figure 7.1). Successive measurements of the interior angles and distances connecting points along the route of the survey are made, with the last line of the traverse closing on the first point. Figure 7.1 illustrates a closed-loop traverse with observed interior angles and line lengths.

The survey drafter interprets the field data, making appropriate adjustments to the angles and lengths to ensure that the traverse closes, and completes a drawing of the traverse.

The bearing of a line defines its direction with respect to the northeast, northwest, southeast, or southwest. A bearing angle defines the quadrant a line falls in, so that a line running 60 degrees and 30 minutes (60d30') counterclockwise from the north falls in the NW quad-

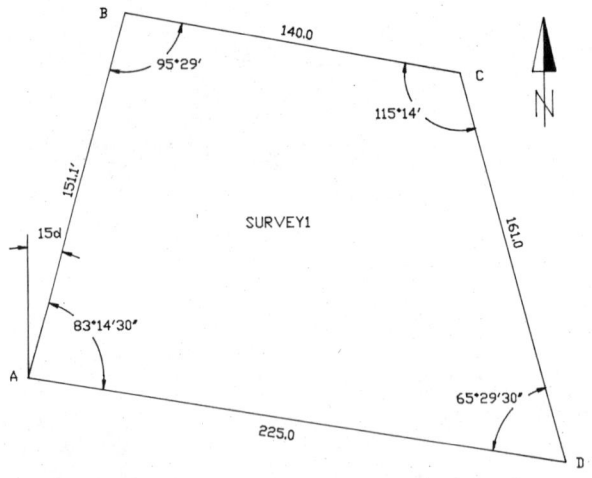

Figure 7.1 Traverse field data.

rant and has a bearing of N60d30'W, whereas a line running 119d30' counterclockwise from the north falls in the SW quadrant and has a bearing of S60d30'W.

The traverse drawing will include a table of the northings and eastings of each station (see Chapter 8). These are the x and y coordinates of each station. The first station is given the coordinates of

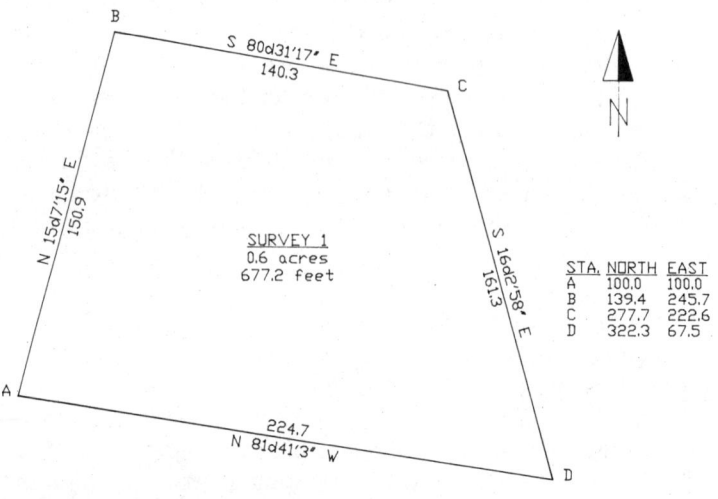

Figure 7.2 Traverse drawing.

100,100 so that it is unlikely any station will have a negative north-ing or easting.

A traverse drawing produced by the final program (including Chapter 8 additions) is illustrated in Figure 7.2.

7.2 Traverse Program

Three secrets of easy programming with AutoLISP are: break the program into a number of small segments, write a function to process each segment, and debug the function before proceeding with the next. Following these principles, the traverse program is composed of a number of user-defined functions invoked by a main function named TRAVERSE. The traverse program does the following:

- Sets system variables and invoke functions
- Inputs data
- Determines the precision of line measurements
- Corrects angles for closure
- Calculates coordinates for each station
- Corrects coordinates for closure
- Sets screen limits
- Draws the traverse
- Adds text to the drawing (see Chapter 8)

The TRAVERSE.LSP program is written using EDLIN as follows:

```
Command: edlin \acad\lisp\traverse.lsp
*i
 1: ; *** TRAVERSE Program ***
 2: ;
 3: ; Interior-angle closed traverse program—adjusts traverse
 4: ; for closure of angles and directions and draws traverse.
 5: ;
 6: ;------------------------
 7: (vmon)    ; Set virtual function pager on.
 8: ;         ** TRAVERSE Function **
 9: (defun traverse ()
10:    ;*** Set system variables
11:    (setvar ''aunits'' 1) ; degrees/minutes/seconds angles
12:    (setvar ''auprec'' 4) ; precision to 1 second
13:    (setvar ''angbase'' 0) ; 0 degrees East
14:    (setvar ''angdir'' 0) ; +'ve angles counterclockwise
15:    ;
16:    ; *** Function calls
17:    ;(input) ; Call INPUT function
18:    ;(prec) ; Call PRECision function
19:    ;(anglerr) ; Call ANGLe ERRor function
20:    ;(calc) ; Call coordinate CALCulation function
```

```
21:  ;(closerr) ; Call coordinate CLOSure ERRor function
22:  ;(drawlim) ; Call DRAWing LIMits function
23:  ;(drawtrav) ; Call DRAW TRAVerse function
24:  ;(addtext) ; Call ADD TEXT function (Chapter 8)
25: )        ; Exit
26: ;-----------------------------
```

Discussion of main program. The VMON command in line 7 of the program is AutoLISP's "virtual function pager" and is used in larger programs in which the available node space (set by SET LISPHEAP in your AUTOEXEC.BAT file) may be insufficient. Once set, AutoCAD will page out infrequently used functions whenever it runs out of memory and automatically read them back in when needed. Only functions that follow the VMON command in the program will be paged. **Note:** Local variables are to be included in the variable list following the function name. They are not included at the early stages of writing the TRAVERSE function because local variables return to their original value when the program is exited, and it is important when debugging a program to be able to list data stored in variables. This must be remembered when writing AutoLISP programs and is another secret of easier programming with AutoLISP.

7.2.1 Angle system variables

AutoCAD system variables governing angles are set in lines 11 to 14, inclusive, using the SETVAR primitive.

AUNITS sets the angle units mode. The following are valid entries:

Setting	Mode	Example
0	Decimal degrees	29.98
1	Degrees/minutes/seconds	29d59'06"
2	Grads	33.3166
3	Radians	0.52333
4	Surveyors units	N29d59'30"E

AUPREC sets the angle unit's decimal place. An integer from 0 to 6 may be entered. The integer 4 sets the precision of angles to four digits to the right of the decimal (to the nearest second).

ANGBASE sets the zero-angle direction with respect to the initial AutoCAD direction of 0 degrees as east. A real number in radians is to be entered. The default east direction for 0 degrees is entered (consequently this line need not be included in the TRAVERSE function). If 0 degrees was to be at the top of the screen, a value of $\pi/2$ would have been assigned to ANGBASE.

Although it is customary in survey work to set 0 degrees at the top of the screen, it is not done in this program because AutoCAD always defines north at the 90 degree location, and it is also customary in traverse work to use north as the top of the drawing. By setting 0 degrees east, AutoCAD will set north at the top of the screen providing the angles are measured counterclockwise.

ANGDIR sets the positive direction for angles. An integer of 1 sets positive angles clockwise, and an integer of 0 sets positive angles counterclockwise.

It is customary to use clockwise as +'ve in traverse work; however, ANGDIR is assigned the integer 0, making counterclockwise positive in the TRAVERSE function. This is done because AutoLISP angle primitives always use counterclockwise as positive (regardless of ANGDIR), and you will find that life is much easier if you accommodate those primitives. Angles may be entered into the program using clockwise as positive providing they are multiplied by -1 in the program.

7.2.2 Function calls

Lines 17 to 24 call functions that perform various segments of the program. Currently they all begin with a semicolon and are comment lines. This is another secret of easier programming in AutoLISP. You will see how it works later. The TRAVERSE function ends with a right parenthesis in line 25.

7.3 Degree-to-Radian and Radian-to-Degree Functions

When working with angles in AutoLISP, it is often necessary to convert degrees to radians and radians to degrees. The following conversion program should be added to your TRAVERSE.LSP file:

```
27: ;
28:      ** Conversion Functions **
29: (defun dtr (a) ; Degrees To Radians
30:    (/ (* a pi) 180)
31: )
32: (defun rdt (r) ; Radians To Degrees
33:    (/ (* r 180) pi)
34: )
35: ;--------------------------
```

Both DTR and RTD take one argument, the angle in degrees to be converted to radians or the angle in radians to be converted to degrees.

7.4 Debugging

The first secret of easier programming with AutoLISP is to break the program into a number of manageable functions. The second is to test each function and debug it before progressing to the next. To test the functions load the TRAVERSE file as follows:

```
Command: (load ''/acad/lisp/traverse'')
```

If you are storing your LISP files on a disk in drive B:, you enter

```
(load ''b:traverse'')
```

If the operation is successful, AutoLISP returns the name of the last function defined in the file: RTD. If AutoCAD is unsuccessful, it will return the name of the file being loaded, followed by an error message and a dump of the current stack contents. Or, if you have insufficient closing parentheses, AutoLISP will return n> indicating that *n* right parenthesis are missing.

Responding to missing parenthesis usually involves typing in the number of right parenthesis indicated. If that doesn't work, try preceding the parenthesis with a quotation mark.

If you receive an error message, look the message up in your *AutoLISP Programmer's Reference* manual. Then edit the TRAVERSE file and locate and correct the error. When the TRAVERSE file is loaded without errors, run the TRAVERSE function by entering:

```
Command: (traverse)
```

If there are no errors in the function, AutoLISP returns 0, the value returned by the ANGDIR system variable in line 14, since it is the last function invoked. If you receive another value or an error, check your program listing. **Note:** If you correct errors in the TRAVERSE file, remember to reload it into the LISP evaluator or you will still be working with the old version of the file.

Test your DTR by entering (**dtr 30**). AutoLISP should return 0.523598 or 0.5236 (Release 10). Check the RTD function by entering (**rtd 0.523598**). AutoLISP should return 30.000000 or 30.0 (Release 10). Do not continue the program until the functions are working correctly.

7.5   Traverse Precision

In the INPUT function the user is to be asked to input the "Decimal places for linear units." The integer entered is bound to AutoCAD's LUPREC system variable. When adjusting the traverse coordinates for closure, however, you need a decimal number representing the allowable closure error within the precision of the data entered. For instance, if the precision of the traverse lengths is 0.01, a closure error of 0.006 does not require that an adjustment be made, whereas an error of 0.06 requires an adjustment to the traverse lengths.

If the precision is 0.01, the integer assigned to LUPREC is 2. The following PREC function gets the integer from LUPREC and checks to see if it is greater than 0. If it is, the REPEAT primitive is used to repeat the division of 1.0 by 10 twice (assume LUPREC is 2), returning the number 0.01, which is the desired precision. This number is bound to the symbol #PREC. **Note:** When writing AutoLISP programs that use a lot of symbols, precede the symbol name with #, e.g., #PREC. This way you will not accidentally be redefining one of AutoLISP's primitive symbols, since none begin with #. The syntax of REPEAT is:

```
(repeat <number><expression>. . .
```

REPEAT evaluates each <expression><number> times and returns the value of the last expression. <number> is any positive integer.

Although the PREC function is not invoked in the TRAVERSE function until after the INPUT function, PREC is being written first. The order of function listings does not matter in a program. The order in which they are invoked is what matters.

Add the following PREC function to your TRAVERSE.LSP file:

```
36: ;
37:      ** Precision (PREC) Function ***
38: (defun prec ()
39:    (setq #prec 1)
40:    (if (> (getvar ''luprec'') 0)
41:      (repeat (getvar ''luprec'')
42:        (setq #prec (/ #prec 10.0))))
43:    )
44: )
45: ;--------------------------
```

The symbol #PREC retains the value bound to it after exiting the PREC function and consequently cannot be entered in the local variable list of this function.

Normally you would reload the TRAVERSE file and check the new function before continuing; however, the PREC function cannot be tested now since it can be invoked only after the INPUT function inputs data into LUPREC.

7.6 INPUT Function

The input function is to have three local symbols—the station identification, interior angle, distance to the next advance station, and a prompt string. Since the data assigned to these symbols changes for each station, they will be defined when creating the function as there is little to be gained during debugging by retrieving their assigned value. If you feel that it might help you locate errors in your function by looking at values assigned to the local variables, place a semicolon in front of each variable definition to make it a comment. When you are through debugging, remove the semicolons.

The data bound to the symbols #LIST (the list of traverse data), #ANGSUM (the sum of interior angles—required in the ANGLERR function), #NORTH, and #0AZ is passed to other functions called by the TRAVERSE function after the INPUT function is exited. Consequently, those functions cannot be listed in the local symbol list. They will later be included in the TRAVERSE function local symbol list because it calls all the other functions, and its local variables retain their bound values until it is exited; then the program ends.

Add the following INPUT function to your TRAVERSE program:

```
46: ;
47:          ** INPUT Function **
48: (defun input (/ #id ; Station identification
49:                 #ang ; Station interior angle
50:                 #dist ; Distance to advance station
51:                 #pr ; Prompt
52:   (textscr) ; Flip to text screen
53:   (prompt ''\n\tENTER THE FOLLOWING TRAVERSE INFORMATION:\n\n'')
54:   (prompt ''\tFormat for entering angles is: nndnn'nn\042'')
55:   (prompt ''\n\tFor example: 50d44'30\042\n'')
56:   (setq #north (dtr 90)) ; North at top of screen
57:   (prompt ''\n\tNORTH is at the TOP of the screen.\n'')
58:   ;  *** Get global data
59:   (prompt ''\nAZIMUTH of 1'st line (clockwise +'ve: '')
60:   (setq #0az (* -1 (getangle))) ; Counterclockwise +'ve
61:   (setq #pr ''\nLinear units type (1 = feet, 2 = metres): '')
62:   (initget 1 ''1 2'')
63:   (if (= 1 (getkword #pr))
64:        (setq #lunits ''ft.'') (setq #lunits ''m''))
65:   (setvar ''luprec'' (setq #lprec
66:            (getint ''\nDecimal places for linear units: '')))
67:   (setq #stats (getint ''\nNumber of stations: '') #list nil)
68:   ;  *** Get data for each station.
69:   (prompt ''\n\nEnter station identifier (3 char's. max)'')
70:   (prompt '' ,interior angle, and dist. to advance station.\n'')
71:   (setq #angsum 0)
72:   (repeat #stats
73:     (setq #id (getstring ''\nStation: ''))
74:     ;      Check if id >3 characters
75:     (while (> (strlen #id) 3)
76:         (princ ''\n\tStation id. cannot exceed 3 char's.'')
77:         (setq #id (getstring ''\nStation: ''))
78:     )
79:     (setq #ang (getangle ''\tAngle: ''))
80:     (setq #angsum (+ #ang #angsum)) ; Sum angles.
81:     (setq #dist (getdist ''\tDistance: ''))
82:     (setq #list (cons (list #id #ang #dist) #list))
83:   )(setq #list (reverse #list))
84: )
85: ; --------------------------
```

Discussion of INPUT function. The TEXTSCR primitive at the beginning of this function flips to AutoCAD's text screen (GRAPHSCR flips
to the graphics screen). Lines 53 to 55, inclusive, use the PROMPT
primitive to inform the user how to input angle data. You are already
familiar with the new-line ("\n") and tab ("\t") control characters used
in the prompt messages. The backslash (\) character is also used to
pass character octal codes to the evaluator in the form "\nnn". In line
54 the prompt message is to include the string nndnn'nn"; however,
the character defining seconds ("), if included, would be interpreted as
the end of the literal string. The octal code for the double-quote character is 042. Therefore, the symbol for seconds can be printed in the
prompt message by its octal code in the form \042. The AutoLISP function (PROMPT "nndnn'nn\042") returns nndnn'nn". This is also done
in line 55.

   In line 56, the user-defined function DTR is used to change 90 degrees to radians. The value returned is bound to the symbol
#NORTH. Since the ANGBASE and ANGDIR system variable set-
tings (lines 13 and 14) set east at 3 o'clock and + 've angles counterclockwise, north is therefore at the top of the screen (AutoCAD always
uses north at 90 degrees).

   Contrary to the ANGDIR setting of 0 (Line 13), which defines counterclockwise angles as positive, the prompt in line 59 indicates to the
user that clockwise angles are + 've. This is to conform to standard
survey practice, and the data input for the azimuth angle (see Section
7.1) set by the GETANGLE primitive in line 60 is multiplied by −1.
For a more thorough discussion of why ANGDIR is set to 0, refer to
Section 7.2.1.

   The INITGET primitive (line 62) establishes options for the next
GETxxx primitive (except GETSTRING and GETVAR) and always returns nil. The syntax of INITGET is:

```
(initget [<bits>] [<string>])
```

The optional <bits> argument is an integer with values as follows:

INITGET bits	Meaning
1	Disallow null input.
2	Disallow zero value input.
4	Disallow negative value input.
8	Do not check screen limits.
16	Return 3-D rather than 2-D points.
32	Dashed rubber-band line or box.

Bits are honored only for GETxxx primitives for which they make sense. The bits are to be added for more than one option. For further information refer to your *AutoLISP Programmer's Reference* manual.

INITGET's optional <string> argument defines a list of keywords to be checked by the next GETxxx primitive. In line 62, the INITGET primitive, (initget 1 "1 2"), establishes the parameters for the GETKWORD primitive in line 63. A null input is disallowed and valid keywords are 1 and 2 (AutoCAD will retry if the input is not a 1 or 2). The GETKWORD prompt has been assigned to the symbol #PR in line 61. If the user enters 1 in response to the GETKWORD primitive in line 63, the string "ft." is bound to the symbol #LUNITS. If 2 is entered, "m" is bound to #LUNITS.

In lines 65 and 66 the GETINT, SETQ, and SETVAR primitives are used to get an integer from the user specifying the number of decimal places, bind it to the symbol #LPREC, and also set AutoCAD's linear units' precision system variable LUPREC.

SETQ and GETINT primitives in line 67 get from the user the number of stations in the traverse and bind that number to the symbol #STATS.

Also in line 67, the symbol #LIST is *unbound* by binding nil to it. This is not necessary for the program. But it is necessary when debugging the function to ensure that previous data bound to #LIST is deleted prior to reinvoking the CONS primitive in line 82 which would add the new entities to the front of the entities in the old list. For the same reason, the symbol ANGSUM is set equal to zero in line 71.

Lines 73 to 83 are repeated #STATS times (by the REPEAT primitive in line 72) in order to get a station identifier, angle, and distance to the next advance station for each station. In line 82, starting at the inside of the expression, the LIST primitive returns a list composed of the station data. Next, the CONS primitive is used to add this list (element) to the front of the current list bound to the symbol #LIST. The list returned by CONS is then bound to the symbol #LIST using the SETQ primitive. When REPEAT is exited, the complete list of traverse station data input is bound to the symbol #LIST.

Since the station i.d. cannot exceed three characters, the WHILE primitive (see Section 5.6.4) is used in lines 75 through 78 to test to see if the length of the string bound to #ID exceeds three characters. If it does, the user is asked to reenter the station identifier. The STRLEN primitive is used to return the length of the string bound to #ID. The syntax of STRLEN is:

```
(strlen <string>)
```

The syntax of CONS is:

```
(cons <new first element> <list>)
```

Because the CONS primitive constructs a list by adding elements to the beginning of the current list, the traverse data list is in reverse order, i.e., (("D" 90 150) ("C" 90 42.5) ("B" 150 76.4) ("A" 30 85)). The REVERSE function is used in line 83 to reverse the list of elements bound to #LIST, i.e., (("A" 30 85) ("B" 150 76.4) ("C" 90 42.5) ("D"90 150)).

7.6.1 Debug input function

Reload the TRAVERSE.LSP file as follows:

```
Command: (load ''/acad/lisp/traverse'')
     or (load ''b:traverse'')
```

If the file is loaded successfully, AutoLISP returns the name of the last function in the file:

```
INPUT
```

If the file is not loaded successfully, edit the file and make the necessary changes. If AutoLISP returns 2> , you are missing 2 closing parentheses. Enter)) or ")) and then edit TRAVERSE.LSP and add the missing parentheses.

The TRAVERSE function does not have to be rerun unless you exited AutoCAD. If you did so, rerun TRAVERSE prior to running INPUT.

Run the INPUT function by entering the following data (see the traverse illustrated in Figure 7.1):

```
Command: (input)
ENTER THE FOLLOWING TRAVERSE INFORMATION:
    Format for entering angles is: nndnn'nn''
    For example: 50d44'30''
    North is at the top of the screen.
AZIMUTH of 1st line (clockwise +'ve): 15d
Linear units type (1 = feet, 2 = meters): 1
Decimal places for linear units: 1
Number of stations: 4

Enter station identifier (3 characters max), interior angle, and
    distance to advance station.

Station: A
    Angle: 83d14'30''
    Distance: 151.1
Station: B
    Angle: 95d29'
    Distance: 140
```

You enter the remainder.

When all of the data is entered, AutoLISP displays the data returned by the last expression in the function [with AutoCAD Release 10 the numbers returned are rounded off, i.e., (("A" 1.45284 151)("B" 1.66645 140.0)...) etc.]:

```
(( ''A'' 1.452841 151.100000)( ''B'' 1.666449 140.000000)( ''C'' 2.011201
161.000000)( ''D'' 1.143045 225.000000))
```

Note that the string data in the list is quoted and that angles are in radians. If your output is different, check your program listing against that in the text. Programming logic errors can often be located by listing variables. For instance, to see what has been assigned to the variable #0AZ, enter:

```
Command: !0az
```

The response should be −0.261799 (−*15 degrees in radians*). If it is not, you have either an error in line 60 of your function, or you entered the wrong azimuth while running the program (Release 10 output is −0.2618 rounded).

The PREC function can be checked now because data has been entered using the INPUT function. Run the PREC function as follows:

```
Command: (prec)
```

AutoCAD returns **0.1**, the data bound to the symbol #PREC at the end of the PREC function. If you have an error, debug your PREC function before continuing. Use the GETVAR primitive to retrieve values assigned to AutoCAD system variables. For example:

```
Command: (getvar luprec)
```

returns **1**.

7.7   ANGLERR Function

The sum of interior angles in a traverse (polygon) with n sides must total: $(n - 2) \times 180$. The difference between the sum of the angles entered and this value is the angle error. Each angle is to be corrected by an amount equal to the angle error divided by the number of stations. For example, if the traverse has four sides (four stations), the sum of angles must equal:

$$(4 - 2) \times 180 = 360 \text{ degrees}$$

And, if the sum of angles is 358d30′0″, each angle must be corrected by adding to it the amount:

$$\frac{360 - 358d30'0''}{4} = 0d22'30''$$

The ANGLERR function is as follows:

```
86: ;
87: ;         ** Angle Error (ANGLERR) function **
88: (defun anglerr (/ #1list #2list #ang)
89: ;         Calculate angle error.
90:   (setq #err (- (* (- #stats 2) 180.0)
91:            (rtd #angsum))); Angle error
```

```
 92:    (setq #corr (dtr (/ #err #stats))) ; Correction
 93:    ;   Apply correction to each station.
 94:    (setq #1list #list #tlist nil)
 95:    (repeat #stats
 96:       (setq #2list (car #1list) #1list (cdr #1list))
 97:       (setq #ang (+ #corr (cadr #2list)))
 98:       (setq #2list (list (car #2list) #ang (caddr #2list)))
 99:       (setq #tlist (cons #2list #tlist))
100:    ) (setq #tlist (reverse #tlist))
101: )
102: ; -------------------------
```

Discussion of ANGLERR function. Local symbols #1LIST, #2LIST, and #ANG are temporary storage areas for traverse data. They are defined prior to debugging since the data assigned to them changes during the running of the function and is of little assistance when debugging. Two other local symbols, #CORR and #ERR, will be added to the list after the program has been debugged.

The angle error and correction are calculated in lines 90 to 92. Note the use of the RTD and DTR functions to convert angles to degrees or radians.

The symbol #LIST has the list of traverse information input bound to it. The ANGLERR function applies the correction (bound to #CORR) to each angle in the list and binds the corrected data to #TLIST. In line 94 the list bound to #LIST is bound to the temporary storage symbol #1LIST, and the symbol #TLIST is unbound by assigning nil to it. If #TLIST is not unbound and the function is rerun during debugging, the CONS function in line 99 will add the new elements to the list of previous data.

7.7.1 CAR and CDR primitives

In order to make corrections to the traverse station angles the angles must be extracted from the list bound to the symbol #LIST. Two functions used to extract data from a list are CAR and CDR. The syntax of CAR and CDR is:

```
(car <list>)

(cdr <list>)
```

CAR returns the *first* element of <list>. CDR returns a *list* containing all but the first element of <list>. For example, given that the symbol ALIST has the following list bound to it, (("A" 23 45)("B" 15 32)("C" 18 12)),

```
(car ALIST)    returns    (''A'' 23 45)
(cdr ALIST)    returns    ((''B'' 15 32)(''C'' 18 12))
```

It is important to note that CAR returns an *element* whereas CDR returns a *list*. Although this is illustrated in the preceding example, it may be more apparent in the following:

(car '(a b c)) returns A, an element and (cdr '(a b c)) returns (B C), a list

AutoLISP supports combinations of CAR and CDR up to four levels deep. Each A represents CAR and D represents CDR; for example, referring to the earlier example and the list bound to ALIST:

Function	Equivalent	Returns
(cadr ALIST)	(car (cdr ALIST))	("B" 15 32)
(cdar ALIST)	(cdr (car ALIST))	(23 45)
(caar ALIST)	(car (car ALIST))	"A"

Study the preceding examples. The logic behind the first is: (cdr ALIST) returns (("B" 15 32)("C" 18 12)), so (cadr ALIST) returns the first element of this new list, or ("B" 15 32).

In lines 95 to 100 of the ANGLERR function, the REPEAT primitive repeats the correction process for each station in the traverse as follows (continuing the traverse example started in Section 7.1); values are rounded to six digits for Release 10:

Line 94. #1LIST is assigned the list of traverse data: (("A" 1.452841 151.100000)("B" 1.666499 140.000000)("C" 2.011201 161.000000)("D" 1.143045 225.000000))

Line 96. (setq #2LIST (car #1LIST)) binds the first element of #1LIST to #2LIST: ("A" 1.452841 151.100000), and (setq #1LIST (car #1LIST)) binds the remainder of #1LIST to #1LIST: (("B" 1.666499 140.000000)("C" 2.011201 161.000000)("D" 1.43045 225.000000))

Line 97. (cadr #2LIST) is equivalent to (car (cadr #2LIST)) and returns 1.455241, the angle in radians of station A. The correction, #CORR, is added to the angle, and the corrected angle is assigned to the symbol #ANG.

Line 98. #2LIST is assigned a list with its first element, "A", being the first element of the previous #2LIST, i.e., (car #2LIST); its second element is the corrected angle bound to the symbol #ANG; and its third element, 151.100000, is the last element of the previous #2LIST, i.e., (caddr #2LIST).

Line 99. A list with the symbol #TLIST is constructed with #2LIST as its *first* element using the CONS primitive. #TLIST is to eventually be assigned the new list of traverse data with corrected angles.

Line 100. The right parenthesis closes the REPEAT primitive (from line 95) which repeats the preceding steps for each station in the traverse. When REPEAT is completed, the list bound to #TLIST is the corrected traverse data in descending station order. The REVERSE primitive reverses the list, placing it in ascending station order.

7.7.2 Debug ANGLERR function

Reload the modified TRAVERSE.LSP file, and correct any errors specified by AutoLISP. If the load is successful, AutoLISP returns the name of the last function evaluated, ANGLERR.

If you have not exited AutoCAD since invoking INPUT, invoke the ANGLERR function by entering (**anglerr**). If the function is correct, AutoLISP will return (rounded to six digits for Release 10):

```
((''A'' 1.455241 151.100000)(''B'' 1.668898 140.000000)(''C'' 2.013601
161.000000)(''D'' 1.145445 225.000000))
```

If you have errors in your function, you may wish to recall data bound to symbols; for instance, !#CORR should return 0.002399, and #err, 0.550000. Do not continue until you have completely debugged the function. If you have difficulty locating a bug in a program, it often helps to have it print data while it is running. For instance, you could insert the following new line 97 in the program:

```
97: (princ ''\n'')(princ #2LIST)(princ ''\n'')(princ #1LIST)
```

This line prints the lists bound to #2LIST and #1LIST during each "repeat." It might illustrate a bug. The line should be deleted after the bug is corrected.

7.8 CALC Function

The CALC function is to calculate x and y coordinates for each station in the traverse. The coordinates of the first station are set at 100,100. The function listing is as follows:

```
104: ;
105: ;                    ** CALC Function **
106: (defun calc (/ #llist #2list #ang #lang #id #dist #coords)
107:    ;   Set angle of line 1
108:    (setq #lang (+ #north #0az))
109:    ;   Extract station 1 list from data list.
110:    (setq #llist (car #tlist) #2list (cdr #tlist))
111:    ;   Extract id and dist from station 1 list.
112:    (setq #id (car #llist) #dist (caddr #llist))
```

```
113:    ;  Start coords list.
114:    (setq #coords (list 100.0 100.0)); 1'st Sta. 100,100
115:         #clist nil)
116:    (setq #clist (cons (list #id #coords) #clist))
117:    ;      Loop through traverse list and set stations.
118:    (repeat (- #stats 1)
119:       ;  Extract next station list from data list.
120:       (setq #1list (car #2list) #2list (cdr #2list))
121:       ; Extract station id.
122:       (setq #id (car #1list))
123:       ;  Set station coords.
124:       (setq #coords (polar #coords #1ang #dist))
125:       ;  Add coords to coords list.
126:       (setq #clist (cons (list #id #coords) #clist))
127:       ;  Extract angle and distance to next station.
128:       (setq #ang (cadr #1list) #dist (caddr #1list))
129:       (setq #1ang (- #1ang (- pi #ang)))
130:    )
131:    ;  Calculate closing station.
132:    (setq #id ''ZZ'') ; Last station id is ZZ.
133:    (setq #coords (polar #coords #1ang #dist) #clerr #coords)
134:    (setq #clist (cons (list #id #coords) #clist))
135:    (setq #clist (reverse #clist))
136:    )
137:    ; --------------------------
```

Discussion of CALC function. Local symbols in the variable list are used as temporary storage areas throughout the function. They are defined now since it will not assist in debugging to list their values.

The symbol #CLIST is used in the function to store the list of traverse coordinates. Since it must retain its assigned data after the function is exited, it is a global variable and is not included in the local symbol list.

In line 108 the angle of the first line of the traverse is calculated as 90 degrees (in radians—bound to #NORTH in line 56) plus the angle bound to the azimuth of the first line (bound to #0AZ in line 60). For the traverse data entered in Section 7.6.1 the data bound to #0AZ is −15 degrees (in radians). The value first bound to #1ANG is then 90 − 15 = 75 degrees (in radians), as illustrated in Figure 7.3.

Since the function is well commented, and the algorithm used to extract station data bound to the symbol #TLIST is similar to that used in the ANGLERR function, it will not be discussed in detail.

In line 112 the first station identifier and distance to the next station is extracted and bound, respectively, to the symbols #ID and #DIST. In Line 114 the coordinates of the first station (100,100) are bound to the symbol #COORDS. A list composed of the first station identifier and coordinates is then constructed and bound to the symbol #CLIST in line 116.

In lines 118 to 130 the REPEAT primitive is used to loop through the sequence of calculations for the remaining stations. The algorithm involves the following:

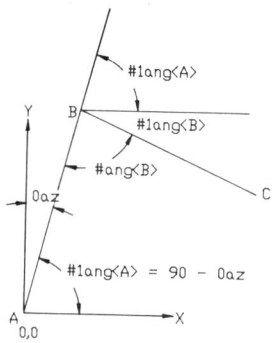

Figure 7.3   Station B coordinates.

Line 120.   Extracts the station traverse data.

Line 122.   Extracts the station identifier from its traverse data and binds it to the symbol #ID.

Line 124.   Calculates the station x,y coordinates using the POLAR primitive (see Section 7.8.1) based on the last station coordinates, the angle bound to #1ang (see Figure 7.3), and distance A-B from the last station and binds the coordinates to the symbol #COORDS. For example, referring to Figure 7.3, the coordinates of station B are calculated as (polar 0,0 #1ang<A> dist<AB>); and the coordinates of station C are (polar B #1ang<B> dist<BC>).

Line 126.   Adds the station and coordinates to the list #CLIST.

Line 128.   Extracts the current station interior angle and binds it to #ANG and extracts the distance to the next station and binds it to #DIST.

Line 129.   Calculates the angle to the next station and binds it to #1ang using the following equation based on Figure 7.3:

#1ang<B> = #1ang<A> – (180 – #ang<B>)   in degrees
#1ang<B> = #1ang<A> – (pi – #ang<B>)   in radians
#1ANG = #1ANG – (pi – #ANG)   the expression

Line 130.   The right parenthesis closes the REPEAT primitive from line 118. The primitives expressions are repeated, or evaluation proceeds to the next expression.

After the REPEAT primitive is exited, the traverse should close on its first point. It is unlikely that it will because of field errors in the traverse lengths (the angles were corrected in the ANGLERR function). Another station identified as ZZ is added to the calculations. Its coordinates are determined following the similar procedures used for the other stations. If its coordinates are 100,100, the traverse has closed on the first station. If not, a correction to each station coordinates is to be made to close the traverse. The ZZ station coordinates are calculated in lines 132 to 134 inclusive. At the end of the expression in line 133 the coordinates of the ZZ station, which are bound to #COORDS, are also bound to the symbol #CLERR, which will be accessed later in the CLOSERR function.

7.8.1 POLAR primitive

The POLAR primitive is used in lines 124 and 133 of the CALC function to calculate the coordinates of a station. The syntax of POLAR is

```
(polar <pt> <angle> <distance>)
```

POLAR returns coordinates of a point at <angle> and <distance> from <pt>. The angle, in radians, is based on the cartesian coordinate system (0 degrees is at 3 o'clock, and counterclockwise rotation is +'ve) regardless of the ANGBASE and ANGDIR settings.

The POLAR primitive is used in the CALC function to return the coordinates of a station. In the first pass of the REPEAT primitive on line 118 the POLAR primitive on line 124 is passed the following data: <pt> is (100 100), the coordinates of station A bound to #COORDS; <angle> is -0.261799, the azimuth of first line bound to #1ANG; and <distance> is 151.100000, the length of first line bound to #DIST. The expression (setq #coords (polar #coords #1ang #dist)) on line 124 is evaluated as:

```
(setq #coords (polar '(100 100) -0.261799 151.10000))
```

It returns (139.107600 245.951400), a list of coordinates of station B, which is then bound to the symbol #COORDS.

7.8.2 Debug CALC function

Reload the TRAVERSE.LSP file and run the CALC function. If the CALC function is successful, AutoLISP returns (for Release 10 numbers are rounded to six digits)

```
''A'' (100.000000 100.000000))(''B'' (139.107600 245.951400))(''C''
(277.23600 233.136000))(''D'' (321.591100 68.366400))(''ZZ''
(98.992860 101.154100))
```

Note that the coordinates of each station are a list and consequently are enclosed in parentheses.

If your functions has errors, correct them before continuing. Remember to add some PRINC expressions if you need help locating errors.

7.9   CLOSERR Function

If the traverse closes, the coordinates of station ZZ will be 100,100 (the same as the coordinates of the first station). If there is a closing error, it is determined in the CLOSERR function and, if it exceeds the precision of the traverse length, an equal correction is made to all station coordinates. The function listing is as follows:

```
138: ;
139: ;      ** CLOSERR function **
140: (defun closerr (/ #1list #2list #xerr #yerr #xadj #yadj)
141: ;          Calc. X & Y error
142:     (setq #xerr (- (car #clerr) 100)
143:           #yerr (- (cadr #clerr) 100))
144:     ;          Compare X and Y error to precision
145:     (if (> (abs #xerr) #prec) (setq #xerr.(/ #xerr #stats))
146:         (setq #xerr 0))
147:     (if (> (abs #yerr) #prec) (setq #yerr (/ #yerr #stats))
148:         (setq #yerr 0))
149: ;          If X or Y error >prec., adjust stat. coords.
150: (if (or (/= #xerr 0) (/= #yerr 0))
151:     (progn
152:         (setq #1list (car #clist) #2list (cdr #clist)
153:               #clist nil)
154:         ;   Do not adjust station 1.
155:         (setq #clist (cons #1list #clist)
156:               #1list (car #2list) #2list (cdr #2list))
157:         ;   Initialize adjustment
158:         (setq #xadj 0.0 #yadj 0.0)
159:         ;      Start adjusting at station 2.
160:         (repeat #stats
161:           (setq #xadj (+ #xadj #xerr) #yadj (+ #yadj #yerr))
162:           (setq #1list (list (car #1list)
163:               (list (- (caadr #1list) #xadj)
164:                     (- (cadadr #1list) #yadj))))
165:         (setq #clist (cons #1list #clist))
166:         (setq #1list (car #2list) #2list (cdr #2list)))
167:     ) (setq #clist (reverse #clist))
168:   )
169: )
170: )
171: ; --------------------------
```

Discussion of CLOSERR function.   In line 133 of the CALC function the list of coordinates for station ZZ is bound to the symbol #CLERR. The coordinates of the first station are 100,100. For the example traverse, the coordinates of station ZZ are 98.992860,101.154100. The closing errors calculated in lines 142 and 143 of the CLOSERR function are as follows:

#Xerr: 98.992860 − 100 = − 1.007140

#Yerr: 101.154100 − 100 = 1.154100

In lines 145 and 147 the x and y errors are divided by the number of stations to obtain the station error. The y station error bound to

#YERR in line 147 is 0.288534, which is printed by adding a PRINC expression in the program. Mathematically, however, 1.154100 / 4 = 0.288525. The discrepancy is caused by the fact that the y coordinate of the ZZ station is returned as 101.154100 but is retained internally with a greater degree of precision (see below). The value returned is truncated at the seventh digit—even though six digits to the right of the decimal are displayed. Strange, but true. **Note:** AutoLISP returns numbers with 7 digits of accuracy (6 for Release 10) but works internally with 14 digits of accuracy and truncates the eighth digit when returning real numbers. Real numbers are also always returned with six digits to the right of the decimal so that (setq a (/ 1.0E4 3)) returns 3333.333000, but (rtos a 2 10) returns 3333.3333333333.

The x and y coordinates of the ZZ station are returned from the list bound to #CLERR using the CAR and CADR functions in lines 142 and 143.

In line 145 the IF and ABS primitives are used to check to see if the absolute value of the x-coordinate error is greater than the precision of the length data (bound to #PREC in the PREC function). If it is, the error per station is calculated by dividing the error by the number of stations and binding the result to the symbol #XERR. If the x-coordinate error does not exceed the precision, 0 is bound to #XERR. A similar procedure is used to determine the y-coordinate station error in lines 147 and 148.

In line 150 and 151 the expression (if (or (/ = #xerr 0) (/ = #yerr 0)) (progn...) is interpreted as: IF the data bound to #XERR is not equal to 0 OR the data bound to #YERR is not equal to 0, THEN evaluate the PROGN expressions bounded by the left parenthesis at line 151 and the right parenthesis at line 169. The PROGN primitive is used to evaluate several expressions, where only one expression is expected by AutoLISP such as, the IF primitive's < then expression >. The IF primitive ends at line 169 and does not have an < else expression >.

In the IF-THEN expression from lines 150 to 169, the x- coordinate and y-coordinate station errors are added to each station's x and y coordinates, respectively, with the exception of the first station, which is to retain the coordinates of 100,100.

For the example traverse, the list bound to #CLIST by the CALC function in Section 7.8.2 is (("A" (100.000000 100.000000)) ("B" (139.107600 245.951400)) ("C" (277.236000 233.136000)) ("D" (321.591100 68.366400)) ("ZZ" (98.992860 101.154100)))

Continuing the example, in line 152 the SETQ and CAR primitives return from #CLIST, the element ("A" (100.000000 100.000000)) and bind it to the symbol #1LIST, and the SETQ and CDR primitives return the list (("B" (139.107600 245.951400) ("C"...))) and bind it to #2LIST. The #CLIST symbol is unbound by binding nil to it.

Since the A-station coordinates are not to be adjusted, the CONS primitive is used in line 155 to construct a list bound to the symbol #CLIST with its first element being the unadjusted data for station A, bound to #1LIST.

In line 155 and 156 the SETQ and CAR primitives return from #2LIST the element ("B" (139.107600 245.951400)) and bind it to #1LIST, and the SETQ and CDR primitives return the list ((("C" (277.236000 223.136000) ("D"...))) and bind it to #2LIST.

An x- and y-coordinate adjustment is to be made to each of the other stations, i.e., B, C, D, and ZZ. Since the station coordinates are based on a traverse line from the preceding station, the corrections are cumulative so that if, for instance, station B correction = 0.1, station C correction is 0.2 and station D correction is 0.3, etc. The symbols to which the x and y adjustments are bound to, #XADJ and #YADJ, are initialized by binding 0 to each in line 158.

The station coordinate correction expressions are repeated for each station (lines 160 through 167) using the REPEAT primitive. For the example traverse the sequence of operations is as follows (the precision illustrated is that returned by AutoLISP rather than that used internally by the LISP evaluator—hence there are some apparent, but not real, mathematical discrepancies):

- From previous lines:

```
#1LIST = (''B'' (139.107600 245.951400))
#2LIST = (((''C'' (277.236000 223.13600))(''D''...)))
#XADJ = 0, #YADJ = 0
#XERR =  - 0.251785, #YERR = 0.288534
```

- Line 161:

```
#XADJ = 0 + ( - 0.251785) =  - 0.251785
#YADJ = 0 + 0.288525 = 0.288534
```

- Lines 162–164:

```
CAR #1LIST = ''B''
CAADR #1LIST = (car (car (cdr #1LIST)))
             = (car (car '((139.107600 245.951400))))
             = (car '(139.107600 245.95140))
             = 139.107600
(- (CAADR #1LIST) #XADJ) = 139.107560 - (- 0.251785)
             = 139.359300
CADADR #1LIST = (car (cdr (car (cdr #1LIST))))
             = (car (cdr (139.107600 245.951400)))
             = (car (245.951400))
             = 245.951400
(- (CADADR #1LIST) #YADJ) = 245.951400 - 0.288534
             = 245.662900
```

Consequently the following list is bound to #1LIST:

```
(''B'' (139.359300 245.662900))
```

- Line 165 constructs a list by adding #1LIST as an element to the front of #CLIST and binds the result to #CLIST returning ((("A" (100.000000 100.000000)) ("B" (139.359300 245.662900)))).

- Line 166 extracts the data for station C from #2LIST and binds it to #1LIST. The data for stations D and ZZ is extracted from #2LIST and bound to #2LIST.

- Line 167 closes the REPEAT from line 148 and repeats the previous expressions for the next station. When all stations have been completed and REPEAT is exited, the list bound to #CLIST is in reverse order of stations. The REVERSE primitive at the end of line 167 is used to reverse the list into ascending station order.

- Line 168 has the closing right parenthesis for the PROGN primitive in line 151.

- Line 169 has the closing right parenthesis for the IF primitive in line 150.

- Line 159 has the closing right parenthesis for the function.

7.9.1 Debug CLOSERR function

Reload the TRAVERSE.LSP file and run CLOSERR. (Note that if you wish to *rerun* CLOSERR, you *must first* rerun CALC since CLOSERR modifies the list bound to #CLIST.) CLOSERR returns the following for the example traverse (Release 10 rounds number to six digits):

```
((''A'' (100.000000 100.000000)) (''B'' (139.359300 245.662900)) (''C''
(277.739500 222.558900)) (''D'' (322.346400 67.5007900)) (''ZZ''
(100.000000 100.000000)))
```

Station ZZ now closes on station A.

7.10 DRAWLIM Function

The DRAWLIM function loops through the list of station coordinates bound to #CLIST and binds the minimum x and y coordinates to the symbols #XMIN and #YMIN and the maximum x and y coordinates to #XMAX and #YMAX.

The traverse width is equal to #XMAX − #XMIN and is bound to the symbol #X (see line 192). The height is bound to the symbol #Y.

The AutoCAD system variable LIMMIN defines the lower left screen limit, and LIMMAX defines the upper right screen limit. The screen width is to be made larger than the traverse dimensions by an amount equal to 1/10 of the traverse total width on the left side (see line

194) and ⅕ of the traverse total width on the right side (see line 196) in order to allow extra space for a north arrow and the table of station northings and eastings (see Chapter 8). For the screen height an amount equal to ¹⁄₁₀ of the total traverse height is added to the top and bottom of the traverse (see lines 194 and 196).

The function listing is as follows:

```
172: ;
173: ;      ** DRAWLIM function **
174: (defun drawlim (/ #1list #2list #xmax #ymax #xmin #ymin #x #y)
175:    ; Set coordinates of first point as max and min.
176:    (setq #1list (car #clist) #2list (cdr #clist))
177:    (setq #xmax (caadr #1list) #ymax (cadadr #1list)
178:       #xmin (caadr #1list) #ymin (cadadr #1list))
179:    ; Loop through list to locate max and min coordinates.
180:    (repeat (- #stats 1)
181:       (setq #1list (car #2list) #2list (cdr #2list))
182:       (if (< (caadr #1list) #xmin)
183:          (setq #xmin (caadr #1list)))
184:       (if (< (cadadr #1list) #ymin)
185:          (setq #ymin (cadadr #1list)))
186:       (if (> (caadr #1list) #xmax)
187:          (setq #xmax (caadr #1list)))
188:       (if (> (cadadr #1list) #ymax)
189:          (setq #ymax (cadadr #1list)))
190:    )
191:    ; Set drawing limits
192:    (setq #x (- #xmax #xmin) #y (- #ymax #ymin))
193:    (setvar ''limmin'' (list
194:       (- #xmin (/ #x 10.0))(- #ymin (/ #y 10.0))))
195:    (setvar ''limmax'' (list
196:       (+ #xmax (/ #x 5.0)) (+ #ymax (/ #y 10.0))))
197:    (command ''zoom'' ''a'')
198: )
199: ; -------------------------
```

Reload the TRAVERSE file and run DRAWLIM. The drawing limits will be set and the invocation of AutoCAD's ZOOM-ALL commands will flip the monitor image to the drawing screen.

7.11 DRAWTRAV Function

The list bound to #CLIST contains the coordinates for each station in the traverse. The DRAWTRAV function is to extract those coordinates from the list and, using the COMMAND primitive, draw the traverse. The function is as follows:

```
200: ;
201: ;      ** DRAWTRAV function **
202: (defun drawtrav (/ #1list #2list #coords)
203:    (setq #1list (car #clist) #2list (cdr #clist))
204:    (setq #coords (cadr #1list))
205:    (command ''pline'' #coords ''0'')
206:       ;  Loop through coords & draw traverse.
```

```
207:    (repeat #stats
208:        (setq #llist (car #2list) #2list (cdr #2list)
209:            #coords (cadr #llist))
210:        (command #coords)
211:    ) (command '''')
212: )
213: ; --------------------------
```

Discussion of function. In lines 203 and 204 the coordinates for the first station are extracted from the list bound to #CLIST and are bound to the symbol #COORDS. The AutoCAD PLINE command is invoked using AutoLISP's COMMAND primitive and the data bound to #COORDS (the coordinates of first point) is returned as the first point of the polyline. The REPEAT primitive is then used to extract the coordinates for the remaining stations of the traverse. Each station then becomes a point in the polyline sequence. The reader should note how the coordinates (bound to #COORDS) are passed to AutoCAD in response to the PLINE requests for points of the traverse in line 210. Remember, the COMMAND primitive is the link between AutoCAD and AutoLISP. The null COMMAND entry in line 211 exits PLINE.

The traverse is drawn using polylines rather than lines because of the versatility of polylines. For instance, the traverse area and perimeter length can be determined by using AutoCAD's AREA command and selecting a point anywhere on the polyline. Station coordinates (polyline vertices) can be easily edited as well using PEDIT.

Reload the TRAVERSE file and run DRAWTRAV.

7.12   Finalizing the TRAVERSE File

Once you have the function debugged, remove the semicolons from the front of the function calls in the TRAVERSE function (except for line 24) so that the functions are invoked by the traverse function.

Next, add the local variables to each function's variable list so that variables revert to their original value, nil, when the function is exited. Local variables named in the main function, TRAVERSE, transfer information to functions called by TRAVERSE and cannot revert to their original value (nil) until the end of the program. The function variable lists are to be modified as follows:

```
(defun traverse (/ #north ; NORTH cartesian angle
                    #lunits ; Length units: ft. or m.
                    #lprec ; Linear units precision
                    #stats ; Number of stations
                    #list ; List of traverse input data
                    #tlist ; Traverse list - angles corr
                    #clist ; List of traverse coordinates
                    #angsum ; Sum of interior angles
                    #0az ; Azimuth of first line
                    #prec ; Length units precision
                    #clerr ; Closure error
```

```
                    )

(defun input (/ #id ; Station identification
                 #ang ; Station interior angle
                 #dist ; Distance to advance station
                 #pr ; Prompt
              )

(defun anglerr (/ #1list #2list #ang #corr #err)
(defun calc (/ #1list #2list #ang #1ang #id #dist #coords)
(defun closerr (/ #1list #2list #xerr #yerr #xadj #yadj)
(defun drawlim (/ #1list #2list #xmax #ymax #xmin #ymin #x #y) (defun
drawtrav (/ #1list #2list #coords)
```

A final listing of the program (including Chapter 8 modifications) is included in Appendix F.

Reload the TRAVERSE.LSP file and run the TRAVERSE function.

Assignment

1. In the CLOSERR function each station's coordinates (excluding the first station) are modified to correct for closing errors. This correction may change the azimuth of the first line from that specified by the user. In practice the azimuth is often assumed to be a known. Consequently the angle (bearing) of line 1 may have to be corrected. Write a function named CHKAZ that is invoked following the CLOSERR function. CHKAZ is to check the angle of line 1 against the specified azimuth. IF the angle does not equal the azimuth, THEN AutoCAD's ROTATE command is to be invoked to rotate the traverse about station #1, thereby correcting the angle of line 1.

2. Write an AutoLISP program to draw a set of stairs. The user is to input the following:

Rise (total stair height)

Desired tread (the horizontal portion of the stair on which you step)

Desired riser (height of one step)

Handrail height ranging from 36 to 42 in

The tread size must fall in the range of 7 to 7 ½ in. The riser (height of on step) must fall in the range of 9 ½ to 10 ½ in.. The slope of the stair must fall in the range of 30 to 35 degrees.

Handrail vertical rails are to be spaced approximately 9 in c/c and are to be anchored to the stair at 60 in c/c.

The program is to follow the format illustrated in this chapter. It is to perform the necessary calculations to design the stair and prepare a list (stored in a list format) of optional tread and riser sizes from which the user is to make a selection. Based on the selection, the program is to draw an elevation (side) view of the stair.

8

Adding Text and Locating Entities

OBJECTIVE   *To extend the TRAVERSE.LSP program from Chapter 7 to add to the traverse drawing—line bearings and lengths, a summary of the traverse area and perimeter, a list of station northings and eastings, and to calculate the relative accuracy ratio of the traverse; also to introduce procedures for accessing AutoCAD entities.*

8.1   ADDTEXT Function

The ADDTEXT function is called by the TRAVERSE function in line 24 (see Chapter 7). ADDTEXT is to:

- Display the screen limits and get the text height from the user

- Print bearings and distances on each traverse line

- Print the station identifications

- Get the traverse title from the user and extract the traverse area and perimeter from the AutoCAD system variable list and to print them

- Calculate and print a list of station northings and eastings

- Print a north arrow on the drawing

- Calculate the traverse relative error

Although ADDTEXT is an extension of the TRAVERSE.LSP file, the author feels it will be less confusing if the EDLIN line numbers in this chapter begin at line 1. Edit your TRAVERSE.LSP file and add the following to the end of the listing (your line numbers will begin from the last number in your file):

```
 1: ;
 2: ;     ** ADDTEXT function **
 3: (defun addtext (/   #txtht   ; Text height
 4:                     #1list   ; List of current station data
 5:                     #2list   ; List of remaining station data
 6:                     #1coord ; Coordinates of current station
 7:                     #2coord ; Coordinates of next station
 8:                     #1id     ; Identifier of current station
 9:                     #2id     ; Identifier of next station
10:                     #0ang    ; Angle of previous line
11:                     #1ang    ; Angle of current line
12:                     #angd    ; Line angle in degrees
13:                     #brg     ; Bearing of a line
14:                     #dist    ; Distance (length) of a line
15:                     #1pt #2pt ; Points for text
16:                     #1stang ; Angle of 1st line
17:                     #per     ; Traverse perimeter
18:     (textscr);           Text screen ''on''.
19:     ; Display screen limits—get text height & dimscale.
20:     (prompt ''\n\nThe screen limits are:'')
21:     (prompt ''\n\tLower left corner '')(princ (getvar ''limmin''))
22:     (prompt ''\n\tUpper right corner '')(princ (getvar ''limmax''))
23:     (initget (+ 1 2 4))
24:     (setq #txtht (getreal ''\n\nSCREEN text height: ''))
25:     (beast)          ; Call BEAring STation text function
26:     (tap)            ; Call Title-Area-Perimeter function
27:     (net)            ; Call Northing-Easting Table
28:     (northar)        ; Call North-ARROW function
29:     (rat)            ; Call Relative-Accuracy-raTio function
30: )
31: ;---------------------------
```

ADDTEXT is a main function that calls a number of subfunctions. The function listing is well commented and will not be discussed in detail. The local symbols in the function's argument list are bindings that are to be transferred to functions called by ADDTEXT. They are determined during the writing of the functions but have been included in the argument list now for clarity. The local symbol #TXTHT has the text height input by the user bound to it (line 24) and is used by functions called by ADDTEXT.

The function begins by displaying the screen limits and requesting input of the text height, which the user determines to suit the intended plot scale based on the screen limits and the plot-sheet size. The INITGET primitive used in line 23 is introduced in Section 7.6. The optional <bits> argument (+ 1 2 4) are: 1—disallow null input, 2—disallow zero value input, and 4—disallow negative value input. The <bits> are honored only for the next GETxxx primitive, which is the GETREAL primitive in line 24.

8.2   Bearing-Station (BEAST) Function

The BEAST function prints the bearing and distance of each traverse line at the midpoint of the line and the station identifier at the station point. This function has no local symbols. Any symbols introduced in

BEAST are to retain their bindings when the function is exited and are consequently listed in the variable list for ADDTEXT. The function listing is as follows:

```
32: ;          ** Bearing-Station (BEAST) Function **
33: (defun beast ()
34:  ;   Get data for first station
35:  (setq #1list (car #clist) #2list (cdr #clist))
36:  (setq #1id (car #1list) #1coord (cadr #1list))
37:  (setq #0ang 99); Set flag for 1'st station
38:  ;   Loop through remaining stations
39:  (repeat (- #stats 1)
40:     ;   Get data for next station
41:     (setq #1list (car #2list) #2list (cdr #2list))
42:     (setq #2id (car #1list) #2coord (cadr #1list))
43:     (brgdst); Call BeaRinG-DiSTance function.
44:     ;   IF not equal to the 1'st station.
45:     (if (/= 99 #0ang) (sta)); Call STAtion function.
46:     ; Prepare for repeat.
47:     (setq #1id #2id #1coord #2coord #0ang #1ang)
48: )
49: ;    Last station.
50: (setq #2coord (cadar #clist))
51: (brgdst); Call BeaRinG-DiSTance function.
52: (sta);       Call STAtion function.
53: ;   Add 1st station identification.
54: (setq #1id (caar #clist) #1coord (cadar #clist))
55: (setq #0ang #1ang #1ang #1stang)
56: (sta);        Call STAtion function.
57: )
58: ;---------------------------
```

A Discussion of BEAST function. A line's bearing and distance are determined and printed by the BRGDST function called by BEAST in line 43. In order to determine the bearing and distance of a line, the coordinates at the *beginning* and *end* of the line are required. This data, along with the station identification, is available in the list bound to the symbol #CLIST.

The coordinates and identifier for the first station are determined in lines 35 and 36 using CAR and CDR primitives. The identifier is bound to the symbol #1ID and the coordinates to #1COORD. In order to locate where a station identification is to be printed on the traverse drawing, the angle of the previous line and the current line are required (see Section 8.2). As a result, the identifier for the first station cannot be printed until the last line is drawn. A flag is set to indicate this is the first line by assigning 99 to the symbol #0ANG in line 37.

In line 39 the REPEAT function is used to repeat a set of expressions for each of the *remaining* stations. In lines 41 and 42 the next station identification is bound to the symbol #2ID and its coordinates are bound to the symbol #2COORD.

The BRGDST function is called in line 43 to calculate and print the current line's bearing and distance. The IF primitive is used in line 45 to check to see if the current station is not the first station, and, if not, the STA function is called to print the station identification.

In line 47 the data for the current *next* station bound to the symbols #2ID and #2COORD is bound to #1ID and #1COORD, respectively, to become data for the new *current* station. Also, the angle of the *current* station, bound to the symbol #1ANG, is bound to the symbol #0ANG to become the angle of the *previous* station. The closing parenthesis for the REPEAT function on line 48 causes evaluation to be repeated for the next station.

The *next* station for the *last* station is the *first* station—station A. In line 50 the coordinates for the first station are bound to the symbol #2COORD, and lines 51 and 52 invoke the BRGDST and STA functions to print the data for the last line of the traverse.

The station identifier for the first station can now be printed. In line 54 the identification and coordinates for the first station are bound to #1ID and #1COORD, respectively. The angle of the first line was calculated in the first pass of the REPEAT primitive by the BRGDST function and bound to the symbol #1STANG. In line 55 the angle of the current line bound to #1ANG is assigned to the symbol #0ANG to become the angle of the previous line; and the angle bound to #1STANG is assigned to #1ANG. The STA function is called in line 56 to print the station identification.

8.3 Bearing-Distance (BRGDST) Function

The BRGDST function calculates and prints the bearing and distance (length) of each line in the traverse at the midpoint of the line. The bearing is printed above the line and the distance is printed below the line. It is called by the BEAST function (see Section 8.2). The listing is as follows:

```
59: ;
60: ;        ** Bearing Distance (BRGDST) Function **
61: (defun brgdst ()
62:  ;       Determine angle and distance of line
63:  (setq #1ang (angle #1coord #2coord)
64:        #dist (distance #1coord #2coord))
65:  ;       If 1st station, save #1ang
66:  (if (= 99 #0ang) (setq #1stang #1ang))
67:  ;          Set Bearing and Distance, and convert to string
68:  (setq #brg (angtos #1ang 4) #txt (rtos #dist 2 #1prec))
69:  ;       Set bearing text location
70:  (setq #pt1 (polar (polar #1coord #1ang (/ #dist 2))
71:                    (+ #1ang (/ pi 2))
72:                    (/ #txtht 2)))
73:  ;       Set distance text location
74:  (setq #pt2 (polar #pt1 (- #1ang (/ pi 2)) (* 2 #txtht)))
75:  ; Write the text
76:  ; Check IF text is upside down: 90
77:  (if (and (> #1ang (/ pi 2)) (< #1ang (*pi 1.5)))
78:      ;   THEN rotate text 180 degrees and move down
```

```
79:    (progn
80:       ; Add 180 degrees angle, convert to degrees
81:       (setq #angd (rtd (+  #lang pi)))
82:       ;   Move text location by #txtht @ 90 degrees
83:       (setq #pt1 (polar #pt1 (+  #lang (/ pi 2)) #txtht))
84:       (setq #pt2 (polar #pt2 (+  #lang (/ pi 2)) #txtht)))
85:    ;    ELSE do not rotate
86:    (setq #angd (rtd #lang))
87: )
88: ;     Print bearing and distance text
89: (command ''text'' ''c'' #pt1 #txtht #angd #brg)
90: (command ''text'' ''c'' #pt2 #txtht #angd #txt)
91: )
92: ;---------------------------
```

Discussion of BRGDST function. The SETQ, ANGLE, and DISTANCE primitives are used in lines 63 and 64 to calculate the angle and distance of the current traverse line from #1COORD to #2COORD and bind them to the symbols #1ANG and #DIST, respectively. The syntax of ANGLE is:

```
(angle <pt1> <pt2>)
```

ANGLE returns the angle in radians between two real coordinate points <pt1> and <pt2>.

The syntax of the DISTANCE primitive is

```
(distance <pt1> <pt2>)
```

DISTANCE returns the distance between the two real coordinate points <pt1> and <pt2>.

In line 66 the IF primitive is used to check to see if the current station is the first station. If it is, the angle bound to #1ANG is bound to the symbol #1STANG for later retrieval.

The angle returned by the ANGLE primitive is in radians based on the setting of the system variables ANGDIR and ANGBASE (current settings are: counterclockwise angles are +'ve, and 0 degrees is east, making north at the top of the screen—see the TRAVERSE function lines 13 and 14). To obtain the bearing of the line, its angle is to be converted to *survey units,* which return an angle as north-east, north-west, south-east or south-west. In line 68 the SETQ and ANGTOS primitives are used to change the angle to a bearing and bind the data to the symbol #BRG. The syntax of the ANGTOS primitive is

```
(angtos <angle> [ <mode> [ <precision> ]])
```

ANGTOS takes a real number <angle> in radians and returns it, edited, as a string. The <mode> argument is an integer indicating the type of editing to be performed, as follows:

ANGTOS mode	Editing format
0	Degrees
1	Degrees/minutes/seconds
2	Grads
3	Radians
4	Surveyor's units

The <precision> selects the number of decimal places desired.

In line 68 the expression (setq #brg (angtos #1ang 4)) returns the angle bound to the symbol #1ANG as a string in *surveyor's units* and binds it to #BRG. Since <precision> is not defined, the current precision of four decimal places is used (see line 12 of the TRAVERSE function—(setvar "auprec" 4)).

The next expression in line 68, (setq #txt (rtos #dist 2 #lprec)), returns the data bound to #DIST as a string in decimal mode with a precision equal to the integer bound to #LPREC (refer to Section 6.3.2 for the syntax of RTOS).

The bearing text location (above the line) is calculated and bound to the symbol #PT1 in lines 70 through 72 using nested POLAR primitives as follows:

```
(polar #1coord #1ang (/ #dist 2))returns the midpoint of the line at angle
#1ANG and distance #DIST/2 from point #1COORD
```

```
(set #pt1 (polar (.. midpoint ..)) (+ #1ang (/ pi 2)) (/ #txtht
2)))returns a point at (#1ANG + 90 degrees) and distance #TXTHT/2 from the
midpoint of the line
```

The distance text is located at an angle of (#1ANG − 90 degrees) and distance (2 × #TXTHT) from #PT1, placing it below the midpoint of the line (see line 74).

If the line falls between 90 and 270 degrees, the text will be printed upside down (try rotating a pencil with the manufacturer's name located on the top when at 0 degrees). This is checked in line 77. If this is so, points #PT1 and #PT2 are rotated by 180 degrees and moved perpendicular (#1ANG + 90 degrees) a distance of #TXTHT. Think about this.

In lines 81 (falls within the IF-THEN) and 86 (falls in the IF-ELSE) the RTD function is used to convert the text angle from radians to degrees for use with AutoCAD's TEXT command.

Finally, the COMMAND primitive is used in lines 89 and 90 to invoke AutoCAD's TEXT command and print the text.

8.4 Station (STA) Function

The STA function is to print the station identifier beside the station location on the traverse drawing. The location of the station is bound

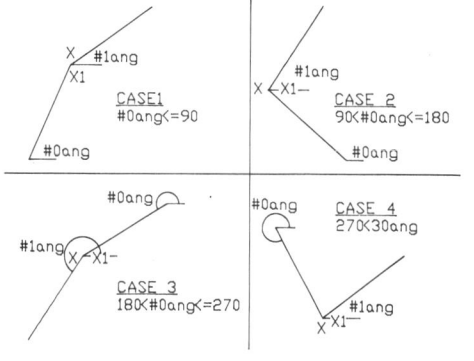

8.1   Station identifier location.

to the symbol #1COORD, and the identifier is bound to the symbol #1ID. The function is composed of a number of IF, AND, and OR primitives to determine where to print the station identification based on the angle of the two intersecting survey lines. The logic is illustrated in Figure 8.1 where X and X1 indicate the available location for printing station identifiers for each case. The station identifier location for case 2, where #0ANG falls between 90 and 180 degrees, is determined in lines 105 to 116 of the function and is discussed in detail following the function listing:

```
 93:  ;
 94:  ;           ** STAtion Function **
 95:  (defun sta ()
 96:    ;   IF #0ang <90
 97:    (if (<=#0ang (/ pi 2))
 98:        (progn
 99:        ; THEN IF #1ang<= 45 or #1ang>  = 180
100:        (if (or (<=#1ang (/ pi 4))(>=#1ang pi))
101:            ; THEN print top side
102:            (progn (setq #pt1 (polar #1coord (/ pi 2) #txtht)))
103:            ; ELSE print bottom side
104:            (setq #pt1 (polar #1coord (* pi 1.5) #txtht)))
105:            (command ''text'' ''c'' #pt1 #txtht 0 #1id))
106: )
107: ; IF 90<#0ang<= 180
108: (if (and (> #0ang (/ pi 2))(<=  #0ang pi))
109:    ;   THEN IF #1ang <= 90 OR #1ang > = 270
110:    (if (or (<=  #1ang (/ pi 2))(>= #1ang (* pi 1.5)))
111:        ; THEN print left side
112:        (progn (setq #pt1 (polar #1coord pi #txtht))
113:            (command ''text'' ''r'' #pt1 #txtht 0 #1id))
114:        ; ELSE print right side
115:        (progn (setq #pt1 (polar #1coord 0 #txtht))
116:            (command ''text'' #pt1 #txtht 0 #1id)))
117: )
118: ; IF 180<#0ang><= 270
119: (if (and (> #0ang pi)(<=  #0ang ((* pi 1.5)))
120:    ;   THEN IF #1ang<= 90 OR # 0ang >= 270
121:    (if (or (<=  #1ang (/ pi 2)) (>= #1ang (* pi 1.5)))
```

```
122:      ;   THEN print left side
123:      (progn (setq #pt1 (polar #1coord pi #txtht))
124:          (command ''text'' ''r'' #pt1 #txtht 0 #1id))
125:      ;   ELSE print right side
126:      (progn (setq #pt1 (polar #1coord 0 #txtht))
127:          (command ''text'' #pt1 #txtht 0 #1id)))
128:      )
129:      ; IF #0ang > 270
130:      (if (> #0ang (* pi 1.5))
131:      ; THEN IF 45<=#1ang<=315
132:      (if (and (>= #1ang (* pi 0.25))(<=  #1ang (* pi 1.75)))
133:      ;    THEN print right side
134:      (progn (setq #pt1 (polar #1coord 0 #txtht))
135:          (command ''text'' #pt1 #txtht 0 #1id))
136:      ;   ELSE print bottom side
137:      (progn
138:          (setq #pt1 (polar #1coord (* pi 1.5) #txtht))
139:          (command ''text'' ''r'' #pt1 #txtht 0 #1id)))
140:      )
141:      )
142:      ;----------------------------
```

Discussion of STA function. This function makes considerable use of the IF, AND, and OR primitives. The syntax of the IF primitive is

```
(if <text exp. > <then exp. > [ <else exp. > ])
```

IF evaluates <test expression> and, if it is not nil, it evaluates a <then expression> and returns the result. Otherwise it evaluates an optional <else expression> and returns the result.

The syntax for the AND primitive is

```
(and <expression> . . . )
```

AND evaluates the <expression>s in sequential order. If any of the expressions evaluates to nil, AND ceases further evaluation and returns nil. Otherwise it returns T.

The syntax for the OR primitive is

```
(or <expression> . . . )
```

OR evaluates the <expression>s in sequential order. If one of the expressions evaluates to nonnil, OR ceases further evaluation and returns T. Otherwise it returns nil.

Lines 108 to 116 of the STA function will be discussed to illustrate the use of the preceding primitives to locate the station identifier for case 2 in Figure 8.1.

Line 108:

```
(if (and (> #0ang (/ pi 2))(<=  #0ang pi))
```

reads .. IF (#0ANG > 90 deg) AND (#0ANG < 180 deg). (This is case 2 in Figure 8.1.)

Line 110: THEN

```
(if (or ( <=#1ang (/ pi 2))(>=#1ang (* pi 1.5)))
```

reads .. IF (#1ANG < = 90 deg) OR (#1ANG > = 270 deg)

Line 112: THEN prints on the *left* side (location X for case 2 in Figure 8.2):

```
(progn (setq #pt1 (polar #1coord pi #txtht))
  (command ''text'' ''r'' #pt1 #txtht pi #lid))
```

The IF primitive expects only one THEN expression, so the PROGN primitive is required to evaluate the expressions. The POLAR primitive returns a point at an angle of 180 degrees (to the left) and #TXTHT units from #1COORD. The point returned is bound to #PT1. The second expression invokes AutoCAD's TEXT command with the right justified option to print the station identifier.

Line 115: ELSE prints on the right side (location X1 for case 2 in Figure 8.1):

```
(progn (setq #pt1 (polar #1coord 0 #txtht))
  (command ''text'' #pt1 #txtht 0 #lid)))
```

This is similar to line 112 but the angle in the POLAR primitive is 0 degrees so the point is to the right of #1COORD. AutoCAD's text command is invoked with the start point at #PT1.

Line 116: The right parenthesis ends the IF primitive from line 108. (Note that there is not an ELSE expression.)

8.4.1 Debug functions

Prior to continuing, run the TRAVERSE and ADDTEXT functions to debug the ADDTEXT, BEAST, BRGDST, and STA functions. Before the functions are run, however, you will have to add semicolons in front of the function calls at lines 26 through 29 since those functions have not been written yet. If your function has bugs, you may want to remove some of the local symbols from the local symbol list in ADDTEXT so that the data assigned to those symbols can be listed from AutoCAD after the function is exited. After the functions are debugged, replace the local symbols removed from the list.

8.5 Title-Area-Perimeter (TAP) Function

The TAP function is to print the title and the traverse area and perimeter in the center of the traverse. The title is input by the user, and the traverse area and perimeter are read from AutoCAD's system variables. When AutoCAD's AREA command is invoked, the area and perimeter read are stored in the system variables AREA and PERIMETER, respectively. The problem, however, is to specify to AutoCAD the area to be read. One way is to designate the corner points of the traverse by reading the coordinates from the list bound to #CLIST. Another way is to pick a point on the polyline defining the traverse. That presents a problem. How do you tell AutoLISP where to select a point on the traverse? *Entity access* provides examination and modification of drawing entities either individually or in groups. Entity access also allows AutoLISP to pass entity names to AutoCAD in response to "Select objects:" wherever "Last" is a valid response.

The TAP function listing is as follows:

```
143: ;
144: ;       ** Title-Area-Perimeter (TAP) Function **
145: (defun tap (/ #title #area #pt1 #lcntr #e)
146:   (textscr)
147:   (setq #title (strcat ''%%u''
148:     (getstring t ''\nEnter traverse title: '') ''%%u''))
149:   (se);   Call SE function to locate polyline
150:   ;   Get traverse area and perimeter.
151:   (command ''area'' ''e'' #e)
152:   (setq #area (getvar ''area'') #per (getvar ''perimeter''))
153:   (if (= #lunits ''ft.'')
154:     ;   THEN units are feet—convert to acres
155:     (setq #area (strcat
156:                 (rtos (/ #area 4.356e4) 2 #lprec) '' acres'')
157:           #per (strcat (rtos #per 2 #lprec) '' feet''))
158:     ;   ELSE units are metres—convert to ha
159:     (setq #area (strcat
160:                 (rtos (/ #area 1.0e4) 2 #lprec) '' ha'')
161:           #per (strcat (rtos #per 2 #lprec) '' metres''))
162:   )
163:   ;   Center and print title, area, per. & linear units
164:   (setq #lcntr (polar #cntr (/ pi 2) #txtht))
165:   (command ''text'' ''c'' #lcntr #txtht 0 #title)
166:   (command ''text'' '''' #area)(command ''text'' '''' #per)
167: )
168: ;---------------------------
```

Discussion of TAP function.   In line 149 the Select Entity (SE) function is called to get the entity name for the polyline (the traverse) from the database (see Section 8.5.1). The entity name is returned bound to the symbol #E. In line 151 the COMMAND primitive is used to invoke AutoCAD's AREA command with the Entity option. The entity selected is the entity whose name is bound to the symbol #E.

When AutoCAD's AREA command is invoked, the defined area and perimeter are bound to the system variables AREA and PERIMETER. The SETQ and GETVAR primitives are used in line 152 to bind the area to #AREA and perimeter to #PER. **Note:** The #PER symbol is not defined as a local symbol since the perimeter is required to calculate the relative accuracy ratio of the perimeter. Consequently, #PER should now be added to the local symbol list for the ADDTEXT function.

In lines 153 through 162 the IF function is used to determine if the units are "ft". If not, they must be "m" (meter) units. If the units are feet, the area is converted to acres by dividing square feet by 43,560. If the units are meters, the area is converted to hectares (ha) by dividing square meters by 10,000. Note the use of the RTOS primitive to convert the real numbers to string data and the use of the STRCAT primitive to string the text together. **Note:** The TAP function's text is to be located at the center of the traverse. Consequently you will have to insert the following three lines into your DRAWLIM function to locate the center point and bind it to the symbol #CNTR:

```
198: ; Locate center point for use in TAP function.
199: (setq #cntr
200:    (list (/ (+ #xmin #xmax) 2)(/ (+ #ymin #ymax) 2)))
```

Note: Also, add the local symbol #CNTR to the local symbol list of the *TRAVERSE* function.

In line 164 of the *TAP* function the POLAR primitive is used to locate the first text point (which is bound to #1CNTR) at an angle of $\pi/2$ (90 degrees) and a distance of #TXTHT (the text height) from the point bound to the symbol #CNTR (the center of the traverse).

The COMMAND primitive is used in line 165 to invoke AutoCAD's TEXT command with the Center option and to print the traverse title. In line 166 the COMMAND primitive is used again to invoke AutoCAD's TEXT command. Notice, however, in this case a null string ("") is used when the text location is requested. This causes the text (the traverse area) to be printed, centered directly below the previous text.

8.5.1   Entity Name and Data Primitives

An AutoCAD drawing consists of entities such as lines, circles, text, attributes, polylines, etc. Each entity is given a unique name by the AutoCAD editor each time the drawing is loaded. The entity names are a sequence of eight hex numbers (eight alphanumeric characters). Linked to the name is all the data necessary to draw the entity.

AutoLISP's entity name and data primitives allow the programmer to select entities by their name and to modify the data defining an entity.

The following is typical entity data for a line:

Entity data list	Description
((- 1 . <Entity name: 60000014>)	Entity name (dotted pair)
(0 . ''LINE'')	Entity type (dotted pair)
(8 . ''0'')	Layer (dotted pair)
(10 3.000000 0.000000 0.000000)	Start point (list)
(11 8.500000 9.000000 0.000000))	End point (list)

The first element in each sublist is a code that allows the sublist to be identified. Some of the typical codes used are summarized in Table 8.1. For a more thorough listing refer to Appendix C of your *AutoCAD Reference Manual*. The start and end points (codes 10 and 11) of the line will be 2-D, rather than 3-D, with Releases 9 and 10 if the FLATLAND system variable is set equal to 1.

TABLE 8.1 Group Codes

Code	Function
- 1	Entity name
0	Entity type: LINE, CIRCLE, POLYLINE, 3DLINE, TEXT
1	Text string
2	A name: Attribute tag, Block name, etc.
3	Prompt string
5	Entity handle (Release 10)
6	Line type name (not shown if default)
7	Text style name (not shown if default)
8	Layer name
10	Primary X coordinates: start point of a line or text, center point of a circle or arc, insertion point, etc.
11–18	Other X coordinates: End point of a line, points of a solid, etc.
20	Primary Y coordinate of 3-D entities.
21–28	Other Y coordinates.
30	Primary Z coordinate of 3-D entities.
31–37	Other Z coordinates.
38	Elevation (with Release 10, FLATLAND = 1)
39	Thickness, if nonzero
40–48	Floating point values: radius, text height, polyline widths, scale factors, etc.

Entity name primitives. Entity names may be passed to AutoCAD in response to any "Select objects:" prompt where "Last" is a valid response. As such they provide the AutoLISP programmer with a means to pass entities to AutoCAD. The following are AutoLISP primitives used to access drawing entity names and the entity database:

(**entnext** [<**ename**>]) If called with no argument <ename>, ENTNEXT returns the first nondeleted entity name in the database. If called with an argument, ENTNEXT returns the first nondeleted entity name *following* <ename>. ENTNEXT can be used to sequentially select entity names from a database by using as the argument <ename> the name of the previous entity (see Section 8.5.2).

(**entlast**)   ENTLAST returns the last nondeleted main entity in the database.

(**entsel** [<**prompt**>]   ENTSEL returns the entity name and the point by which it was selected. This allows AutoLISP to perform operations such as BREAK, TRIM, and EXTEND.

(**handent** <**handle**>)   Release 10 only. AutoCAD's HANDLE command can be used to assign a unique identifier to every entity in the drawing. Although an entity's name can change from one editing session to another, the handle does not. The LIST command may be used to list the entity's handle. Given the <handle> argument, the HANDET function returns the entity name.

Entity data primitives. These primitives retrieve and modify entity data:

(**entdel** <**ename**>)   The entity specified by ENTDEL is deleted from the database if it is currently in the drawing, and it is undeleted if it has been deleted previously in this editing session.

(**entget** <**ename**>)   The entity with the name <ename> is retrieved from the database and returned as a list.

(**entupd** <**ename**>)   Although ENTMODE updates the database, it does not change the screen. ENTUPD is used to change the screen after the database is modified. See Chapter 9 for more primitives that retrieve and modify data.

8.5.2   Select entity (SE) function

Following is the listing for the SE function:

```
169: ;
170: ;      ** Select Entity (SE) Function **
171: (defun se ()
172:   (setq #e (entnext))
173:      (while (/= ''POLYLINE'' (cdr (assoc 0 (entget #e)))))
174:         (setq #e (entnext #e))
175:   )
176: )
177: ;----------------------------
```

Discussion of SE function. The SETQ and ENTNEXT primitives are used in line 172 to return the entity name of the first nondeleted entity in the database and bind it to the symbol #E.

In line 173 the ENTGET primitive returns a list containing the defined data for the entity whose name is bound to the symbol #E. In the entity list, the entity type is in a sublist with a 0 as the code (first) character (refer to Table 8.1). The ASSOC primitive is used to search the entity list for an item (sublist) with 0 as the key element and to return the item (sublist). The syntax of the ASSOC primitive is:

```
( assoc <item><alist>)
```

ASSOC searches <alist for <item> as the key element and returns the <alist> entry. If <item> is not found as a key in <alist>, ASSOC returns nil. For example:

```
(setq abc (list '(cat fast) '(dog slow) '(2 number)))
(assoc 'cat abc) returns: (cat fast)
(assoc 2 abc) returns: (2 number)
(assoc 'mouse abc) returns: nil
```

Continuing with line 173, ASSOC searches the list bound to #E looking for a sublist with 0 as the first element. The structure of entity lists is such that there will always be a sublist with 0 as the first element since the 0 code is associated with the entity type, e.g., (0 . "LINE"). This entity sublist is referred to as a dotted pair. The CDR primitive in the expression returns the second element of the dotted pair, e.g., "LINE". **Note:** The syntax of the CDR primitive (see Section 7.7.1) is that it normally returns a list composed of all but the first element of its <list>. When the <list> is a dotted pair, however, the CDR primitive returns the second element without enclosing it in a list.

The WHILE primitive (see Section 5.6.4) is interpreted in line 173 to read: WHILE the data returned by the CDR primitive is not equal (/ =) to "POLYLINE", the next expression is evaluated and then the test expression is reevaluated. As a result, if the entity type associated with the code 0 is not "POLYLINE", line 174 is evaluated.

Line 174 uses the SETQ and ENTNEXT primitives to return the entity name of the *next* nondeleted entity in the database and bind it to the symbol #E. Note that ENTNEXT is called with an argument #E, the name of the last entity returned, so it will return the entity name *following* the previous entity. The WHILE test expression is then repeated. This process continues until the entity type "POLYLINE" is located or the last entity in the database is evaluated. Since the entity type "POLYLINE" is in the database, the SE function is exited with the polyline's name (hex number) bound to the symbol #E.

The entity name bound to the symbol #E is used in line 151 of the TAP function to select the polyline in the traverse drawing using AutoCAD's AREA-Entity command as follows:

```
(command ''area'' ''e'' #e)
```

8.6 Northing/Easting Table (NET) Function

The NET function reads the station identifier, coordinates from the list bound to the symbol #CLIST, and prints a table listing each station's northing and easting. The northing is the station's X coordinate and the easting is the station's Y coordinate. The listing is as follows:

```
178: ;
179: ;      ** Northing/Easting Table (NET) Function **
180: (defun net (/ #1list #2list #id #nrth #east
181:          #1loc #2loc #3loc)
182: (setq #1loc (list (- (car (getvar ''limmax''))(* #txtht 20))
183:                (+ (cadr (getvar ''limmin''))
184:                   (* #txtht (+ #stats 20))))
185:       #2loc (polar #1loc 0 (* #txtht 4))
186:       #3loc (polar #2loc 0 (* #txtht 6)))
187: ;     Print heading
188: (command ''text'' #1loc #txtht 0 ''%%uSTA.%%u'')
189: (command ''text'' #2loc #txtht 0 ''%%uNORTH%%u'')
190: (command ''text'' #3loc #txtht 0 ''%%uEAST%%u'')
191: ; Print data
192: (setq #2list #clist)
193: (repeat #stats
194:   (setq #1list (car #2list) #2list (cdr #2list))
195:        #1loc (polar #1loc (* pi 1.5) (* 1.5 #txtht))
196:        #2loc (polar #2loc (* pi 1.5) (* 1.5 #txtht))
197:        #3loc (polar #3loc (* pi 1.5) (* 1.5 #txtht))
198:        #id (car #1list); string data
199:        #nrth (rtos (caadr #1list) 2 #1prec); real-string
200:        #east (rtos (cadadr #1list) 2 #1prec)); real-string
201:   (command ''text'' #1loc #txtht 0 #id)
202:   (command ''text'' #2loc #txtht 0 #nrth)
203:   (command ''text'' #3loc #txtht 0 #east)
204: )
205: )
206: ;--------------------------
```

Discussion of NET function. In lines 182 through 186 the start locations of the table headings STA., NORTH, and EAST are calculated and bound to the symbols #1LOC, #2LOC, and #3LOC, respectively. The x coordinate of #1LOC is determined in line 182 by subtracting the product of 20 times the text height from the upper right screen limit x coordinate (where 20 is based on 13 letters in the headings plus spaces plus extra). The y coordinate of #LOC1 is determined by subtracting the product of the text height times the sum of 15 plus the number of stations multiplied by 1.5 from the upper right screen limit y coordinate (1.5 times the text height is the vertical spacing of the text). The number 15 is selected by the Author. The LIST function binds these two coordinates together as a list, which is bound to #1LOC.

The reader should be familiar with the procedure used between lines 193 to 200 to extract the data from the list bound to #CLIST. The POLAR function is used to locate the next station data directly below the previous station data. Note that the RTOS function is used to convert the coordinates to string data with the desired precision before printing.

8.7   North Arrow (NORTHAR) Function

The points for the north arrow are calculated in terms of the text height so that it is scaled to suit the drawing. The points are identified in Figure 8.2. The function listing is as follows:

```
207: ;
208: ;          ** NORTH Arrow Function **
209: (defun northar (/ #pt1 #pt2 #pt3 #pt4 #pt5 #pt6 #ntxtht)
210:   (setq #pt1 (getpoint ''\nLocate tip of NORTH arrow.'')
211:         #pt2 (polar #pt1 (+  (* 1.5 pi) (atan 0.3)) (* #txtht 5))
212:         #pt3 (polar #pt2 pi (* #txtht 1.5))
213:         #pt4 (polar #pt3 pi (* #txtht 1.5))
214:         #pt5 (polar #pt1 (* pi 1.5) (* #txtht 10))
215:         #pt6 (polar #pt5 (/ pi 2) #txtht))
216:   (command ''pline'' #pt1 #pt2 #pt4 #pt1 #pt5)(command '''')
217:   (setvar ''fillmode'' 1)
218:   (command ''solid'' #pt1 #pt2 #pt3)
219:   (command '''')(command '''')
220:   (setq #ntxtht (* 2.5 #txtht))
221:   (command ''text'' ''c'' #pt6 #ntxtht 0 ''N'')
222:   (command ''text'' ''0,0'' #txtht 0 '' '')
223:   (command ''redraw'')
224: )
225: ;----------------------------
```

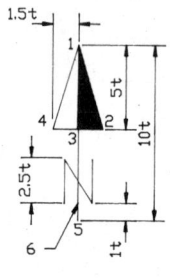

t = TXTHT

8.2   North arrow.

8.9   Relative Accuracy Ratio (RAT) Function

The relative accuracy ratio of a traverse is a ratio of the perimeter divided by the hypotenuse of the closing error of the traverse. The perimeter of the traverse was calculated in the TAP function and bound to the symbol #PER. The hypotenuse of the closing error has not been calculated. As a result, the following lines are to be inserted into the CLOSERR function of the TRAVERSE.LSP file:

```
144: ;    Calc. hypotenuse for relative accuracy ratio
145: (setq #relacc (sqrt (+  (* #xerr #xerr) (* #yerr #yerr))))
```

The hypotenuse is calculated by the pythagorean theory and is bound to the symbol #RELACC.

The listing of the RAT function is as follows:

```
226: ;
227: ;           ** Relative Accuracy Ratio Function **
228: (defun rat ()
229:   (setq #relacc (/ (atof #per) #relacc)
230:     #relacc (strcat '’\nRELATIVE ACCURACY of TRAVERSE is 1:’’
231:             (rtos #relacc 1 0)))
232:   ;    Print the relative accuracy ratio
233:   (princ #relac) (princ)
234: )
```

When you have completed debugging the TRAVERSE.LSP file, the system variable CMDECHO should be set to 0 so that AutoCAD commands executed by the AutoLISP COMMAND primitive are not echoed to the screen. By default, CMDECHO is set to 1 and all AutoCAD commands are echoed. Add the following line to your TRAVERSE.LSP file to turn off the echo to the screen of AutoCAD commands in the function:

```
8: (setvar ’’cmdecho’’ 0) ; Set command echo off.
```

The complete listing of TRAVERSE.LSP file is printed in Appendix F.

Assignment

1. Extend the stair program from assignment 1 in Chapter 7 by writing functions to dimension the stair rise and run and to list a table showing the number of risers, stair tread width, and riser.

2. Write a function to be added to the TRAVERSE.LSP file that will allow the drafter to change the text height and rerun the ADDTEXT function. The new function will have to erase everything in the drawing except the traverse. Use AutoCAD's ERASE and WINDOW commands to select all entities in the drawing; then use the REMOVE command and your SE function to remove the traverse from the

selection. Remember that AutoLISP primitives cannot be invoked from within the COMMAND primitive.

3. How could the TRAVERSE program be modified so that instead of entering the screen text height the drafter enters the plot scale? The program would then use that scale to determine the text height. Assume that the desired plot text height is 2.5 mm. Show the changes to be made to the program.

Entity Database Access

OBJECTIVE   *To write AutoLISP functions to manipulate data in a drawing entity data base utilizing entity name and selection-set primitives and to read the symbol table.*

9.1 Function to Locate Text, LOCNAME

When working with large drawings, it is often necessary to rapidly locate specific data or zoom on a particular area. For instance, consider the problem of a map containing a number of townships. The drafter is asked to locate a certain township and print a copy of it. The following LISP program requests the name (of the township) to be located, searches the drawing database for TEXT entities, and then searches for the (township) name. If the name is found, its coordinates are read from the database and that area of the drawing is zoomed. It is assumed that the township name will be written in uppercase text on the drawing. The LOCNAME.LSP program is

```
 1:   ; LOCNAME Locates a name on a drawing
 2:   ; and zooms by 0.5 on the location.
 3:   ; The name on the drawing must be in upper case.
 4:   ;
 5:   (defun locname (/T n en flag lst loc)
 6:      (setq n (strcase (getstring T ''Name to locate: '')))
 7:         flag 0 loc nil ; Set exit flag to 0, bind nil to LOC.
 8:         en (entnext) ; Get first entity name.
 9:         lst (entget en)); retrieve entity from database.
10:   (while (= flag 0) ; Search while flag is 0.
11:      ; If a TEXT entity is located:
12:      (if (= ''TEXT'' (cdr (assoc 0 lst)))
13:         ; then if this data matches the name,
14:         (if (= n (cdr (assoc 1 lst)))
15:            ; get its location and set flag to 1 <exit>.
16:            (setq loc (cdr (assoc 11 lst))
17:               flag 1)
18:         )
19:      )
```

```
20:     ; Look at the next entity.
21:     (if (null (setq en (entnext en)))
22:         ; If no next entity set exit flag.
23:         (setq flag 1)
24:         ; Else repeat search for TEXT entity <flag =0>.
25:         (setq lst (entget en))
26:     )
27:     ) ; Exit while-loop when flag /= 0.
28:     (if (null loc) ; If no location was found.
29:       (progn (princ ''\nNOT FOUND.\n'')()) ; Then name not found.
30:       (command ''zoom'' ''c'' loc 0.5) ; Else found, so zoom.
31:     )
32: )
```

Discussion of LOCNAME function. The name of the township to locate is requested in line 6 using the GETSTRING primitive with the optional T (see Section 4.3.3). Since the township name is in uppercase text on the drawing, the STRCASE primitive is used to change the name entered to uppercase text. In line 8 of the LOCNAME function the ENTNEXT primitive is used without an argument to get the entity name of the first entity in the drawing database. The entity name found is bound to the symbol EN and, in line 9, the SETQ and ENTGET primitives are used to retrieve the entity definition data from the database and bind the list to the symbol LST. For a TEXT entity the definition data may appear as illustrated in Table 9.1 (see also Section 8.5.1).

Next, the WHILE primitive is used to loop through the database from lines 10 to 27 while the symbol FLAG has zero bound to it. Note that in line 7 the value 0 is initially bound to the symbol FLAG.

In line 12 of the loop the list bound to LSP is analyzed. The ASSOC

TABLE 9.1   TEXT Entity List

Entity data list	Description
((-1 . <Entity name: 6000012C>))	Entity name (dotted pair)
(0 . "TEXT")	Entity type (dotted pair)
(8 . "TOWNSHIP")	Layer name (dotted pair)
(10 1125.1 4158.1 0.0)	Text start point coordinates
(40 . 46.8)	Text height (dotted pair)
(1 . "GARSON")	Text (dotted pair)
(50 . 0.0)	Rotation angle (dotted pair)
(41 . 1.0)	X scale factor (dotted pair)
(51 . 0.0)	Oblique angle (dotted pair)
(7 . "STANDARD")	Text style (dotted pair)
(71 . 0)	Gen. flag[1] (dotted pair)
(72 . 1)	Just'n.[2] (dotted pair)
(11 1257.9 4158.1 0.0))	Align. pt.[2] (list)

[1]Generation flags: 0 normal; 2 text is backward; 4 text is upside down.

[2]Text justification: 0 left justified; 1 baseline centered C"; 2 right justified "R"; 3 aligned "A"; 4 fully centered "M"; 5 fit "F".

In group 11 the text alignment point is dependent on the justification code.

primitive retrieves the entry associated with the group code 0 in the definition data list. For example if the list bound to LST is as illustrated in Table 9.1, ASSOC returns the dotted pair (0 . "TEXT"). The CDR primitive then returns the second element of the dotted pair, i.e., "TEXT". If the item returned is not "TEXT", the IF primitive, from line 12, is exited at line 20 and evaluation continues to line 21.

If the element returned by the CDR primitive in line 12 is "TEXT", the IF primitive directs evaluation to line 14 where the CDR and ASSOC primitives are used to retrieve the entry associated with the group code 1 from the entity bound to LST. As illustrated in Table 9.1, the entry bound to group code 1 in the definition data for a TEXT entity is the text string.

In line 14 the IF primitive is used to determine if the text string is equal to the name bound to the symbol N. If it is, evaluation proceeds to line 16 where the ASSOC and CDR primitives are used to retrieve the entry associated with the group code 11 (the text alignment point—see Table 9.1), which is then bound to the symbol LOC. Since the name requested has been found, the exit flag is set by binding 1 to the symbol FLAG.

On exiting the IF primitive(s), evaluation proceeds to the following expressions:

```
(if (null (setq en (entnext en)))    line 21
    (setq flag 1)                    line 23
    (setq lst (entget en))           line 25
```

The ENTNEXT function is invoked with the entity name bound to EN as its argument. Since the name of the entity just analyzed is currently bound to EN, the name of the next entity in the database is returned by ENTNEXT. If there are no more entities in the database, nil is returned. The SETQ primitive is used to bind the item returned to the symbol EN.

The IF and NULL primitives are used to determine if nil is returned. If it is, *then* evaluation proceeds to the next line, line 23, where the exit flag is set by binding 1 to the symbol FLAG; *else* evaluation proceeds to line 25 where the ENTGET and SETQ primitives are used to bind to the symbol LST the entity whose name is bound to EN.

The WHILE primitive in line 10 is bound by the right parenthesis in line 27. When evaluation reaches line 27, the test expression, (= flag 0), of the WHILE primitive is reevaluated. If T is returned, the escape flag, which is set by binding 1 to the symbol FLAG in line 17 or 23, was not set and the expressions in the WHILE loop are reevaluated. If nil is returned, the escape flag was set. This indicates that either the name searched for was found in line 17 or there are no more entities in the database and the flag was set in line 23.

When the WHILE primitive is exited at line 28, the expression (if (null loc)) is used to determine if data is bound to the symbol LOC. Since the symbol LOC was initialized by binding nil to it in line 7, if data is bound to it, that data will be the coordinates of the text searched for—see line 16.

If there is no data bound to the symbol LOC, the NULL primitive returns T and the *<then-expression>* on line 29 is invoked, i.e., (progn (princ "\nNOT FOUND.\n")()). The PROGN primitive is required because the IF primitive normally evaluates one *then expression* and there are two expressions to be evaluated, i.e., (princ "\nNOT FOUND.\n") and ().

If there is data bound to the symbol LOC, the NULL primitive returns nil, and the *<else-expression>* on line 30 is evaluated. The COMMAND primitive is used to execute the AutoCAD ZOOM CENTER command. The desired center point is the coordinates bound to the symbol LOC, and the magnification is 0.5.

Assignment. Boot AutoCAD and complete a drawing containing a number of rectangles each containing an original name in uppercase text. Then load the LOCNAME function and use it to locate and zoom on specific names on the drawing. You may wish to change the magnification of the zoom in the function.

9.2   Entity Selection Sets

In the previous section AutoCAD entities are accessed by using the ENTNEXT primitive to get the *entity name,* which is used as a pointer to the entity.

A *selection set* is a collection of entity names. Selection sets should not be used frivolously since they consume AutoCAD's temporary file slots. Refer to your manual for information if you have problems. The following primitives are used to perform various operations on selection sets (refer to your *AutoLISP Programmer's Reference* for more information on selection sets):

(ssget [<mode>] [<pt1> [<pt2>]]).   SSGET returns a selection set. The optional <mode> argument is a string specifying the type of entity selection to be performed. This may be "W" (window), "C" (crossing), "L" (last), or "P" (previous). The <pt1> and <pt2> arguments are points relative to the selection. If a "W" or "C" argument is used, the corner points <pt1> and <pt2> *must* be supplied.

If SSGET is used with no arguments, the user is prompted through AutoCAD's general "Select objects:" mechanism. Examples of SSGET are

```
(ssget)                    Prompts user to "Select objects:
```

```
(ssget ''L'')                    Selects last entity in database
(ssget ''W'' '(0,0)'(3,3))       Selects entities in the window from 0,0 to 3,3.
(ssget '(3 4))                   Selects entities passing through 3,4.
(ssget ''C'' '(1 1) '(2 2)       Selects the entities crossing the window from
                                   1,1 to 2,2.
```

(ssget "X" <filter-list>) (Release 10). SSGET is a special mode of the SSGET primitive that is used to scan the entire drawing and create a selection set of all main entities that match specified criteria in the <filter-list>.
The following expression binds to the symbol SS a selection set consisting of all the text on the Township layer of a drawing:

```
(setq ss (ssget ''X'' (list (cons 0 ''TEXT'') (cons 8 ''TOWNSHIP''))))
```

Table 9.2 lists group codes currently accepted by SSGET "X".

TABLE 9.2   SSGET "X" Group Codes

Code	Meaning
0	Entity type
2	Block name for Block references
6	Linetype name
7	Text style name for Text and Attribute definitions
8	Layer name
39	Thickness
62	Color number
66	Attributes
210	3-D extrusion direction vector

(sslength <ss>). SSLENGTH returns an integer which is the number of entities in selection set <ss>. If the number exceeds 32767, it is returned as a real.

(ssname <ss> <i>). SSNAME returns the entity name of the <i>th element of the selection set <ss>. If <i> is negative or greater than the highest numbered entity in the selection set, nil is returned.

9.2.1   LOOK function

The LOOK function uses selection set manipulation primitives to allow the drafter to select a group of entities in a AutoCAD drawing and to look at the definition data for each entity selected. The LOOK.LSP function is

```
1: ; LOOK displays definition data for selected entities.
2: ;
3: (defun look (/ ss num defdat i ne)
4:    (setq ss (ssget)) ; Obtain selection-set
5:    (setq num (sslength ss) i 0) ; Number of entities
```

```
 6:   ; Display definition data for each entity in the set.
 7:   (repeat num
 8:      (setq ne (ssname ss i)
 9:          defdat (entget ne))
10:      (prin1 defdat) (terpri)
11:      (getstring ''Press RETURN to continue.\n'')
12:      (setq i (+ i 1))
13:   )
14: )
```

Discussion of LOOK function. The SSGET primitive is used in line 5 to obtain a selection set. Since no optional arguments are used, AutoCAD's "Select objects:" prompt will be displayed to prompt the user to select objects on the monitor. The drafter may select objects using any of the standard selection options such as Window, Last, etc. The selection set is bound to the symbol SS by the SETQ primitive.

Next, the SSLENGTH primitive is used to return the number of entities in the selection set. The integer returned is bound to the symbol NUM, which is used in line 7 with the REPEAT primitive to loop through the expressions from lines 8 to 12, displaying the definition data for each entity in the selection set.

In line 5 the integer 0 is bound to the symbol I. During the first pass of the loop, the SSNAME primitive on line 8 returns the entity name of the 0th element of the selection set bound to the symbol SS, which is then bound to the symbol NE. Note that the first element in the selection set has the index 0 not 1.

In lines 9 and 10 the ENTGET and PRIN1 primitives are used to retrieve the list of definition data for the entity name bound to the symbol NE and to display the data. Notice the use of the TERPRI primitive to return a new line.

The user is then prompted to "Press RETURN to continue" by the GETSTRING primitive. When Return is pressed, the index I is incremented by 1 in line 12. The right parenthesis in line 13 closes the REPEAT primitive.

Assignment. Boot AutoCAD and draw the following entities:

- A CIRCLE on Layer FIRST, color RED, center at 2,3 and 1.5 unit diameter.

- A LINE on Layer SECOND, line type HIDDEN, from 4,4,0 to 5,5,2 (Release 10) or 4,4 to 5,5 (earlier versions).

- Use DIM to dimension the line.

- A POLYLINE with coordinates 1,1,0 and 3,3,5 (Release 10) or 1,1 and 3,3 (earlier versions). Start width 0.2 and end width 0.3.

- TEXT print "HELLO" at 3.5,3.5 using the Middle option.

- BLOCK with an ATTRIBUTE—visible, not constant, tag "APPLE", prompt "Change fruit:", location 6.5,6.5. Invoke and enter the text "ORANGE".

Load the LOOK function. If you have a line printer connected to your microcomputer, press Ctrl-Q so that data displayed on the prompt line is echoed to the line printer. Invoke the LOOK function and use the window option to select all entities on the monitor.

List the codes for the following:

- CIRCLE center, diameter, layer color
- LINE line type, layer name, star, and end points
- Dimension text
- POLYLINE start point, start width, end width, end point
- TEXT string, start point, alignment point, rotation
- ATTRIBUTE tag string, prompt string, text start point

9.3 Entity Definition Data Manipulation

It is often useful to be able to change properties of an entity by modifying its definition data in the database. The following primitives are useful in such programs:

(entmode <elist>) ENTMODE is passed an entity definition data list, <elist>, updates the database, and returns <elist>. All objects referenced by ENTMODE such as line type and Shape and Block names must have been previously defined. An exception to this is Layer. Also, an entities type handle cannot be changed.

(subst <newitem> <olditem> <list>) SUBST searches <list> for <olditem> and returns a copy of <list> with <newitem> substituted in place of every occurrence of <olditem>. If <olditem> is not found, <list> is returned unchanged.

(entupd <ename>) ENTUPD is required to update subentities such as a vertex on a Polyline or a Block attribute when they have been modified with ENTMODE. ENTUP does not have to be used when main entities have been modified. The argument <ename> is the entity name of any part of the Polyline or Block.

9.3.1 Text layer change function—CHGLAY

The CHGLAY function allows the user to change the layer that text on a drawing resides on. It is as follows:

```
 1:  ; CHGLAY program changes the layer text resides on.
 2:  ;
 3:  (defun chglay (/ newname old8 new8 ss num ne lst i)
 4:    (prompt ''\nEnter name of NEW layer: '')
 5:    (setq newname (strcase (getstring)))
 6:    (command ''LAYER'' ''N'' newname) (command '''')
 7:    (prompt ''\n\nEnter W to window text to be changed.\n'')
 8:    (setq ss (ssget)) ; Select selection-set.
 9:    (setq num (sslength ss) i 0) ; get number of entities
10:    (repeat num
11:      (setq ne (ssname ss i)) ; get entity name
12:      (setq lst (entget ne)) ; get definition data list
13:      (if (= ''TEXT'' (cdr (assoc 0 lst)))
14:        (progn
15:          (setq old8 (assoc 8 lst)); old dotted pair
16:          (setq new8 (cons 8 newname)); new dotted pair
17:          (setq lst (subst new8 old8 lst)); substitute
18:          (entmod lst)) ; update the entity
19:      )(setq i (+ 1 i))      ; end IF & increment index
20:    )                        ; and repeat.
21: )
```

Discussion of CHGLAY function. In line 4 the user is prompted to enter the new layer name that the text is to be moved to. The name entered is changed to uppercase text by the STRCASE primitive in line 5, and is bound to the symbol NEWNAME. Note that the GETSTRING primitive does not include the optional flag argument T; therefore, the input may not contain blanks.

Although the ENTMODE command can create a new layer, the layer is created in line 6 using AutoCAD commands instead. The user is then prompted in line 7 to enter W to window the text to be changed.

In line 8 the SETQ and SSGET primitives are used to get the selection set and bind it to the symbol SS.

The SSLENGTH primitive is used in line 9 to determine the number of entities in the selection set bound to the symbol SS. The integer returned is bound to the symbol NUM and used with the REPEAT primitive to create a loop encompassing lines 10 through 19.

In line 9 the integer 0 is bound to the symbol I which is used as an index for the SSNAME primitive in line 11. On the first repeat, the SSNAME primitive returns the entity name for the 0th item in the selection set bound to SS. The entity name returned is bound to the symbol NE.

The SETQ and ENTGET primitives are used in line 12 to get the definition data for the entity name bound to NE and bind the list to the symbol LST. For example, the definition data bound to the symbol LST may appear as follows (Release 10 output will be rounded):

```
((-1 . <Entity name: 60000014>) (0. ''TEXT'') (8. ''LAYR-1'') (10
1.859521 7.024989) (40 . 0.200000) (1 . ''Hello'') (50 . 0.000000) (41 .
1.000000) (51 . 0.000000) (7 . ''STANDARD'') (71 . 0) (72 . 0) (11
0.000000 0.000000))
```

The expression (if (= "TEXT" (cdr (assoc 0 lst)) in line 13 uses the ASSOC and CDR primitives to return the item associated with 0 group in the definition data list bound to the symbol LST. The second element in the dotted pair with a group code of 0 is the entity type (see Table 9.1). If the entity type returned is "LINE", evaluation proceeds to line 14; otherwise evaluation proceeds to line 19 and exits the IF primitive.

If the entity type is "LINE", the PROGN primitive in line 14 invokes the evaluation of the group of expressions from lines 15 to 18:

```
14:     (progn
15:         (setq old8 (assoc 8 lst))
16:         (setq new8 (cons 8 newname))
17:         (setq lst (subst new8 old8 lst))
18:         (entmod lst))
```

In line 15 the ASSOC primitive searches the list (definition data) bound to the symbol LST for the element associated with key element (group code) 8. The second element in the dotted pair with the group code 8 is the layer name (see Table 9.1). The entry returned is bound to the symbol OLD8. For instance, for the definition data bound to the symbol LST in the preceding example, the item returned and bound to the symbol OLD8 would be (8 . "LAYR-1").

The CONS primitive is used in line 16 to construct a new list composed of the integer 8 and the atom bound to the symbol NEWNAME. The syntax of the CONS primitive is:

```
(cons <new first element> <list>)
```

When the CONS <list> is an atom (see Section 4.4.1), the list returned is a dotted pair. If, for example, the string "LAYR-2" is bound to the symbol NEWNAME, the CONS primitive in line 16 returns (8 . "LAYR-2"). The SETQ primitive is used to bind the dotted pair returned to the symbol NEW8.

In line 17 the SUBST primitive is used to substitute the item (dotted pair) bound to the symbol NEW8 for the item (dotted pair) bound to the symbol OLD8 in the list (definition data) bound to the symbol LST. The SETQ primitive is then used to bind the modified list to the symbol LST. For the preceding examples the list bound to the symbol LST will now be as follows: ((- 1 . <Entity name: 60000014>) <0 . "TEXT") >(8 . "LAYR-2") (10 1.859521 7.024989) (40 . 0.200000) (1 . "Hello") (50 . 0.000000) (41 . 1.000000) (51 . 0.000000) (7 . "STANDARD") (71 . 0) (72 . 0) (11 0.000000 0.000000))

In the last line of the PROGN primitive's expressions (line 18) the ENTMODE primitive is passed the modified list that is bound to the symbol LST to update the database for the entity whose name is specified in the −1 group in the list. For the previous example the entity name is <**Entity name: 60000014**>.

On exiting the IF primitive (line 19) the index I for the SSNAME primitive is incremented by 1 and evaluation proceeds to line 20, which contains the closing parenthesis for the REPEAT primitive on line 10. The REPEAT primitives's expressions are then repeated. The number of repeats is defined by the integer bound to the symbol NUM, which is the number of entities in the selection set (line 9).

After all entities in the selection set have been searched, evaluation proceeds to line 21 and the function is complete. All text entities in the selection set will now reside on the new layer specified.

Assignment

1. Write a function that requests a new text height from the user and searches the entire database for text, modifying the current text height to the new text height.

2. Write a function that deletes all entities residing on a specified layer, input by the user, in a selection set.

9.4 Symbol Table Access

The TBLNEXT and TBLSEARCH primitives are used to access (read-only) AutoCAD's layer, line type, named view, text style, and block *definition symbol table*. The syntax of these primitives is discussed below.

(**tblnext** <**symbol type**> [**T**]).   TBLNEXT is used to scan the entire *symbol table* for a specific symbol type such as "LAYER", "LTYPE", "VIEW", "STYLE", and "BLOCK". With Release 10 add "UCS" and "VPORT".

The first time TBLNEXT is invoked, it returns the first entry for the *symbol type* specified. The next time it returns the second entry, etc. This sequential search continues, even if the drawing is exited and then reloaded, until there are no more entries in the table and nil is returned.

If the optional T argument is included, TBLNEXT restarts the search at the beginning of the table. For example, (tblnext "LAYER") returns the first layer entry in the symbol table, (tblnext "LAYER") returns the second layer entry, and (tblnext "LAYER" T) restarts the search at the beginning of the table and returns the *first* LAYER entry.

The entry returned by TBLNEXT is a list of dotted pairs, for example:

```
Command: (tblnext ''layer'') returns:
((0. ''LAYER'')                       Symbol type
 (2 . ''0'')                          Symbol name
 (70 . 0)                             Flags
 (62 . 7)                             Color number (-ve if off)
 (6 . ''CONTINUOUS''))                Line type
```

```
Command: (tblnext ''block'') returns:
((0 . ''BLOCK'')                              Symbol type
 (2 . ''WIDGET'')                             Symbol name
 (70 . 0)                                     Flags
 (10 8.500000 1.000000 0.000000)             Insertion point[1]
 (-2 . <Entity name: 600000078>))            First entity name
```

(tblsearch <symbol type><symbol name>[T]). TBLSEARCH is used to scan the symbol table searching for a *<symbol type>* with the *<symbol name>*. If the symbol type and the symbol name specified are found, a list of dotted pairs is returned. If no such entry is found, nil is returned. For example, (tblsearch "block" "widget") returns the list of dotted pairs in the preceding example. Blocks with names other than "WIDGET" are ignored.

The entity name in the -2 group returned by TBLNEXT and TBLSEARCH can only be passed to the ENTGET and ENTNEXT primitives.

Although normally TBLSEARCH has no effect on TBLNEXT, if the optional (Release 10 only) flag T is set and a nonnil value is returned by TBLSEARCH, TBLNEXT's entry counter is adjusted so that the next TBLNEXT call returns the entry following the one returned by TBLSEARCH.

9.4.1 Function to list layers—SRCHLAY

The following function uses the TBLNEXT primitive to scan the symbol table of a drawing for layers with names beginning with a specified string. The layer names beginning with the specified strings are printed on the monitor. The SRCHLAY function is:

```
 1:  ; SRCHLAY searches the symbol table for Layers
 2:  ; beginning with specified strings in their name.
 3:  ;
 4:  (defun SRCHLAY (/ strg ent nam lgth)
 5:    (setvar ''cmdecho'' 0)(textscr)
 6:    (initget 1)
 7:    (prompt ''\nThis function locates layer names'')
 8:    (prompt ''\nbeginning with specified strings.\n'')
 9:    (prompt ''\n\tENTER THE STRING TO SEARCH FOR: '')
10:    (setq strg (strcase (getstring)))
11:    (setq lgth (strlen strg))
12:                        ; Look at the first layer.
```

---

[1]The Insertion point is that selected when creating the block.

```
13:    (setq ent (tblnext ''layer'' T))
14:         (chkname)        ; Look for the string.
15:                          ; Look for other layers.
16:         (while (not (null (setq ent (tblnext ''layer''))))
17:                          ; If found then look for string.
18:             (chkname)
19:         )                ; Close While.
20: )                        ; Exit function
```

Discussion of SRCHLAY function. The INITGET primitive in line 6 is used to disallow null input to the GETSTRING primitive in line 10. The string entered by the user is changed to uppercase text with the STRCASE primitive and then bound to the symbol STRG.

In line 11 the SETQ and STRLEN primitives are invoked to determine the length of the string bound to STRG—the layer-name string to be searched for—and bind the integer returned to the symbol LGTH.

The TBLNEXT primitive is used to scan the symbol table for the entry LAYER. Since the T argument is included, the search starts at the beginning of the symbol table. TBLNEXT returns a list which is bound to the symbol ENT by the SETQ primitive. The list may appear as follows:

```
((0 . ''BLOCK'') (2 . ''FLOOR-1'') (70 . 0) (10 1.859521 5.251822
0.000000) (-2 . <Entity name 40000018>))
```

The 2 group contains the symbol name (block name) that is to be examined. A function called CHKNAME, invoked in line 14, will compare characters in the symbol name with the string bound to the symbol STRG and print the names of layers where a match is found. The function will be discussed later.

In line 16 the TBLNEXT primitive is invoked without the T argument:

```
(while (not (null (setq ent (tblnext ''layer'')))))
```

As a result, the search for the specified string in the layer names continues, starting at the second entry in the symbol table—which is returned and bound to the symbol ENT. If the entry returned is nonnil, the NULL primitive returns nil, which in turn is evaluated by the NOT primitive, which returns T. Since the WHILE primitive is passed a T, the expressions in lines 16 to 19 are reevaluated.

The expressions following the WHILE function are comment lines except for line 18 where the CHKNAME function is called.

When the end of the symbol table is encountered, the TBLNEXT primitive returns nil, the NULL primitive returns T, the NOT primitive returns nil, and the WHILE function expressions are not reevaluated. Evaluation continues at line 20, thereby exiting the function.

CHKNAME function. The CHKNAME function is to locate the layer name in the list and determine if the specified string is part of the name. The function is as follows:

```
21: (defun chkname ( )
22:        ; Does the name match that looked for?
23:    (if (=  (substr (cdr (assoc 2 ent)) 1 lgth) strg)
24:                ; If yes then print the name.
25:    (progn
26:        (setq nam (cdr (assoc 2 ent)))
27:            (prinlist (list ''Layer name: '' nam ''\n'')))
28:    )
29: )
```

In line 23 the ASSOC function searches the list bound to the symbol ENT and returns a list which is the 2 group in the entry from the symbol table. As illustrated in the discussion of the SRCHLAY function, the list bound to ENT may appear as follows:

```
((0 . ''BLOCK'') (2 . ''FLOOR-1'') (70 . 0) (10 1.859521 5.251822
0.000000) (-2 . <Entity name 40000018>))
```

For the entry illustrated the dotted pair returned by the ASSOC primitive is: **(2 . "FLOOR-1")**.

The CDR primitive is used to return the layer name from the dotted pair, i.e., **"FLOOR-1"**, which is passed to the SUBSTR primitive. The syntax of SUBSTR is as follows:

```
(substr <string><start<[length])
```

SUBSTR returns a substring of <string>, starting at the <start> character position and continuing for [length] characters. If the [length] argument is not included, the substring continues to the end of the <string>.

The string passed to the SUBSTR primitive in line 23 is the layer name. The start argument is 1 and the end argument is the integer bound to the symbol LGTH, which is the length of the string to be located—line 11 of the SRCHLAY primitive. If the integer 5 is bound to the symbol LGTH, the string returned by SUBSTR for the previous example is **"FLOOR"**.

The IF primitive is then used to evaluate if the string returned by SUBSTR is equal to the string bound to the symbol STRG. If it is, the expressions in lines 25 through 28, which are within the PROGN primitive parenthesis, are evaluated. If it is not, evaluation passes to line 29 where the function is exited.

The reader should be familiar with all of the expressions enclosed by the PROGN primitive. Note the use of the PRINLIST function developed in Section 5.4 to print the layer name.

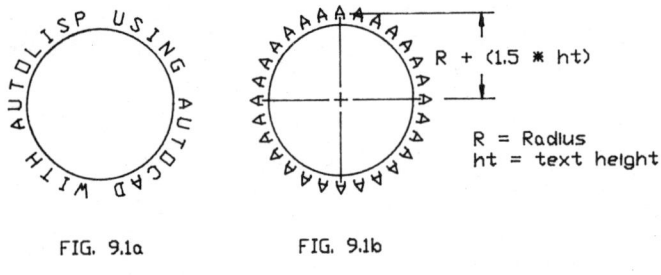

FIG. 9.1a   FIG. 9.1b

Figure 9.1   (*a*) Circular text and (*b*).

The PRINLIST function must be added to the file:

```
30: (defun prinlist (args / a)
31:   (foreach a args (princ a))()
32: )
```

Assignment

1. Boot AutoCAD and begin a drawing to test the SRCHLAY function. Create a number of new layers, naming three of them FLOOR-1, FLOOR-2, and FLOOR-3. Test your SRCHLAY function by searching for layers with names beginning with the string FLOOR.

2. Expand the SRCHLAY function to write all the layer names to a computer file. The entries in the file are to be collated in the file in alphabetical order. The name of the file is to be the same as the drawing with the extension .BLN. The file may be printed to a line printer from DOS by using the TYPE command, i.e.,

```
C:\>type name.BLN >prn
```

3. Write a function that will draw a circle and write text around the circle as illustrated in Figure 9.1.
   The pseudocode is as follows:

Define the function
Change to the text screen
Input: Circle diameter
        Text height
        Text (advise user to include *all* spaces)
Determine the length of the text string
Change to graph screen
Get the circle center
Calculate the midpoint coordinates (in terms of the circle center point) of a letter A located 1½ text heights above the circle circumference at 90 degrees [see Figure 9.1(*b*)]—bind the coordinates to PT1
Draw the circle

Print a single A at PT1

Get the entity name for A

Draw an circular array of A's using the number of items as the text length [Figure 9.1(b)]

Initialize a counter REPEAT for each item of text:

Extract a character from the text using AutoLISP's SUBSTR primitive (see below)

Change an A defined by the entity name determined earlier to a character extracted from the text

Get the entity name for the next A in the array and

repeat

The text will be printed in reverse; therefore, the AutoLISP SUBSTR function should extract letters from the text in reverse. How can this be done? The syntax of the SUBSTR primitive is:

```
(substr <string><start>[length])
```

SUBSTR returns a substring of <string> starting at the <start> character position and continuing for [length]. If [length] is not specified, the substring continues to the length of <string>. For example:

```
(substr ''abcd'' 2)          returns ''bcd''
(substr ''abcd'' 1 2)        returns ''ab''
(setq a ''abcd)(substr a 2 1) returns ''b''
```

If present, <start> and <length> must be positive integers. To extract the text from <string> in reverse order, consider starting <start> as the length of the string (see STRLEN) and decrementing <start> with each pass of the REPEAT function.

Three-Dimensional Drawing

OBJECTIVE   *To write AutoLISP functions to draw 3-D Entities.*

10.1 Introduction

Three-dimensional capabilities were first added to AutoCAD in Ver. 2.5 with the ability to assign an elevation and thickness to any 2-D object thereby producing an *extruded plane.* The extruded plane made it simple to produce planar faces, but since the only points visible to AutoCAD on the plane lay on the initial elevation, it was difficult to connect other entities to the extruded lines or intersections. Also, the planes could lie only in the Z-Z axis; therefore lines or planes could not be drawn in three dimensions with an X,Y,Z position.

With Ver. 2.6 AutoCAD added the 3DLINE and 3DPLANE commands. The 3DLINE command allows the drafter to draw a line with X,Y,Z coordinates for each end point. The 3DFACE command allows the drafter to draw a face, or plate, in space by defining three or four corners in any orientation. Each corner of the face, or plate, requires X,Y,Z coordinates.

Release 10 introduced a major change in how 3-D objects are viewed and drawn. With this release, AutoCAD is transformed from a 2-D drawing system with some 3-D capabilities to a full 3-D drawing system. All entities are now defined in 3-D space; however, this does not add complexities to 2-D drawings since the Z coordinate can usually be ignored and AutoCAD assumes a default value of 0.

Release 10 coordinates are a list of three reals, x,y,z, and Ver. 2.6 coordinates are usually a list of two reals, x,y; consequently, the AutoLISP programmer must be careful if a 2-D AutoLISP function is to be usable with both releases. Making an AutoLISP program compatible often is as simple as using the CADR primitive rather than the LAST primitive (which returns the last element in a list) to retrieve the y coordinate from a list.

Release 10 can be made to behave like earlier releases by setting the FLATLAND system variable to 1. The default value is 0. When FLATLAND is set to 1, points entered are treated as 2-D lists, unless a specific 3-D command is being used. FLATLAND is intended to be a "bridge" only and will be removed in the next major update of AutoCAD.

10.2   Cone Construction—Ver. 2.6 to Release 10

An AutoLISP function is to be written to draw a cone using the 3-D commands available with Ver. 2.62 of Release 9. This function will also work with Release 10 without having to set FLATLAND to 1. The AutoCAD ELEV command and the ELEVATION system variable will be dropped with the next major update of AutoCAD, however.

A 3-D cone is easily drawn in plan view (the x,y axis) by initially drawing a triangular face with its base at elevation 0 and its vertex at the desired height (in the z axis) of the cone. The circular array command is used to rotate the face around its vertex, thus creating the other faces of the cone. This creates a cone with a polygon base rather than a circular base, as illustrated in Figure 10.1. If the vertex angle of the face is reasonably small, however, the base will appear circular. An angle of 15 degrees is usually sufficient.

10.2.1   Cone function

A cone may be drawn by mathematically constructing the initial triangular face and using AutoCAD's ARRAY command to rotate the face about the vertex.

In the following, Xn is the X coordinate of point n; Yn is the Y coordinate of point n; and Zn is the Z coordinate of point n, where n is point a, b, or c as illustrated in Figure 10.2. Hence Xa is the X coor-

Figure 10.1   3-D cone.

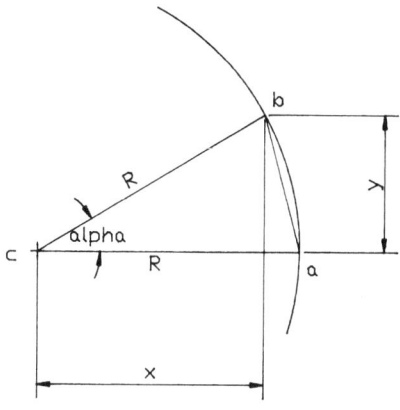

Figure 10.2   Cone face.

dinate of point a, Yb is the Y coordinate of point b, etc.

The initial cone face is constructed using the following procedure (see also Figure 10.2):

$$x = R \times \cos \alpha \qquad y = R \times \sin \alpha$$

In order to draw the cone, the following is required:

X,Y coordinates of point c

The radius, R, of the base

The base elevation

The height of the cone

Coordinates for points a and b are calculated as follows:

Xa = Xc + R
Ya = Yc
Xb = Xc + x
Yb = Yc + y
Za = Zb = base elevation
Zc = base elevation + height

The function that is to draw the cone is to begin by assigning the initial face vertex angle of 15 degrees (in radians) to the symbol AL-PHA (see Figure 10.2). The angle is converted to radians using: radians = degrees $\times$ π / 180. GETxxx primitives are used to request data from the user. The function is

1: ;   ** CONE Function **

```
2: (defun cone (/ radius center baselev ht)
3:   ; Vertex angle is set as 15 degrees.
4:   (setq alpha (* 15 (/ pi 180)))
5:   (setq center (getpoint ''Cone center point (X,Y): ''))
6:   (setq radius (getreal ''\nRadius: ''))
7:   (setq baselev (getreal ''\nBase elevation: ''))
8:   (setq ht (getreal ''\nHeight: ''))
```

The cone center point is a list (Xc Yc) requested from the user and assigned to the symbol CENTER in line 5. With Release 10 the list is (Xc Yc 0) since the default Z coordinate is 0.

Point A on the 3-D face (see Figure 10.2) is a list of three real coordinates (Xa,Ya,Za) and is created as follows:

```
9:  (setq a (list
10:   (+ (car center) radius)
11:   (cadr center)
12:   baselev))
```

In line 5 of the function the center point of the cone base is bound to the symbol CENTER as a list (Xc Yc) – (Xc Yc 0) with Release 10. The CAR primitive is used in Line 10 to return the first element of the list bound to CENTER, Xc. The element Xc is added to the radius to determine Xa.

The expression (cadr center) in line 11 is equivalent to (car (cdr center)). The CDR primitive returns a list composed of all elements of the object list except for the first element, hence (cdr center) returns (Yc) or (Yc 0). The CAR primitive returns the first element of its object list so that (car (cdr center)) returns Yc. Ya is numerically equal to Yc.

Finally, Za is the base elevation BASELEV. The LIST primitive returns a list (Xa Ya Za) which is assigned to the symbol A by the SETQ primitive in line 9.

Point c on the 3-D face in Figure 10.2 has the coordinates (Xc,Yc,Zc). The symbol CENTER has bound to it the list (Xc Yc) or (Xc Yc 0), and Zc is equal to the base elevation plus the cone height entered by the user. The next line of the function is to assign the list (Xc Yc Zc) to the variable C.

```
13: (setq c (list
14:   (car center)
15:   (cadr center)
16:   (+ baselev ht)))
```

Why will the following not work in place of the preceding expression?

```
13: (setq c (list
14:   center
15:   (+ baselev ht)))
```

The preceding expression binds to the symbol C, the list ((Xc Yc) Zc) or ((Xc Yc 0) Zc)). Why? How does the correct version differ?

The next line of the function is to bind the list (Xb Yb Zb) to the symbol B, where Xb = Xc + (radius × cos α), Yb = Yc + (radius × sin α) and Zc = base elevation:

```
17: (setq b list
18:    (+ (car center) (* radius (cos alpha)))
19:    (+ (cadr center) (* radius (sin alpha)))
20:    baselev)
```

Review the preceding expression and ensure that you understand how each of the functions is applied to get the desired list.

The symbols A, B, and C have each been assigned a list composed of the coordinates of points a, b, and c, respectively, which define the corners of the 3-D face illustrated in Figure 10.2. The AutoCAD 3DFACE command is now used to draw the 3-D face and requires as input the data assigned to the symbols A, B, and C. The command is invoked as follows:

```
21:  (command ''3dface'' a b c a)
22:  (command '''')
```

Line 22 is required to exit AutoCAD's 3DFACE command.

Finally, the cone is drawn using AutoCAD's ARRAY command to rotate the face about its vertex, point c. When the command is invoked, it requires the following information. *Do not enter this data.* It is here only to illustrate what is required in the LISP program.

```
ARRAY <return> Select objects: L (Last) <return>
Select objects: <return>Rectangular/Polar array (R/P):
P <return>Center point of array: !center <return>
Number of items: null <return>Angle to fill
(+  = ccw,- = cw)<360>: 360 <return>Angle between items: 15
<return>Rotate objects as they are being copied <Y>: Y <return>
```

When the ARRAY command is invoked in the AutoLISP program, it will have to include all of the entries specified above:

```
(command ''array'' ''L'' ''P'' center '''' 360 15 ''Y'')
```

Note that string data is enclosed in quotation marks.

The final listing of the CONE function is as follows:

```
1:        ** CONE Function **
2:   (defun cone (/ radius center baselev ht)
3:     (setq alpha (* 15 (/ pi 180)))
4:     (setq center (getpoint ''Cone center point (X,Y): ''))
5:     (setq radius (getreal ''\nRadius: ''))
6:     (setq baselev (getreal ''\nBase elevation: ''))
7:     (setq ht (getreal ''\nHeight: ''))
8:     (setq a (list
9:        (+ (car center) radius)
10:    (cadr center)
11:    baselev))
12:   (setq c (list
13:     (car center)
```

```
14:      (cadr center)
15:      (+ baselev ht)))
16:    (setq b (list
17:      (+ (car center) (* radius (cos alpha)))
18:      (+ (cadr center) (* radius (sin alpha)))
19:      baselev))
20:  (command ''3dface'' a b c a)
21:  (command '''')
22:  (command ''array'' ''L'' ''P'' center '''' 360 15 ''Y'')
23: )
```

Boot AutoCAD and run the CONE function. To get an inverted cone, enter a base elevation of 0 and a height of -3.

Assignment. Write an AutoLISP function in a file named TRCONE.LSP to draw a truncated cone (see Figure 10.3). The program will be similar to your CONE.LSP function; however, the initial 3-D face will have four points—two defining its base edge and two defining its top edge. The calculation for the top edge points is similar to that for the base edge points. All that varies is the radius. Data to be requested from the user is:

Cone center point

Base radius

Base elevation

Cone height

Height to the cutoff (from the base)

10.3   Sphere Function—Ver. 2.6 to Release 10

A dome can be constructed from a cone and truncated cones fitted together. A sphere is two domes fitted together. The following AutoLISP function draws a sphere as illustrated in Figure 10.4. Review the program in detail to understand the procedure. The sphere is drawn using 30-degree segments both vertically and horizontally.

Figure 10.3   Truncated cone.

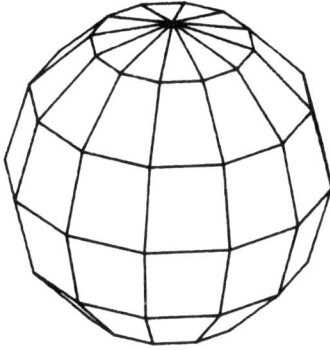

Figure 10.4 3-D sphere.

The symbols used in the function are illustrated in Figure 10.5. The hatched face illustrates the application of the symbols to draw one face of the sphere.

```
;        ** SPHERE Function **
(defun sphere    (/ rad ; Sphere radius
            xy         ; Center X,Y coordinates
            degv       ; Ver segment angle in degrees
            degh       ; Hor segment angle in degrees
            angh angv ; Ver and Hor angle in radians
            a1 b1      ; Lower corners of 3-D face
            a2 b2      ; upper corners of 3-D face
            r1 r2      ; radius at upper and lower seg's
            z)         ; center elevation
    (setvar ''cmdecho'' 0)
    (setq xy (getpoint ''Sphere X,Y center point: ''))
    (setq rad (getreal ''\nRadius: ''))
    (setq z (getreal ''\nCenter elevation: ''))
    (setq degv 0 degh 30)
    (setq angh (* degh (/ pi 180)))
    ;     Draw top half of sphere.
    (drwface base)
    ;     Draw bottom half of sphere
    (setq rad (* -1 rad) degv 0)
    (drwface base)
)
;     ** Draw Face (DRWFACE) Function **
; DRWFACE function to draw sphere faces.
  (defun drwface (base)
    (while ( <= degv 60)
      (setq angv (* degv (/ pi 180)))
      (setq r1 (* rad (cos angv)))
      (setq r2 (* rad (cos (+ angv (* 30 (/ pi 180))))))
      (setq a1 (list
          (+ (car xy) r1)
          (cadr xy)
          (+ z (* rad (sin angv)))))
    (setq b1 (list
          (+ (car xy) (* r1 (cos angh)))
          (+ (cadr xy) (* r1 (sin angh)))
          (+ z (* rad (sin angv)))))
```

```
(setq a2 (list
    (+ (car xy) r2)
    (cadr xy)
    (+ z (* rad (sin (+ angv (* 30 (/ pi 180))))))))
(setq b2 (list
    (+ (car xy) (* r2 (cos angh)))
    (+ (cadr xy) (* r2 (sin angh)))
    (+ z (* rad (sin (+ angh (* 30 (/ pi 180))))))))
(command ''3DFACE'' b2 b1 a1 a2)
(command '''')
(command ''array'' ''L'' '''' ''P'' xy '''' 360 30 ''Y'')
(setq degv (+ degv 30))
)
)
```

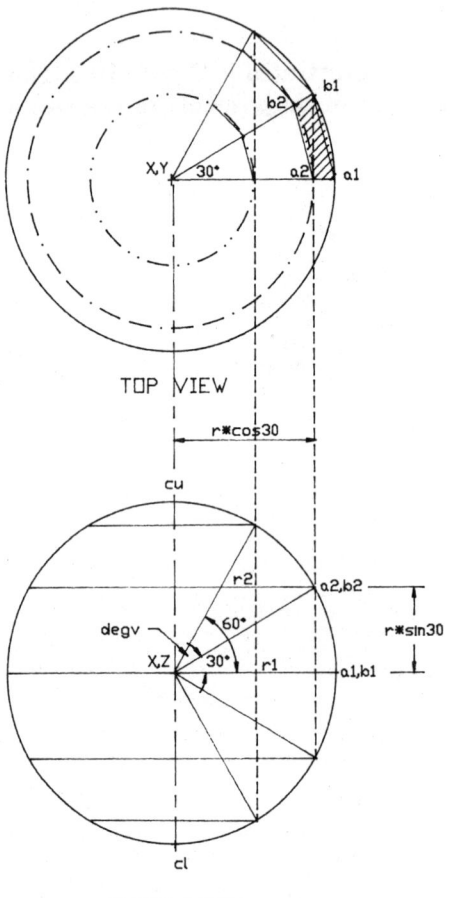

TOP VIEW

r*cos30

FRONT VIEW

Figure 10.5 Sphere construction.

Assignment

1. Modify the sphere program to allow the user to input the segments as either 10, 15, 20, or 30 degrees.

2. Modify the sphere program to draw a dome. The modification is done in a few lines.

10.4   Release 10 Coordinate Systems

AutoCAD works with a fixed World Coordinate System and an arbitrary User Coordinate System:

World Coordinate System (WCS).   The WCS is a fixed cartesian coordinate system with its x axis along the bottom of the screen and its y axis along the side of the screen. The origin, point 0,0,0, is on the lower left corner of the x,y plane, and the positive z axis projects out from the screen. Negative coordinates may be used. Positive rotational angles about an axis are based on the right-hand rule. For example, a positive rotation about the z axis is determined by pointing the thumb of your right hand in the positive direction of the axis, out of the screen, and curling your fingers. The direction of your fingers indicates positive rotation about the z axis, i.e., counterclockwise.

User Coordinate System (USC).   A UCS is a coordinate system which may be defined in any plane. The UCS x and y axis, which are always 90 degrees apart, form the *construction plane,* and the z axis projects perpendicular from that plane. The axis may be rotated at any angle, based on the right-hand rule.

The origin always remains fixed on the WCS; however, on the UCS the origin is at a location specified by the user when the UCS is defined. For instance, if you are drawing a bin that has sloping sides and a "true view" of a sloping side is required, a UCS might be defined on the plane of the bin's side. A plan view of the UCS would then represent a true view of the side of the bin on which the UCS was defined.

When inputting data to AutoCAD, points may be specified with respect to the current UCS (i.e., point 3,4,5) or they may be specified with respect to the WCS by preceding the coordinate with an asterisk (i.e., point *7,9,8 or *@3<60. Two lists which are numerically different for each coordinate system may define the same point on the object.

Although the UCS was developed to facilitate 3-D drawings, it is also quite useful for 2-D drawings. For example, orthographic drawings are generally drawn with three views—a top view, front view, and a right-side view. The WCS origin might be the lower left corner of the screen. When working on the right-side view, it might be easier to input coordinates if a UCS with its origin in the lower left corner of *that* view is defined.

10.5 Viewing 3-D Objects

The screen can be divided into up to 4 different viewports (16 on a 32-bit workstation) with each viewport displaying a different UCS view of the object. As changes are made to the object in one viewport, they are immediately reflected in the other viewports. The views can be named and restored as required.

The dynamic preview command, DVIEW, allows the drafter to view an object in three-dimensional space from any angle, with any focal point, and with a variety of focal lengths similar to telephoto or wide-angle camera lenses. The object can be viewed from within, and sections of the object can be clipped from the view. This command also allows you to view the object in perspective. The DVIEW command is meant for viewing objects, not for drawing or editing.

10.6 AutoLISP Primitive Differences with Release 10

Table 10.1 lists AutoLISP primitives described in earlier chapters that either return 3-D points or can be supplied a 3-D point for input with Release 10 of AutoCAD. The use of these primitives in earlier chapters is still acceptable. If a 2-D point is entered where a 3-D point is expected, Release 10 uses the current elevation (usually 0) as a default z coordinate. Also, programs in earlier chapters use the CADR

TABLE 10.1   AutoLISP Primitive Changes with Release 10

Primitive	Section	Change
ANGLE	8.3	3-D points supplied are projected onto current construction plane.
DISTANCE	8.3	Returns a 3-D point.
GETANGLE	6.5.5	The angle returned is with respect to the current construction plane.
GETDIST	5.3.1	<pt> is an optional 2-D or 3-D base point in the current UCS.
GETPOINT	4.3.3	<pt> is an optional base point in the current UCS.
POLAR	7.8.1	The point returned is with respect to the current UCS. <pt> may be supplied as a 3-D point. <angle> is always with respect to the current construction plane.

primitive to extract the y coordinate, so a list composed of x,y,z will not affect the output.

10.7   Chute Program

An AutoLISP program to use AutoCAD's viewports to draw a top view, a front view, a true view of a sloping side, and a 3-D isometric view of a square chute follows:

```
 1:  ;         *** CHUTE Program ***
 2:  ; This function draws 4 views of a square chute
 3:  ; with top and bottom lip sides of 250 mm.
 4:  ;
 5:  (defun chute (/ #top #bot #ht a b c d e f g h)
 6:      (setvar ''cmdecho'' 0) ;Command echo off
 7:      ; *** Set system variables
 8:      (setvar ''lunits'' 2)  ;Degree units—mm
 9:      (setvar ''luprec'' 0)  ;0 digits to right of decimal
10:      (chutein)              ;Get input
11:      (chutelim)             ;Set limits
12:      (chutedrw)             ;Draw plan view of chute
13:      (chuteprt)             ;Create viewports
14: )
15: ;--------------------------
16: ;
17: ;        ** CHUTEIN—Input data **
18: (defun chutein (/ #init)
19:     (setq #init '(initget (+ 1 2 4 8)))
20:     (eval #init)
21:     (setq #top (getreal ''Enter top width in mm: ''))
22:     (eval #init)
23:     (setq #bot (getreal ''Enter bottom width in mm: ''))
24:     (eval #init) (setq #ht 0)
25:     (while (> 750 (setq #ht
26:       (getreal ''\nEnter total height in mm (>= 750): '')))
27:       (princ ''\n\tREDO—Total height must be > 750 mm'')
28:     )
29: )
30: ;--------------------------
31: ;
32: ;        ** CHUTELIM—Set limits **
33: (defun chutelim ()
34:     (setvar ''limmin'' (list
35:     (* -1 (/ #top 4)) (* -1 (/ #ht 4))))
36:     (setvar ''limmax'' (list
37:     (* 1.25 #top) (* 1.25 #ht)))
38:     (command ''zoom'' ''all'')
39: )
40: ;--------------------------
41: ;
42: ;        ** CHUTEDRW—Draw chute **
43: (defun chutedrw (/ z n)
44:     (setq a (list 0 0 0)
45:          b (list #top 0 0)
46:          c (list #top #top 0)
47:          d (list 0 #top 0)
48:          z (- 0.0 (- #ht 500)) n (/ (- #top #bot) 2)
```

```
49:          e (list n n z)
50:          f (list (+ n #bot) n z)
51:          g (list (+ n #bot) (+ n #bot) z)
52:          h (list n (+ n #bot) z))
53:   ; Draw top
54:   (setvar ''thickness'' 250)
55:   (command ''line'' a b c d ''c'')
56:   ; Draw bottom
57:   (setvar ''thickness'' -250)
58:   (command ''line'' e f g h ''c'')
59:   (setvar ''thickness'' 0)
60:   ; Draw sides
61:   (command ''3dface'' a e f b c g h d a e '''')
62: )
63: ;--------------------------
64: ;
65: ;        ** CHUTEPRT—Create viewports **
66: (defun chuteprt ()
67:   (setvar ''ucsicon'' 3)              ;UCS icon on at origin
68:   (command ''vports'' 4)              ;Create 4 viewports
69:   (setvar ''cvport'' 6)               ;Current vwport—6—TOP
70:   (command ''ucs'' ''s'' ''top'') ;Save UCS
71:   (command ''zoom'' ''e'')(command ''zoom'' ''.75x'')
72:   (setvar ''cvport'' 9)               ;Current vwport—9—FRONT
73:   (command ''ucs'' ''x'' 90)          ;Rotate UCS x-axis 90
74:   (command ''ucs'' ''s'' ''front'')  ;Save UCS
75:   (command ''plan'' ''u'' ''front'') ;Display UCS
76:   (command ''zoom'' ''.75x'')
77:   (setvar ''cvport'' 3)               ;Current vwport—3
78:   (command ''vpoint'' ''rotate'' ''-30'' ''-30'')
79:   (command ''view'' ''s'' ''iso'')    ;Save view—ISO
80:   (command ''hide'')
81:   (setvar ''cvport'' 1)               ;Current vwport—1—AUX1
82:   (setq bt (trans b 0 1)              ;Transpose WCS to Front
83:         ct (trans c 0 1)
84:         ft (trans f 0 1))
85:   (command ''ucs'' 3 bt ct ft)        ;Define UCS on side
86:   (command ''ucs'' ''x'' 180)         ;Rotate UCS 180
87:   (command ''ucs'' ''s'' ''aux'')    ;Save UCS
88:   (command ''plan'' ''u'' ''aux'') ;Display UCS
89:   (command ''zoom'' ''.75x'')
90:   (command ''hide'')
91: )
```

Discussion of chute function. The controlling function, from lines 5 through 14, calls five subfunctions: CHUTEIN inputs data about the chute to be drawn, CHUTELIM sets the screen limits, CHUTEDRW draws the top view of the chute, and CHUTEPRT creates the four screen viewports and draws a front view, an isometric, and a true view of a side of the chute.

Discussion of the program is limited to general explanations and to new primitives not introduced in earlier chapters. The reader should study the program carefully and refer to previous chapters if further clarification is necessary.

The WHILE primitive is used in line 25 to print the expression in line 27 while the chute height entered by the user is less than 750 mm. This value is an arbitrary minimum limit on the total bin height since the top and bottom sections of the chute are 250 mm high.

Although four views are to be displayed on the monitor—one in each viewport—the actual drawing only includes one view. This will be clarified later.

The initial view drawn in the WCS is a top view of the bin. To create other views the construction plane is shifted to the plane desired by defining a UCS.

The WCS screen limits are 2-D points defined in the CHUTELIM function, lines 33 through 39. The x coordinate of lower left corner of the screen is set as −¼ times the width of the top of the chute; and the y coordinate is −¼ times the height of the chute. The x and y coordinates of the top right corner of the screen are 1.25 times the chute width and height, respectively.

The origin of the WCS, point 0,0,0, is to be at the lower left corner of the top view of the chute at the point where the sloping side and the top sides meet.

The top and bottom lip of the chute are to be drawn as extruded lines, and the sides are to be drawn as 3-D faces.

The CHUTEDRW function draws the top view of the chute in the WCS. Prior to the chute being drawn, the corner points of the sloping sides, illustrated in Figure 10.6, are calculated in lines 44 through 52. The top lip of the bin is then drawn using lines extruded 250 mm up from the sloping sides (lines 54 and 55). The bottom lip is drawn using

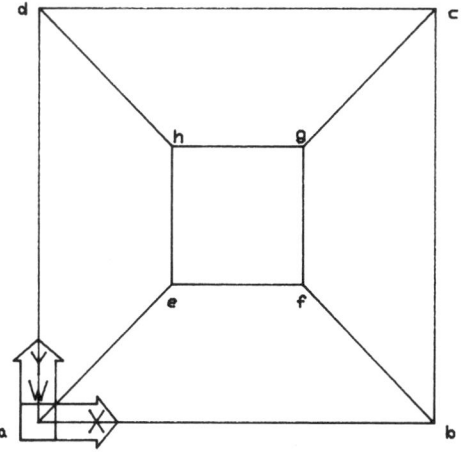

Figure 10.6 WCS—Top view of chute.

lines extruded 250 mm down from the bottom of the sloping sides (lines 57 and 58). In line 59 the thickness is set to 0 so that there are no extruded lines when other entities are drawn.

The sides of the bin are drawn using AutoCAD's 3DFACE command in line 61. Note the order of the points entered to draw all the faces sequentially. Review the sequence using Figure 10.6.

10.7.1   Coordinate system icon

AutoCAD uses a "coordinate system icon' (see the X-Y arrows in Figures 10.6 and 10.7) to show the orientation of the current construction plane. The "W" in the icon indicates that the plane is on the WCS. A " + " is displayed in the icon if the icon is at the UCS origin. If the UCS is being viewed from above (its positive Z direction), a box is formed at the base of the icon. When a view direction is on the edge of

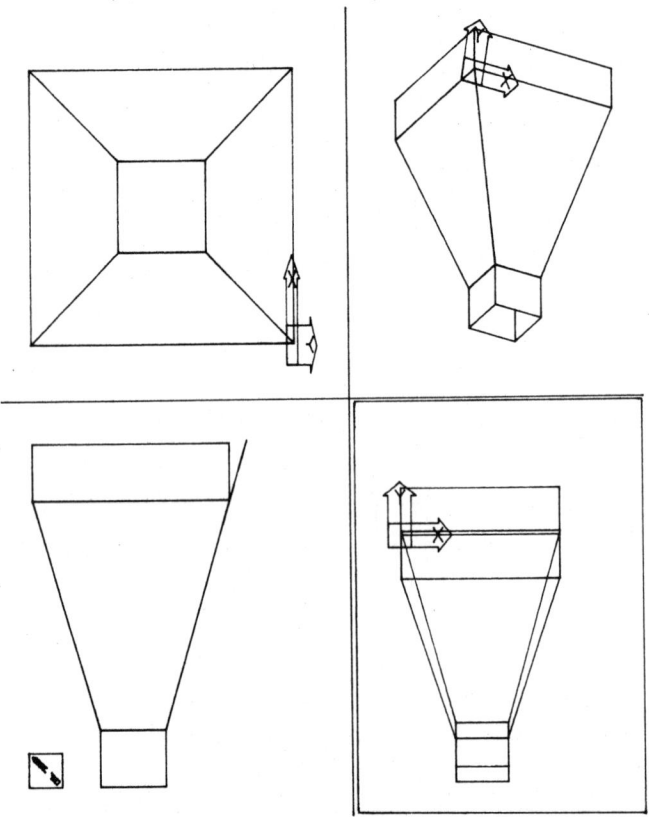

Figure 10.7   Screen viewports.

a UCS, the icon is replaced by a broken pencil as illustrated in the front view in Figure 10.7.

The CHUTEPRT function which begins on line 66 of the program is to create the viewports and draw the required views. In line 67 the SETVAR function is used to set the system variable UCSICON to 3 (see Appendix B) so that the icon is floated to the UCS origin if possible. If the origin is off screen or the icon cannot be positioned at the origin without being clipped, it is displayed in the lower left corner of the viewport.

10.7.2 Viewports

AutoCAD's VPORTS command is used in line 68 to divide the screen into four viewports. Each viewport will have a copy of the screen that was current when the viewport was created, i.e., the top view of the chute.

Each viewport has an identification number. The lower right one is number 1, the upper right one is number 3, the upper left one is number 6, and the lower left one is number 9. In line 69 the upper left viewport is made the current viewport by setting the system variable CVPORT to 6. This viewport is to display the top view of the chute, which happens to be the current view. The UCS is the WCS and does not have to be changed. AutoCAD's UCS command and the Save option are used in line 70 to save the UCS with the name Top. This program would operate the same if the UCS was not saved; however, if a UCS has been saved, it can be recalled using the UCS Recall option at a later time without having to redefine it.

In line 71 the view is zoomed to the extent of the viewport and then to .75X. This provides a reasonable-size view.

In line 72 the lower left viewport is set as the current viewport and is where the front view of the chute is to be displayed. AutoCAD's UCS command and the X option are used in line 73 to rotate the *icon* about the x axis by 90 degrees. Using the right-hand rule, place your thumb in the direction of the x axis (see Figure 10.6). A positive rotation is in the direction your fingers point. A 90-degree rotation about the x axis will point the y axis out of the screen so that the x,y plane is on the front view of the chute, which is the desired view. The UCS is then saved with the name Front. Although a new UCS has been defined, the view of the chute has not been updated. This is done by invoking AutoCAD's PLAN command with the Ucs option and the UCS to be shown in plan is the Front view (see line 75). When a plan view is drawn, it is drawn to the extent of the viewport. A .75X zoom is then invoked to display a reasonable-size view.

In line 77 the top right viewport is made current. This view is to display an isometric view of the chute. AutoCAD's VPOINT command and the Rotate option are used to rotate the viewpoint −30 from the x axis in the x-y plane of the current UCS and −30 from the x-y plane (along the z axis). The viewpoint is always directed toward the UCS origin. Our viewpoint is therefore 30 degrees below the front view (the current UCS) and 30 degrees out from the screen as illustrated in Figure 10.7. Since the UCS was not changed, the view is saved using AutoCAD's VIEW command with the Save option and the name Iso on line 79. The HIDE command is then invoked to eliminate the "hidden" lines from the screen.

If you want to continue drawing or modify this view, you must define a UCS since the VPOINT command is used only to display a view.

10.7.3 Translating points between coordinate systems

Viewport 1 is to contain a true view of a sloping side of the bin, so a UCS is to be defined on the plane of a side. This is easy to do with AutoCAD's UCS command and the 3 option, which allows you to select three points defining the plane, i.e., the points bound to the symbols B, C, and F (see Figure 10.6). But, points B, C, and F are points on the WCS whereas the current coordinate system is a UCS named Front (see line 74). Consequently, prior to using those points, they must be translated to the current UCS. The TRANS AutoLISP primitive translates a point (or a displacement) from one coordinate system to another. The syntax of TRANS is as follows:

```
(trans <pt> <from> <to> [T])
```

The <pt> argument is a 3-D point in the coordinate system specified by a code in the <from> argument, which is to be translated to a coordinate system specified by a code in the <to> argument. If the optional [T] argument is present, <pt> is treated as a 3-D displacement rather than a point. The <to> and <from> arguments can be any of the following:

Code	Coordinate system
0	WCS
1	Current UCS
2	Display Coordinate System (DCS—see below)

The DCS is a coordinate system relative to the current viewing direction.

Prior to their use in the current UCS, Front, points B, C, and F are translated from the WCS (Code 0) to the current UCS (Code 1) using the TRANS primitive in lines 82, 83, and 84. The translated points are bound to the symbols BT, CT, and FT. AutoCAD's UCS command with the 3 option is then used to define the new UCS. Since point F is below the previous UCS, the x axis is now pointing down on the plane of the side. It is rotated 180 degrees in line 86 so that it points up. The UCS is saved as Aux. The remaining expressions should be clear to you.

Save the function in a file named CHUTE. Load it and run the CHUTE function. After your function is debugged, add the expression (setvar "cmdecho" 0) to the beginning so that AutoCAD commands are not echoed to the screen.

10.7.4 UCS and BLOCK command.

When a block is created, the UCS in effect at the time of creation becomes the WCS for the block, with its origin as the block's insertion base point. When the block is inserted into a drawing, the block's coordinate system is aligned parallel to the UCS in effect in the drawing. As a result, multiview drawings may be easily created by aligning a UCS with the desired view and then saving the view as a Wblock for insertion into the multiview drawing.

Assignment

1. Modify the CHUTE program to draw chutes with rectangular openings. The user is to enter the width and length of the top and bottom openings, the chute height, and the location of the bottom opening with respect to the left front corner of the top.

2. Add a function to the CHUTE program to dimension the top and front views of the chute following standard dimensioning procedures.

3. Write a function that a drafter can invoke to create three viewports on the screen. (You can determine the viewport identification numbers by using AutoCAD to create the desired three viewports and then using the function (getvar "cvport") to return the number of the current viewport.) The top left viewport is to contain a top view of the object, the lower left is to contain a front view, and the right viewport is to contain an auxiliary view. The function is to prompt the user to pick three points on the object, defining the plane of the auxiliary view.

Appendix

AutoCAD Scale and Text Heights

Table A1 - AutoCAD Scale & Text Heights

A. - Drawing units: FEET (AutoCAD Decimal Units)

Drawing Scale	HATCH	LTSCALE	3/32" TEXT TXT	DMSCALE	1/8" TEXT TXT	DMSCALE	3/16" TEXT TXT	DMSCALE
1/8"=1'0"	8.00	6.00	0.75	4.17	1.00	5.56	1.50	8.33
3/16"=1'0"	5.33	4.00	0.50	2.78	0.67	3.70	1.00	5.56
1/4"=1'0"	4.00	3.00	0.38	2.08	0.50	2.78	0.75	4.17
5/16"=1'0"	3.20	2.40	0.30	1.67	0.40	2.22	0.60	3.33
3/8"=1'0"	2.67	2.00	0.25	1.39	0.33	1.85	0.50	2.78
1/2"=1'0"	2.00	1.50	0.19	1.04	0.25	1.39	0.38	2.08
5/8"=1'0"	1.60	1.20	0.15	0.83	0.20	1.11	0.30	1.67
3/4"=1'0"	1.33	1.00	0.13	0.69	0.17	0.93	0.25	1.39
7/8"=1'0"	1.14	0.86	0.11	0.60	0.14	0.79	0.21	1.19
1"=1'0"	1.00	0.75	0.09	0.52	0.13	0.69	0.19	1.04
1.5"=1'0"	0.67	0.50	0.06	0.35	0.08	0.46	0.13	0.69
2"=1'0"	0.50	0.38	0.05	0.26	0.06	0.35	0.09	0.52
1/4 size	0.33	0.25	0.03	0.17	0.04	0.23	0.06	0.35
1/2 size	0.17	0.13	0.02	0.09	0.02	0.12	0.03	0.17
Full size	0.08	0.06	0.01	0.04	0.01	0.06	0.02	0.09

B. - Drawing units: AutoCAD Architectural or Engineering Units

Drawing Scale	HATCH	LTSCALE	3/32" TEXT TXT	DMSCALE	1/8" TEXT TXT	DMSCALE	3/16" TEXT TXT	DMSCALE
1/8"=1'0"	96.00	72.00	9.00	50.00	12.00	66.67	18.00	100.00
3/16"=1'0"	64.00	48.00	6.00	33.33	8.00	44.44	12.00	66.67
1/4"=1'0"	48.00	36.00	4.50	25.00	6.00	33.33	9.00	50.00
5/16"=1'0"	38.40	28.80	3.60	20.00	4.80	26.67	7.20	40.00
3/8"=1'0"	32.00	24.00	3.00	16.67	4.00	22.22	6.00	33.33
1/2"=1'0"	24.00	18.00	2.25	12.50	3.00	16.67	4.50	25.00
5/8"=1'0"	19.20	14.40	1.80	10.00	2.40	13.33	3.60	20.00
3/4"=1'0"	16.00	12.00	1.50	8.33	2.00	11.11	3.00	16.67
7/8"=1'0"	13.71	10.29	1.29	7.14	1.71	9.52	2.57	14.29
1"=1'0"	12.00	9.00	1.13	6.25	1.50	8.33	2.25	12.50
1.5"=1'0"	8.00	6.00	0.75	4.17	1.00	5.56	1.50	8.33
2"=1'0"	6.00	4.50	0.56	3.13	0.75	4.17	1.13	6.25
1/4 size	4.00	3.00	0.38	2.08	0.50	2.78	0.75	4.17
1/2 size	2.00	1.50	0.19	1.04	0.25	1.39	0.38	2.08
Full size	1.00	0.75	0.09	0.52	0.13	0.69	0.19	1.04

C. - Drawing units: Engineering (Feet) (AutoCAD Decimal Units)

Drawing Scale	HATCH	LTSCALE	3/32" TEXT TXT	DMSCALE	1/8" TEXT TXT	DMSCALE	3/16" TEXT TXT	DMSCALE
1:3000	250.00	187.50	23.44	130.21	31.25	173.61	46.88	260.42
1:2500	208.33	156.25	19.53	108.51	26.04	144.68	39.06	217.01
1:2000	166.67	125.00	15.63	86.81	20.83	115.74	31.25	173.61
1:1500	125.00	93.75	11.72	65.10	15.63	86.81	23.44	130.21
1:1250	104.17	78.13	9.77	54.25	13.02	72.34	19.53	108.51
1:1000	83.33	62.50	7.81	43.40	10.42	57.87	15.63	86.81
1:750	62.50	46.88	5.86	32.55	7.81	43.40	11.72	65.10
1:600	50.00	37.50	4.69	26.04	6.25	34.72	9.38	52.08
1:500	41.67	31.25	3.91	21.70	5.21	28.94	7.81	43.40
1:400	33.33	25.00	3.13	17.36	4.17	23.15	6.25	34.72
1:300	25.00	18.75	2.34	13.02	3.13	17.36	4.69	26.04
1:200	16.67	12.50	1.56	8.68	2.08	11.57	3.13	17.36
1:100	8.33	6.25	0.78	4.34	1.04	5.79	1.56	8.68
1:50	4.17	3.13	0.39	2.17	0.52	2.89	0.78	4.34
1:25	2.08	1.56	0.20	1.09	0.26	1.45	0.39	2.17
1:20	1.67	1.25	0.16	0.87	0.21	1.16	0.31	1.74

A. - Drawing units: METRES

Drawing Scale	HATCH	LTSCALE	2.5 mm TEXT TXT	DIMSCALE	3 mm TEXT TXT	DIMSCALE	4 mm TEXT TXT	DIMSCALE
1:10	0.25	0.19	0.03	0.14	0.03	0.17	0.04	0.22
1:20	0.51	0.38	0.05	0.28	0.06	0.33	0.08	0.44
1:30	0.76	0.57	0.08	0.42	0.09	0.50	0.12	0.67
1:40	1.02	0.76	0.10	0.56	0.12	0.67	0.16	0.89
1:50	1.27	0.95	0.13	0.69	0.15	0.83	0.20	1.11
1:100	2.54	1.91	0.25	1.39	0.30	1.67	0.40	2.22
1:200	5.08	3.81	0.50	2.78	0.60	3.33	0.80	4.44
1:250	6.35	4.76	0.63	3.47	0.75	4.17	1.00	5.56
1:300	7.62	5.72	0.75	4.17	0.90	5.00	1.20	6.67
1:400	10.16	7.62	1.00	5.56	1.20	6.67	1.60	8.89
1:500	12.70	9.53	1.25	6.94	1.50	8.33	2.00	11.11
1:750	19.05	14.29	1.88	10.42	2.25	12.50	3.00	16.67
1:1000	25.40	19.05	2.50	13.89	3.00	16.67	4.00	22.22
1:2000	50.80	38.10	5.00	27.78	6.00	33.33	8.00	44.44
1:5000	127.00	95.25	12.50	69.44	15.00	83.33	20.00	111.11

B. - Drawing units: MILLIMETRES

Drawing Scale	HATCH	LTSCALE	2.5 mm TEXT TXT	DIMSCALE	3 mm TEXT TXT	DIMSCALE	4 mm TEXT TXT	DIMSCALE
1:1	25	19	2.5	14	3.0	17	4.0	22
1:2	51	38	5.0	28	6.0	33	8.0	44
1:3	76	57	7.5	42	9.0	50	12.0	67
1:4	102	76	10.0	56	12.0	67	16.0	89
1:5	127	95	12.5	69	15.0	83	20.0	111
1:10	254	191	25.0	139	30.0	167	40.0	222
1:20	508	381	50.0	278	60.0	333	80.0	444
1:50	1270	953	125.0	694	150.0	833	200.0	1111
1:100	2540	1905	250.0	1389	300.0	1667	400.0	2222
1:200	5080	3810	500.0	2778	600.0	3333	800.0	4444
1:250	6350	4763	625.0	3472	750.0	4167	1000.0	5556
1:300	7620	5715	750.0	4167	900.0	5000	1200.0	6667
1:400	10160	7620	1000.0	5556	1200.0	6667	1600.0	8889
1:500	12700	9525	1250.0	6944	1500.0	8333	2000.0	11111
1:750	19050	14288	1875.0	10417	2250.0	12500	3000.0	16667

B

AutoCAD System Variables—Release 10

Variable name	Example	Meaning
ACADPREFIX	""	Directory name specified by ACAD environment variable. (read only)
ACADVER	10	AutoCAD version (read only)
AFLAGS	0	Attribute modes (sum of): 1=Invisible, 2=Constant, 3=Verify
ANGBASE	0	Angle 0 direction.
ANGDIR	0	1=clockwise, 0=counterclockwise
APERTURE	10	Object snap target height in pixels.
AREA	0.0000	Area computed by AREA, LIST or DBLIST. (read only)
ATTDIA	0	Attribute entry: 1=dialog box, 2=prompts
ATTMODE	1	Attribute display mode: 0=off, 1=normal, 2=on.
ATTREQ	1	Attribute values: 0=use defaults, 1=enable prompts
AUNITS	0	Angular units mode:0=decimal degrees, 1=degrees/minutes/seconds, 2=grads, 3=radians, 4=surveyors units.
AUPREC	0	Angular units decimal places
AXISMODE	0	Axis: 1=on, 0=off
AXISUNIT	0.00,0.00	Axis spacing: X,Y
BACKSZ	0.0	Back clipping plane offset.
BLIPMODE	1	Marker blips: 1=on, 0=off
CDATE	19880811.112308251	Date/time: YEARMODY.HRMISEmsec (read only)
CECOLOR	"BYLAYER"	Current entity color. (read only)
CELTYPE	"BYLAYER"	Current entity linetype. (read only)
CHAMFERA	0.00	First chamfer dist.
CHAMFERB	0.00	Second chamfer dist.
CLAYER	"BORDER1"	Current layer. (read only)
CMDECHO	1	When AutoLISP's COMMAND function is used, prompts and input are echoed if 1 and not echoed if 0.
COORDS	0	0=coordinate display updated on picks only, 1=display of absolute coordinates is continuously updated, 2=distance and angle from last point are displayed when a distance or angle is requested.
CVPORT		ID number of current viewport.
DATE	2447385.47443859	Julian date/time. (read only)
DIMALT	0	Alternated dimension units: 0=off, 1=on
DIMALTD	2	Alternate dimension units decimal places.
DIMALTF	25.40	Alternate units scale factor.
DIMAPOST	""	Character string to be edited following an alternate dimension. (read only)
DIMASO	1	Associative dimensioning: 0=off, 1=on
DIMASZ	0.18	Dimension arrow size.
DIMBLK	""	Name of block to be drawn instead of normal arrow. (read only)
DIMBLK1	None	Name of user-specified 1'st arrow block.
DIMBLK2	None	Name of user-specified 2'nd arrow block.
DIMCEN	0.09	Dimension center mark size/type: 0=no center marks, -=center lines, +=centermark.
DIMDLE	0.00	Dimension line extension.
DIMDLI	0.38	Dimension line increment.
DIMEXE	0.18	Extension line extension.
DIMEXO	0.06	Extension line offset.
DIMFLAC	1.00	Global scale factor for linear dimension measurements.
DIMLIM	0	Generate dimension limits as default text: 0=off, 1=on
DIMPOST	""	Dimension string to be editied following dimension measurements.
DIMRND	0.00	Rounding value for dimensions.
DIMSAH	Off	Separate arrow heads: On=use DIMBLK1 & DIMBLK2, Off=use DIMBLK.

DIMSCALE	1.00	Overall dimension scale factor.
DIMSE1	0	Suppress extension line 1: 0=off 1=on
DIMSE2	0	Suppress extension line 2: 0=off 1=on
DIMSHO	0	Redefine dimension entities while dragging (if DIMASO is on): 0=off, 1=on
DIMSOXD	Off	Suppress outside-extension dimension lines.
DIMTAD	1	Dimension text above dimension line: 0=off, 1=on
DIMTIH	0	Dimension text inside horizontal: 0=off, 1=on
DIMTIX	Off	Text forced inside extension lines.
DIMTM	0.00	Dimension minus tolerance.
DIMTOFL	Off	Dimension text outside force dimension line.
DIMTOH	0	Dimension text outside horizontal: 0=off, 1=on
DIMTOL	0	Append dimension tolerances to default text: 0=off, 1=on
DIMTP	0.00	Dimension plus tolerance
DIMTSZ	0.00	Dimension tick size (if 0, arrows are drawn).
DIMTVP	0	Dimension text vertical position.
DIMTXT	0.18	Dimension text height.
DIMZIN	3	Dimension zero-inch editing: 0=omit zero feet and precisley zero inches, 1=include zero feet and precisley zero inches, 2=include zero feet, 3=include precisely zero inches 4=suppress leading 0 in decimal dim's. 8=suppress trailing zeros in decimal dim's. 12=suppress leading & trailing zeros.
DISTANCE	0.00	Distance computed by DIST, LIST or DBLIST. (read only)
DRAGMODE	2	0=no dragging, 1=on if requested, 2=auto.
DRAGP1	10	Regen-drag input sampling rate.
DRAGP2	25	Fast-drag input sampling rate.
DWGNAME	"misc\advg"	Drawing name (read only)
DWGPREFIX	"C:\ACAD\MISC\"	Drive/directory prefix for drawing (read only)
ELEVATION	0.00	Current 3D elevation
EXPERT	0	1=suppress certain "Are you sure?" prompts, 0=issue normal prompts.
EXTMAX	283.00,184.45	Upper right "drawing uses" extents (read only)
EXTMIN	0.00,0.00	Lower left "drawing uses" extents (read only)
FILLETRAD	0.00	Fillet radius
FILLMODE	1	Fill mode: 0=off, 1=on
FLATLAND	0	1=DXF & AutoLISP operate as prior to Release 10 0=DXF & AutoLISP use Release 10 capabilities.
FRONTZ	0.0	Front clipping plane offset for current viewport.
GRIDMODE	0	Grid: 0=off, 1=on
GRIDUNIT	0.00,0.00	Grid spacing: X,Y
HANDLES	0	Entity handles: 1=on, 0=disabled (read only)
HIGHLIGHT	1	Object selection highlighting: 0=off, 1=On
INSBASE	0.00,0.00	Insertion base point set by BASE command.
LASTANGLE	0	End angle of last arc entered. (read only)
LASTPOINT	0.00,0.00	Referenced by @ during keyboard point entry.
LASTPT3D	0.00,0.00,0.00	Last 3D point (to be disabled with Release 11)
LENSLENGTH	1	Length of lens (mm) in perspective view (read only).
LIMCHECK	0	Limits checking: 0=off, 1=on
LIMMAX	283.00,183.00	Upper right drawing limits.
LIMMIN	0.00,0.00	Lower left drawing limits.
LTSCALE	1.0000	Global linetype scale factor.
LUNITS	2	Linear units mode: 1=scientific, 2=decimal, 3=engineering, 4=architectural
LUPREC	2	Linear units decimal places or denominator.
MENUECHO	0	0=echo all menu items and system prompts, 1=suppress echo of menu items (^P toggles prompts on or off), 2=suppress printing of system prompts during menu,C90 4=disable ^P toggle of menu item echoing.
MENUNAME	/ACAD/PROTO1	Current loaded menu file (read only).

MIRRTEXT	1	MIRROR reflects text: 0=off, 1=on
ORTHOMODE	0	Orhogonal mode: 0=off, 1=on
OSMODE	0	Object snap mode (sum of): 1=Endpoint, 2=Midpoint, 4=Center, 8=Node, 16=Quadrant, 32=Intersection, 64=Insert, 128=Perpendicular, 256=Nearest, 512=Quick
PDMODE	0	Point display mode.
PDSIZE	0.0000	Point display size
PERIMETER	0.00	Perimeter computed by AREA, LIST or DBLIST (read only)
PICKBOX	3	Object selection target height in pixels.
POPUPS	1	Dialog boxes, menu bar, pull-down menus, icon menus 1=available, 0=not available.
QTEXTMODE	0	Quick text mode: 0=off, 1=on
REGENMODE	1	REGENAUTO: 0=off, 1=on
SCREENSIZE	567.00,165.00	Graphic screen size in pixels: X,Y (read only)
SKETCHINC	0.10	Sketch record increment.
SKPOLY	0	Sketch generates lines if 0, polylines if 1.
SNAPANG	0	Snap/grid rotational angle in radians.
SNAPBASE	0.00,0.00	Snap/grid origin point.
SNAPISOPAIR	0	Current isometric plane: 0=left, 1=top, 2=right
SNAPMODE	0	Snap mode: 0=off, 1=0n
SNAPSTYL	0	Snap style: 0=standard, 1=isometric
SNAPUNIT	1.00,1.00	Snap spacing: X,Y
SPLFRAME	0	Display control of polygon for spline fit polylines, definining mesh of surface fit polygon mesh & invisible edge of 3D face. 1= display, 0=no display
SPLINESEGS	8	Number of line segments for each spline patch.
SPLINETYPE	5	PEDIT spline curve generated: 5=quadratic B-spline, 6=cubic B-spline
SURFTAB1	6	Number of tabulations generated by RULESURF & TABSURF, and mesh density in M direction for REVSURF & EDGESURF.
SURFTAB2	6	Mesh density in N direction for REVSURF & EDGESURF.
SUFRTYPE	5	Surface fitting performed by PEDIT & Smooth 5=quadratic B-spline, 6=cubic B-spline, 8=Bezier.
SURFU	6	Surface density in M direction.
SURFV	6	Surface density in N direction.
TARGET	0.0,0.0,0.0	Location of target point for current viewport, in UCS.
TDCREATE	2447524.0	Time and date of drawing creation (read only).
TDINDWG	0.0072108	Total drawing editing time (read only).
TDUPDATE	2447524.0	Time and date od last update/save (read only).
TDUSRTIMER	0.00835961	User elapsed time (read only).
TEMPREFIX	""	Directory name configured for placement of temporary files. (read only)
TEXTEVAL	0	0=all responses to prompts for text strings and attribute values taken literally, 1=text starting with "(" or "!" evaluated as an AutoLISP expression,
TEXTSIZE	0.20	Text height.
TEXTSTYLE	"STANDARD"	Name of current text style.
THICKNESS	0.00	3D thickness
TRACEWID	0.05	Trace width.
UCSICON	1	Coordinate system icon: 0=off, 1=on in lower left corner of viewport, 3=float icon to UCS origin.
UCSNAME	""	Name of current coordinate system (read only)
UCSORG	0.0,0.0,0.0	Origin point of current coordinate system in worlc coordinates.
UCSXDIR	1.0,0.0,0.0	X-direction of current UCS (read only).
UCSYDIR	0.0,1.0,0.0	Y-direction of current UCS (read only).
USERL1-5	nil	5 variables for storage & retreval of integers by 3'rd party developers
USERR1-5	nil	5 variables for storage & retreval of real numbers by 3'rd party developers.
VIEWCTR	141.5,98.83	Center of current view. (read only)
VIEWDIR	0.0,0.0,1.0	Current viewport viewing direction in world coordinates (read only).
VIEWMODE	0	View mode for current viewport, sum of: 1=perspective view, 2=front clipping,

		4=back clipping, 8=UCS "follow mode", 16=front clipping not at "eye".
VIEWSIZE	197.65	Current view height in drawing units. (read only)
VIEWTWIST	0.0	Height of view in current viewport (read only).
VPOINTX	0.00	X component of current 3D view point. (read only)
VPOINTY	0.00	Y component of current 3D view point. (read only)
VPOINTZ	1.00	Z component of current 3D view point. (read only)
VSMAX	283.00,197.65	Upper right corner of current viewport's virtual screen. (read only)
VSMIN	0.00,0.00	Lower left corner of current viewport's virtual screen. (read only)
WORLDUCS	1	Current UCS same as world coordinate system: 1=yes, 0=no.
WORLDVIEW	0	DVIEW & VPOINT command input relative to: 1=UCS changed to WCS, 0=UCS.

C

File Management

One of the first problems new (and experienced) microcomputer users in a business encounter is how to deal with the number of files created. In Chapter 1 a procedure for dealing with AutoCAD files and drawing files is discussed. The procedure of logging onto a directory or drawing subdirectory, however, can be made much easier by the use of a file management program. The following routines illustrate a file management process you might wish to adopt.

C.1 Program Selection Menu

The Program Selection Menu lists the programs available for the user to select from. It will be created using EDLIN. If you are unfamiliar with EDLIN, refer to Appendix H.

The Program Selection Menu named PSM.DOC follows. For illustration purposes the menu provides for the selection of only three programs. You can expand the menu as required once you understand the principles. Use the Tab key to add the spaces to the menu.

```
C:\>EDLIN PSM.DOC
New File
*I
    1: PROGRAM SELECTION MENU
    2:
    3:  !-------------------------------------!
    4:  ! PROGRAM                      ENTER  !
    5:  !-------------------------------------!
    6:  !                                     !
    7:  ! AUTOCAD . . . . . . . . . . . CAD # !
    8:  !                                     !
    9:  ! LOTUS . . . . . . . . . . . . . 1   !
   10:  !                                     !
   11:  ! WORDPERFECT . . . . . . . . . . 2   !
   12:  !                                     !
   13:  ! MENU. . . . . . . . . . . . . . 0   !
   14:  !                                     !
   15:  ! # = Project Name                    !
   16:  !                                     !
   17:  !-------------------------------------!
   18: ^C
*E
```

To display the PSM.DOC file a batch file named 0.BAT (zero.bat) is created. This file uses the DOS TYPE command to list the contents of the file:

```
C:\>edlin 0.bat
New file
*i
    1: echo off
    2: cls
    3: type psm.doc
    4: ^C
*e
```

The 0.bat file is automatically run when the computer is booted by adding it to the AUTOEXEC.BAT file. Use the TYPE command to list that file prior to adding to it:

```
C\>type autoexec.bat
```

If you completed the tasks outlined in Sections 2.2.1 and 2.2.2, your AUTOEXEC.BAT file may appear as follows:

```
ECHO OFF
CLS
DATE
TIME
PROMPT $P$G
SET LISPHEAP=40000
SET LISPSTACK=5000
SET ACADFREERAM=24
```

Using EDLIN, add the following line to the AUTOEXEC.BAT file (Begin insertion after the last line in the file. If there are eight lines, enter 9I.):

```
C:\>EDLIN AUTOEXEC.BAT
End of input file
*9i
    9: 0
   10: C
*e
```

When the computer is booted, the AUTOEXEC.BAT file is executed. In line 9 of the file, the batch file named 0 is run. The 0.BAT file clears the screen and types the Program Selection Menu file (PSM.DOC) on the screen.

C.2   Program Batch Files

When the Program Selection Menu is displayed, the user runs AutoCAD by entering cad 101nm87 (assuming the project number is 101NM87), Lotus by entering 1, Word Perfect by entering 2, and redisplays the PSM Menu by entering 0.

Assuming the Lotus files are stored in a subdirectory named Lotus, and Lotus is loaded by entering Lotus, the 1.BAT file may appear as follows:

```
cls
cd \lotus
lotus
cd \
0
```

When the user enters 1, the 1.BAT file is executed as follows:

The screen is cleared

The directory is changed to the LOTUS subdirectory

Lotus is loaded

When Lotus is exited, control returns to the batch file and the remaining two commands are executed:

The directory is changed to the root directory

The 0.bat file is loaded to redisplay the Program Selection Menu.

Write a similar batch file named 2.BAT to load Word Perfect, or some other program you have on your system.

If the batch file is to change the current directory without running a program in the new directory, it would contain only the CLS and CD\xxxx commands. The 0.BAT file should be placed in that directory so the user can return to the root directory and load the Program Selection Menu by entering 0.

C.2.1 AutoCAD Program Batch File

The batch file used to load AutoCAD is based on the assumption that your AutoCAD files are stored in a subdirectory named ACAD and your drawings are to be stored in subdirectories of ACAD named by the project number. The file name is CAD.BAT. The listing is as follows:

```
cls
path \;\system;\acad
cd \acad
if not exist %1 md %1
cd %1
acad
cd \
0
```

The PATH command in the second line of the batch file tells DOS that, if a file cannot be located in the current directory, then other directories to search are the root directory, the system subdirectory, and the ACAD subdirectory. Note that the two paths specified are separated by a semicolon.

The %1 symbol used in the fourth and fifth lines of the file is a "replaceable parameter." DOS replaces the symbol with the parameter you included when you entered the batch command. For instance, if you selected the CAD option from the Program Selection Menu by typing CAD 101NM87, the symbol %1 is replaced by 101NM87 in the batch file.

The format of the DOS IF NOT command used in the fourth line of the menu is:

```
if not <condition> <command>
```

If the <condition> is not true, the <command> is carried out. In this case the <condition>: exist <filename> checks whether the named file exists in the current directory. If the file does not exist, the command md <filename> is carried out—a new subdirectory of the current directory is made using the file name specified. If you selected the CAD option from the Program Selection Menu by entering CAD 101NM87, the batch file would do the following:

Clear the screen.

Tell DOS to check the root directory, \, the system subdirectory, and the ACAD subdirectory if a file is not located in the current directory.

Change the current directory to the ACAD subdirectory.

Check to see if the 101NM87 file (or subdirectory) exists in the current directory. If it does not exist, a new subdirectory named 101NM87 is made; if the file exists, the md command is not executed.

The current directory is changed to 101NM87.

The ACAD program is executed—note that since the current directory is 101NM87, ACAD will not be found in the current directory but will be found in the ACAD directory, hence the need for the PATH command earlier in the batch file.

When ACAD is exited, control returns to the batch file, the current directory is changed to the root directory, and the 0.BAT file is loaded.

PROTO1—From Chapter 4

PROTO1.MNU

```
 1  ***SCREEN
 2  [ -PLOT- App. D1 - PROTO1.MNU from Chapter 6]
 3  [ -SHEET-]
 4  [ A4-HOR ]^C^Clayer;make;border;color;green;border;;limits;+
 5  0,0;277,180;zoom;all;line;0,0;277,0;277,180;0,180;c;+
 6  insert;/acad/proto/title;277,0;;;;\\\\\\\\\\\\block;+
 7  b2;0,0;w;-1,-1;278,181;;(setq w 277 h 180);$s=si
 8  [ A3-HOR ]^C^Clayer;make;border;color;green;border;;limits;+
 9  0,0;390,277;zoom;all;line;0,0;390,0;390,277;0,277;c;+
10  insert;/acad/proto/title;390,0;;;;\\\\\\\\\\\\block;+
11  b2;0,0;w;-1,-1;391,278;;(setq w 390 h 277);$s=si
12  [ A-HOR ]^C^Clayer;make;border;color;green;border;;limits;+
13  0,0;10,7.25;zoom;all;line;0,0;10,0;10,7.25;+
14  0,7.25;c;insert;/acad/proto/title;10,0;.039;;;+
15  \\\\\\\\\\\\block;b2;0,0;w;-.1,-.1;10.1,7.3;;+
16  (setq w 10.0 h 7.25);$s=i
17  [ B-HOR ]^C^Clayer;make;border;color;green;border;;limits;+
18  0,0;15.75,10;zoom;all;line;0,0;15.75,0;+
19  15.75,10;0,10;c;insert;/acad/proto/title;+
20  15.75,0;.039;;;;\\\\\\\\\\\\block;b2;0,0;+
21  w;-.1,-.1;15.8,10.1;;(setq w 15.75 h 10.05);$s=i
22
23  [ACAD_MNU]^C^Cmenu;acad;
24
25  quit
26  end
27  save
28
29
30  [MULTISCL]^C^Cmenu;/acad/proto/proto2;
31
32
33
34
35  **si
36  [ -DWG- ]
37  [-UNITS-]
38  [metres](setq txt 2.5 conv 25.4 unts 2 precise 2);$s=m
39  [ mm ](setq txt 2.5 conv 25.4 unts 2 precise 0);$s=mm
40
41  [ROOTMENU]$s=SCREEN
42
43
44
45
46
47
48
49
50
51
```

```
52
53
54
55  **m
56  [-SCALE-]
57  [1:10  ](setq f 0.01);script;/acad/proto/proto1;
58  [1:20  ](setq f 0.02);script;/acad/proto/proto1;
59  [1:50  ](setq f 0.05);script;/acad/proto/proto1;
60  [1:100 ](setq f 0.1);script;/acad/proto/proto1;
61  [1:200 ](setq f 0.2);script;/acad/proto/proto1;
62  [1:250 ](setq f 0.25);script;/acad/proto/proto1;
63  [1:300 ](setq f 0.3);script;/acad/proto/proto1;
64  [1:400 ](setq f 0.4);script;/acad/proto/proto1;
65  [1:500 ](setq f 0.5);script;/acad/proto/proto1;
66  [1:1000](setq f 1);script;/acad/proto/proto1;
67  [1:2000](setq f 2);script;/acad/proto/proto1;
68
69  [1:n ](setq f1 (getreal "Scale Factor 1: "));\+
70  (setq f (/ f1 1000));script;/acad/proto/proto1;
71
72
73  [-LAST-]$s=
74  [ROOT-MNU]$s=SCREEN
75
76  **mm
77  [-SCALE-]
78  [1:1   ](setq f 1);script;/acad/proto/proto1;
79  [1:2   ](setq f 2);script;/acad/proto/proto1;
80  [1:5   ](setq f 5);script;/acad/proto/proto1;
81  [1:10  ](setq f 10);script;/acad/proto/proto1;
82  [1:20  ](set1 f 20);script;/acad/proto/proto1;
83  [1:50  ](setq f 50);script;/acad/proto/proto1;
84  [1:100 ](setq f 100);script;/acad/proto/proto1;
85  [1:200 ](setq f 200);script;/acad/proto/proto1;
86  [1:250 ](setq f 250);script;/acad/proto/proto1;
87  [1:300 ](setq f 300);script;/acad/proto/proto1;
88  [1:400 ](setq f 400);script;/acad/proto/proto1;
89  [1:500 ](setq f 500);script;/acad/proto/proto1;
90  [1:1000](setq f 1000);script;/acad/proto/proto1;
91  [1:2000](setq f 2000);script;/acad/proto/proto1;
92  [1:n   ](setq f (getreal "Scale factor 1: "));\+
93  script;/acad/proto/proto1;
94
95  [-LAST-]$s=
96  [ROOTMENU]$s=SCREEN
97  **i
98  [ -DWG- ]
99  [-UNITS-]
100
101 [arch/eng](setq txt (/ 3.0 32) conv 1);$s=ae
102
```

```
103  [civ-eng](setq txt (/ 3.0 32) conv 1 unts 2 +
104  precise (getint "Number of digits to right of decimal: "));\+
105  $s=c
106
107  [mech-eng](setq txt / 3.0 32) conv 1 unts 2 +
108  precise (getint "Number of digits to right of decimal: "));\+
109  $s=mm
110
111  [ROOTMENU]$s=SCREEN
112
113
114
115
116
117
118
119
120
121  **a
122  [-SCALE-]
123  [3/32"=1'](setq f 128);script;/acad/proto/proto1;
124  [1/8" =1'](setq f 96);script;/acad/proto/proto1;
125  [3/16"=1'](setq f 64);script;/acad/proto/proto1;
126  [1/4" =1'](setq f 48);script;/acad/proto/proto1;
127  [3/8"=1'](setq f 32);script;/acad/proto/proto1;
128  [1/2" =1'](setq f 24);script;/acad/proto/proto1;
129  [3/4" =1'](setq f 16);script;/acad/proto/proto1;
130  [1" = 1'](setq f 12);script;/acad/proto/proto1;
131  [1 1/2"=1'](setq f 8);script;/acad/proto/proto1;
132  [ 3" = 1'](setq f 4);script;/acad/proto/proto1;
133  [ 6" = 1'](setq f 2);script;/acad/proto/proto1;
134  [Fullsize](setq f 1);script;/acad/proto/proto1;
135
136  [ n" = 1'](setq f1 (getreal "Decimal scale Factor n = "));\+
137  (setq f (/ 12 f1));script;/acad/proto/proto1;
138
139  [-LAST-]$s=
140  [ROOTMENU]$s=SCREEN
141
142  **c
143  [-SCALE-]
144  [1"= 1'  ](setq f 1);script;/acad/proto/proto1;
145  [1"= 5'  ](setq f 5);script;/acad/proto/proto1;
146  [1"= 10' ](setq f 10);script;/acad/proto/proto1;
147  [1"= 15' ](setq f 15);script;/acad/proto/proto1;
148  [1"= 20' ](setq f 20);script;/acad/proto/proto1;
149  [1"= 30' ](setq f 30);script;/acad/proto/proto1;
150  [1"= 50' ](setq f 50);script;/acad/proto/proto1;
151  [1"= 100'](setq f 100);script;/acad/proto/proto1;
152  [1"= 200'](setq f 200);script;/acad/proto/proto1;
153  [1"= 300'](setq f 300);script;/acad/proto/proto1;
```

```
154  [1"= 400'](setq f 400);script;/acad/proto/proto1;
155  [1"= 500'](setq f 500);script;/acad/proto/proto1;
156
157  [1"= n'  ](setq f (getreal "Scale Factor n = "));\+
158  script;/acad/proto/proto1;
159
160  [-LAST-]$s=
161  [ROOTMENU]$s=SCREEN
162
163  **ae
164  [ SELECT ]
165  [ UNITS  ]
166
167  [ARCHITEC](setq unts 4);$s=arch
168  [example:](prompt "Units appear as 1'-3 1/2")
169
170  [Engineer](setq unts 3 precise +
171  (getint "Number of digits right of inch decimal: "));\$s=a
172  [example:](prompt "Units appear as 1'-3.5 ")
173
174
175  [-LAST-]$s=
176
177
178
179
180
181
182
183
184  **arch
185  [ SELECT ]
186  [SMALLEST]
187  [FRACTION]
188  [  TO   ]
189  [ DISPLAY]
190
191  [ none](setq precise 0);$s=a
192  [ 1/2" ](setq precise 1);$s=a
193  [ 1/4" ](setq precise 2);$s=a
194  [ 1/8" ](setq precise 3);$s=a
195  [ 1/16"](setq precise 4);$s=a
196  [ 1/32"](setq precise 5);$s=a
197  [ 1/64"](setq precise 6);$s=a
198
199
200  [-LAST-]$s=
201
202
203
```

PTOTO1.SCR

Release 9 and 10

```
1   (setq x (* f w) y (* f h))
2   (setq p (list x y))
3   limits 0,0 !p zoom all
4   insert b2 0,0 !f !f 0
5   (setq stxt (* f txt)) setvar textsize !stxt
6   (setvar "ltscale" (* 0.75 conv f))
7   (setvar "dimscale" (/ stxt 0.18))
8   layer set 0
9
10  setvar lunits !unts setvar luprec !precise setvar coords 1
11  menu acad
```

Version 2.62

```
1   (setq x (* f w) y (* f h))
2   (setq p (list x y))
3   limits 0,0 !p zoom all
4   insert b2 0,0 !f !f 0
5   (setq stxt (* f txt)) setvar textsize !stxt
6   (setvar "ltscale" (* 0.75 conv f))
7   (setq dims (/ stxt 0.18))
8   dim dimscale !dims exit
9   layer set 0
10
11  text 0,0 !stxt 0 .
12  erase 1
13
14  setvar lunits !unts setvar luprec !precise setvar coords 1
15  menu acad
```

PROTO1 and PROTO2—
From Chapter 6

PROTO1.MNU

```
 1  ***SCREEN
 2  [ -PLOT-  App. E1, PROTO1. MNU from Chapter 4]
 3  [ -SHEET-]
 4  [ A4-HOR ]^C^Clayer;make;border;color;green;border;;limits;+
 5  0,0;277,180;zoom;all;line;0,0;277,0;277,180;0,180;c;+
 6  insert;/acad/proto/title;277,0;;;;\\\\\\\\\\\\block;+
 7  b2;0,0;w;-1,-1;278,181;;(setq w 277 h 180);$s=si
 8  [ A3-HOR ]^C^Clayer;make;border;color;green;border;;limits;+
 9  0,0;390,277;zoom;all;line;0,0;390,0;390,277;0,277;c;+
10  insert;/acad/proto/title;390,0;;;;\\\\\\\\\\\\block;+
11  b2;0,0;w;-1,-1;391,278;;(setq w 390 h 277);$s=si
12  [ A-HOR ]^C^Clayer;make;border;color;green;border;;limits;+
13  0,0;10,7.25;zoom;all;line;0,0;10,0;10,7.25;+
14  0,7.25;c;insert;/acad/proto/title;10,0;.039;;;+
15  \\\\\\\\\\\\block;b2;0,0;w;-.1,-.1;10.1,7.3;;+
16  (setq w 10.0 h 7.25);$s=i
17  [ B-HOR ]^C^Clayer;make;border;color;green;border;;limits;+
18  0,0;15.75,10;zoom;all;line;0,0;15.75,0;+
19  15.75,10;0,10;c;insert;/acad/proto/title;+
20  15.75,0;.039;;;\\\\\\\\\\\\block;b2;0,0;+
21  w;-.1,-.1;15.8,10.1;;(setq w 15.75 h 10.0);$s=i
22
23  [ACAD_MNU]^C^Cmenu;acad;
24
25  quit
26  end
27  save
28
29
30
31
32
33
34
35  **si
36  [ -DWG- ]
37  [-UNITS-]
38  [metres]^C^C(setq txt 2.5 conv 25.4 unts 2 precise 2);$s=m
39  [ mm ]^C^C(setq txt 2.5 conv 25.4 unts 2 precise 0);$s=mm
40
41  [ROOTMENU]$s=SCREEN
42
43
44
45
46
47
48
49
50
51
```

```
52
53
54
55  **m
56  [-SCALE-]
57  [1:10  ](setq f 0.01);script;/acad/proto/proto1;
58  [1:20  ](setq f 0.02);script;/acad/proto/proto1;
59  [1:50  ](setq f 0.05);script;/acad/proto/proto1;
60  [1:100 ](setq f 0.1);script;/acad/proto/proto1;
61  [1:200 ](setq f 0.2);script;/acad/proto/proto1;
62  [1:250 ](setq f 0.25);script;/acad/proto/proto1;
63  [1:300 ](setq f 0.3);script;/acad/proto/proto1;
64  [1:400 ](setq f 0.4);script;/acad/proto/proto1;
65  [1:500 ](setq f 0.5);script;/acad/proto/proto1;
66  [1:1000](setq f 1);script;/acad/proto/proto1;
67  [1:2000](setq f 2);script;/acad/proto/proto1;
68
69  [1:n ](setq f1 (getreal "Scale Factor 1: "));\+
70  (setq f (/ f1 1000));script;/acad/proto/proto1;
71
72
73  [-LAST-]$s=
74  [ROOT-MNU]$s=SCREEN
75
76  **mm
77  [-SCALE-]
78  [1:1   ](setq f 1);script;/acad/proto/proto1;
79  [1:2   ](setq f 2);script;/acad/proto/proto1;
80  [1:5   ](setq f 5);script;/acad/proto/proto1;
81  [1:10  ](setq f 10);script;/acad/proto/proto1;
82  [1:20  ](set1 f 20);script;/acad/proto/proto1;
83  [1:50  ](setq f 50);script;/acad/proto/proto1;
84  [1:100 ](setq f 100);script;/acad/proto/proto1;
85  [1:200 ](setq f 200);script;/acad/proto/proto1;
86  [1:250 ](setq f 250);script;/acad/proto/proto1;
87  [1:300 ](setq f 300);script;/acad/proto/proto1;
88  [1:400 ](setq f 400);script;/acad/proto/proto1;
89  [1:500 ](setq f 500);script;/acad/proto/proto1;
90  [1:1000](setq f 1000);script;/acad/proto/proto1;
91  [1:2000](setq f 2000);script;/acad/proto/proto1;
92  [1:n  ](setq f (getreal "Scale factor 1: "));\+
93  script;/acad/proto/proto1;
94
95  [-LAST-]$s=
96  [ROOTMENU]$s=SCREEN
97  **i
98  [ -DWG- ]
99  [-UNITS-]
100
101 [arch/eng](setq txt (/ 3.0 32) conv 1);$s=ae
102 [example]^P(prompt "Units appear as 1'3-1/2 or 1'-3.5 ");^P
```

```
103
104  [civ-eng](setq txt (/ 3.0 32) conv 1 unts 2 +
105  precise (getint "Number of digits to right of decimal: "));\+
106  $s=c
107  [example]^P(prompt "Decimal feet units. Scale 1 in. = x ft.  ");^P
108
109  [mech-eng](if (not meng) (load "/acad/lisp/meng"));+
110  (meng);\\$s=mm
111  [example]^P(prompt "Decimal inch units.  Scale is 1:x  ");^P
112
113  [ROOTMENU]$s=SCREEN
114
115
116
117
118
119
120  **a
121  [-SCALE-]
122  [3/32"=1'](setq f 128);script;/acad/proto/proto1;
123  [1/8" =1'](setq f 96);script;/acad/proto/proto1;
124  [3/16"=1'](setq f 64);script;/acad/proto/proto1;
125  [1/4" =1'](setq f 48);script;/acad/proto/proto1;
126  [3/8"=1'](setq f 32);script;/acad/proto/proto1;
127  [1/2" =1'](setq f 24);script;/acad/proto/proto1;
128  [3/4" =1'](setq f 16);script;/acad/proto/proto1;
129  [1" = 1' ](setq f 12);script;/acad/proto/proto1;
130  [1 1/2"=1'](setq f 8);script;/acad/proto/proto1;
131  [ 3" = 1'](setq f 4);script;/acad/proto/proto1;
132  [ 6" = 1'](setq f 2);script;/acad/proto/proto1;
133  [Fullsize](setq f 1);script;/acad/proto/proto1;
134
135  [ n" = 1'](setq f1 (getreal "Decimal scale Factor n = "));\+
136  (setq f (/ 12 f1));script;/acad/proto/proto1;
137
138  [-LAST-]$s=
139  [ROOTMENU]$s=SCREEN
140
141  **c
142  [-SCALE-]
143  [1"= 1' ](setq f 1);script;/acad/proto/proto1;
144  [1"= 5' ](setq f 5);script;/acad/proto/proto1;
145  [1"= 10' ](setq f 10);script;/acad/proto/proto1;
146  [1"= 15' ](setq f 15);script;/acad/proto/proto1;
147  [1"= 20' ](setq f 20);script;/acad/proto/proto1;
148  [1"= 30' ](setq f 30);script;/acad/proto/proto1;
149  [1"= 50' ](setq f 50);script;/acad/proto/proto1;
150  [1"= 100'](setq f 100);script;/acad/proto/proto1;
151  [1"= 200'](setq f 200);script;/acad/proto/proto1;
152  [1"= 300'](setq f 300);script;/acad/proto/proto1;
153  [1"= 400'](setq f 400);script;/acad/proto/proto1;
```

```
154  [1"= 500'](setq f 500);script;/acad/proto/proto1;
155
156  [1"= n'   ](setq f (getreal "Scale Factor n = "));\+
157  script;/acad/proto/proto1;
158
159  [-LAST-]$s=
160  [ROOTMENU]$s=SCREEN
161
162  **ae
163  [ SELECT ]
164  [ UNITS  ]
165
166  [Architec](setq unts 4);$s=arch
167  [example:]^P(prompt "Units appear as 1'-3 1/2  ");^P
168
169  [Engineer](setq unts 3 precise +
170  (getint "Number of digits right of inch decimal: "));\$s=a
171  [example:]^P(prompt "Units appear as 1'-3.5 ");^P
172
173
174  [-LAST-]$s=
175
176
177
178
179
180
181
182
183  **arch
184  [ SELECT ]
185  [SMALLEST]
186  [FRACTION]
187  [   TO   ]
188  [ DISPLAY]
189
190  [ none](setq precise 0);$s=a
191  [ 1/2" ](setq precise 1);$s=a
192  [ 1/4" ](setq precise 2);$s=a
193  [ 1/8" ](setq precise 3);$s=a
194  [ 1/16"](setq precise 4);$s=a
195  [ 1/32"](setq precise 5);$s=a
196  [ 1/64"](setq precise 6);$s=a
197
198
199  [-LAST-]$s=
200
201
202
```

PROTO1.SCR

```
Release 9 and 10
1   (if (= ans "F") (setq f (* f (/ 1.0 12))))
2   (setq x (* f w) y (* f h))
3   (setq p (list x y))
4   limits 0,0 !p zoom all
5   insert b2 0,0 !f !f 0
6   (setq stxt (* f txt)) setvar textsize !stxt
7   (setvar "ltscale" (* 0.75 conv f))
8   (setvar "dimscale" (/ stxt 0.18))
9   layer set 0
10
11  (if (not txtht) (load "/acad/lisp/txtht"))
12  (txtht)
13  setvar lunits !unts setvar luprec !precise setvar coords 1
14  (if (not dwgdata) (load "/acad/lisp/dwgdata"))
15  (dwgdata)
16  (if (not dwgdata1) (load "/acad/lisp/dwgdata1"))
17  (dwgdata1)
18  menu acad
```

PROTO1.SCR—Version 2.62

```
Version 2.62
1   (if (= ans "F") (setq f (* f (/ 1.0 12))))
2   (setq x (* f w) y (* f h))
3   (setq p (list x y))
4   limits 0,0 !p zoom all
5   insert b2 0,0 !f !f 0
6   (setq stxt (* f txt)) setvar textsize !stxt
7   (setvar "ltscale" (* 0.75 conv f))
8   (setq dims (/ stxt 0.18))
9   dim dimscale !dims exit
10  layer set 0
11
12  (if (not txtht) (load "/acad/lisp/txtht"))
13  (txtht)
14  text 0,0 !stxt 0 .
15  erase 1
16
17  setvar lunits !unts setvar luprec !precise setvar coords 1
18  (if (not dwgdata) (load "/acad/lisp/dwgdata"))
19  (dwgdata)
20  (if (not dwgdata1) (load "/acad/lisp/dwgdata1"))
21  (dwgdata1)
22  menu acad
```

TXTHT.LSP

```
TXTHT.LSP

;TXTHT function
;provides SMALL, MEDIUM & LARGE texts for PROTO1.SCR
;
(defun txtht ()
  (if (< txt 2.5)
    (setq small (* f (/ 3.0 32))
        medium (* f (/ 1.0 8))
        large (* f (/ 3.0 16)))
    (setq small (* f 2.5)
        medium (* f 3.0)
        large (* f 4.0))
  )
)
```

PROTO1.MNU

```
 1  ***SCREEN
 2  [-PLOT-  App. E3 - PROTO2.MNU]
 3  [-SHEET-]
 4  [A4-HOR]^C^Clayer;make;border1;color;green;border1;new;border,+
 5  btext0,btext1;freeze;border,btext0,btext1;;limits;0,0;277,180;+
 6  zoom;all;line;0,0;277,0;277,180;0,180;c;insert;/acad/proto/title1;+
 7  277,0;;;;\\\\\\\\\\\\(setvar "textsize" 2.5);$s=insrt
 8  [A3-HOR]^C^Clayer;make;border1;color;green;border1;new;border,+
 9  btext0,btext1;freeze;border,btext0,btext1;;limits;0,0;390,277;+
10  zoom;all;line;0,0;390,0;390,277;0,277;c;insert;/acad/proto/title1;+
11  390,0;;;;\\\\\\\\\\\\(setvar "textsize" 2.5);$s=insrt
12  [A-HOR]^C^Clayer;make;border1;color;green;border1;new;border,+
13  btext0,btext1;freeze;border,btext0,btext1;;limits;0,0;+
14  10,7.25;zoom;all;line;0,0;10,0;10,7.25;0,7.25;c;+
15  insert;/acad/proto/title1;10,0;.039;;;\\\\\\\\\\\\\+
16  (setvar "textsize" (/ 3.0 32));$s=insrt
17  [B-HOR]^C^Clayer;make;border1;color;green;border1;new;border,+
18  btext0,btext1;freeze;border,btext0,btext1;;limits;0,0;+
19  15.75,10;zoom;all;line;0,0;15.75,0;15.75,10;0,10;+
20  c;insert;/acad/proto/title1;15.75,0;.039;;;\\\\\\\\\\\\\+
21  (setvar "textsize" (/ 3.0 32));$s=insrt
22
23  [INSERT]$s=insrt
24
25  [DataList](if (not datalist)(load "/acad/lisp/datalist"));(datalist)
26
27  [ACAD_MNU]menu;acad
28
29  quit
30  end
31  save
32
33
34  [next]$s=insrt
35
36
37
38  **insrt
39  [INSERT](if (not dwgin) (load "/acad/lisp/dwgin"));+
40  (dwgin)
41
42  MOVE
43  ERASE
44  FILES
45
46  [ -TEXT- ]
47  [ small ](if (< (getvar "textsize") 1) (setq tex (/ 3.0 32))(setq tex 2.5));+
48  text;\!tex;\\
49  [ medium](if (< (getvar "textsize") 1) (setq tex (/ 1.0 8))(setq tex 3.0));+
50  text;\!tex;\\
51  [ large ](if (< (getvar "textsize") 1) (setq tex (/ 3.0 16))(setq tex 4.0));+
```

```
52  text;\!tex;\\
53
54  [LTSCALE](if (< (getvar "textsize") 1) (setvar "ltscale" (/ 3.0 4))+
55  (setvar "ltscale" (* 25.4 (/ 3.0 4))))
56  [DIMSCALE](setq dims (/ (getvar "textsize") 0.18));dim dimscale !dims exit
57
58  [DataList](if (not datalist)(load "/acad/lisp/datalist"));(datalist)
59
60  [ROOTMENU]$s=SCREEN
61  [ACAD_MNU]menu;acad;
62
63  quit
64  end
65  save
```

F

Traverse Program

```
;        *** TRAVERSE Program  Ver, 1,0 ***
;
; Interior-angle closed traverse program - adjusts traverse
; for closure of angles and directions, and draws traverse,
;
;------------------------------------------------------------------
(vmon)    ;Set virtual function pager on,
(setvar "cmdecho" 0) ; Set command echo off,
;       ** TRAVERSE Function **
(defun traverse (/ #north ; NORTH cartesian angle
            #lunits ; Length units, ft, or m,
            #lprec  ; Linear units precision
            #stats  ; Number of stations,
            #list   ; List of traverse input data,
            #tlist  ; List of trav, data - angles corr,
            #clist  ; List of traverse coordinates
            #angsum ; Sum of interior angles,
            #0az    ; Azimuth of 1'st line,
            #prec   ; Length units precision,
            #clerr  ; Closure error,
            #cntr   ; Center of traverse area,
            #relacc); Relative accuracy ratio of traverse,
    ;
    ; *** Set system variables
    (setvar "aunits" 1)  ; units - degrees/minutes/seconds
    (setvar "auprec" 4)  ; precision - 1 second
    (setvar "angbase" 0) ; 0 degrees East
    (setvar "angdir" 0)  ; angles +'ve counterclockwise
    ;
    ; *** Function Calls
    (input)    ; Call INPUT function,
    (prec)     ; Call PRECision function,
    (anglerr)  ; Call ANGLe ERRor correction function,
    (calc)     ; Call coordinate CALCulation function,
    (closerr)  ; Call coordinate CLOSure ERRor function,
    (drawlim)  ; Call DRAWing LIMits function,
    (drawtrav) ; Call DRAW TRAVerse function,
    (addtext)  ; Call ADD TEXT function,
)      ; Exit
; ----------------------------------------------------------------
;
;       ** Conversion functions **
(defun dtr (a)   ; Degrees to radians,
  (/ (* a pi) 180)
)
(defun rtd (r)   ; Radians to degrees,
  (/ (* r 180) pi)
)
; ----------------------------------------------------------------
;
;       ** Precision (PREC) Function **
(defun prec ()
  (setq #prec 1)
  (if (> (getvar "luprec") 0)
      (repeat (getvar "luprec")
        (setq #prec (/ #prec 10,0)))
  )
)
; ----------------------------------------------------------------
;
;       ** INPUT Function **
(defun input (/ #id   ; Station identification,
```

```
              #ang    ; Station interior angle,
              #dist   ; Distance to advance station,
              #pr)    ; Prompt
    (textscr)        ; Flip to text screen,
    (prompt "\n\tENTER THE FOLLOWING TRAVERSE INFORMATION:\n\n")
    (prompt "\tFormat for entering angles is: nndnn'nn\042")
    (prompt "\n\tFor example: 50d44'30\042\n")
    (setq #north (dtr 90))        ; North at top of screen,
    (prompt "\n\tNORTH is at the top of the screen,\n")
    ;    *** Get global data
    (prompt "\nAZIMUTH of 1'st line (clockwise +'ve): ")
    (setq #0az (* -1 (getangle))) ; Change counterclockwise +'ve,
    (setq #pr "\nLinear units type (1=feet, 2 = metres): ")
    (initget 1 "1 2")
    (if (= "1" (getkword #pr))
       (setq #lunits "ft,") (setq #lunits "m"))
    (setvar "luprec" (setq #lprec
          (getint "\nDecimal places for linear units: ")))
    (setq #stats (getint "\nNumber of stations: ") #list nil)
    ;    *** Get data for each station,
    (prompt "\n\nEnter station identifier (3 characters max), interior angle,")
    (prompt "\nand distance to advance station,\n") (setq #angsum 0)
    (repeat #stats
      (setq #id (getstring "\nStation: "))
      ; Check if id > 3 characters
      (while (>= (strlen #id) 3)
        (princ "\n\tStation identifier cannot exceed 3 characters,")
        (setq #id (getstring "\nStation: "))
      )
      (setq #ang (getangle "\tAngle: "))
      (setq #angsum (+ #ang #angsum))    ; Sum angles,
      (setq #dist (getdist "\tDistance: "))
      (setq #list (cons (list #id #ang #dist) #list))
    ) (setq #list (reverse #list))
  )
  ; -----------------------------------------------------------
  ;
  ;
  ;       ** Angle Error (ANGLERR) Function **
  (defun anglerr (/ #1list #2list #ang #corr #err)
  ;    Calculate angle error,
    (setq #err (- (* (- #stats 2) 180,0)
          (rtd #angsum)))  ; Angle error
    (setq #corr (dtr (/ #err #stats)))  ; Correction
    ;    Apply correction to each station,
    (setq #1list #list #tlist nil)
    (repeat #stats
      (setq #2list (car #1list) #1list (cdr #1list))
      (setq #ang (+ #corr (cadr #2list)))
      (setq #2list (list (car #2list) #ang (caddr #2list)))
      (setq #tlist (cons #2list #tlist))
    ) (setq #tlist (reverse #tlist))
  )
  ; -------------------------------------------------------------
  ;       ** CALC Function **
  (defun calc (/ #1list #2list #ang #1ang #id #dist #coords)
    ; Set angle of line 1
    (setq #1ang (+ #north #0az))
    ; Extract station 1 list from data list,
    (setq #1list (car #tlist) #2list (cdr #tlist))
    ; Extract id and dist from station 1 list,
    (setq #id (car #1list) #dist (caddr #1list))
    ; Start coords list,
```

```
(setq #coords (list 100,0 100,0)    ; Sta. 1 set to 100,100
   #clist nil)
(setq #clist (cons (list #id #coords) #clist))
; Loop through traverse list and set stations.
(repeat (- #stats 1)
   ;    Extract next station list from data list.
   (setq #1list (car #2list) #2list (cdr #2list))
   ;    Extract station id.
   (setq #id (car #1list))
   ;    Set station coords.
   (setq #coords (polar #coords #1ang #dist))
   ;    Add coords to coords list.
   (setq #clist (cons (list #id #coords) #clist))
   ;    Extract angle and distance to next station.
   (setq #ang (cadr #1list) #dist (caddr #1list))
   (setq #1ang (- #1ang (- pi #ang)))
)
; Calculate closing station.
(setq #id "ZZ")   ; Last station id is ZZ.
(setq #coords (polar #coords #1ang #dist) #clerr #coords)
(setq #clist (cons (list #id #coords) #clist))
(setq #clist (reverse #clist))
)
; -----------------------------------------------------------------
;
;        ** Closing Error (CLOSERR) Function **
(defun closerr (/ #1list #2list #xerr #yerr #xadj #yadj)
   ;    Calc. X & Y error
   (setq #xerr (- (car #clerr) 100)
      #yerr (- (cadr #clerr) 100))
   ;    Calc. hypotenuse for relative accuracy ratio calculation
   (setq #relacc (sqrt (+ (* #xerr #xerr)(* #yerr #yerr))))
   ;    Compare X and Y-error to precision
   (if (> (abs #xerr) #prec) (setq #xerr (/ #xerr #stats))
      (setq #xerr 0))
   (if (> (abs #yerr) #prec) (setq #yerr (/ #yerr #stats))
      (setq #yerr 0))
   ;    If X or Y error > prec., adjust stat. coords.
   (if (or (/= #xerr 0) (/= #yerr 0))
      (progn
         (setq #1list (car #clist) #2list (cdr #clist) #clist nil)
         ; Do not adjust station 1.
         (setq #clist (cons #1list #clist)
            #1list (car #2list) #2list (cdr #2list))
         ; Initialize adjustment.
         (setq #xadj 0,0 #yadj 0,0)
         ; Start adjusting at station 2.
         (repeat #stats
            (setq #xadj (+ #xadj #xerr) #yadj (+ #yadj #yerr))
            (setq #1list (list (car #1list)
               (list (- (caadr #1list) #xadj)
                  (- (cadadr #1list) #yadj))))
            (setq #clist (cons #1list #clist))
            (setq #1list (car #2list) #2list (cdr #2list))
         ) (setq #clist (reverse #clist))
      )
   )
)
; -----------------------------------------------------------------
;
;        ** Drawing Limits (DRAWLIM) Function **
(defun drawlim (/ #1list #2list #xmax #ymax #xmin #ymin #x #y)
```

```
; Set coordinates of first point as max and min.
(setq #1list (car #clist) #2list (cdr #clist))
(setq #xmax (caadr #1list) #ymax (cadadr #1list)
    #xmin (caadr #1list) #ymin (cadadr #1list))
; Loop through list to locate max and min coordinates.
(repeat (- #stats 1)
  (setq #1list (car #2list) #2list (cdr #2list))
  (if (< (caadr #1list) #xmin)
      (setq #xmin (caadr #1list)))
  (if (< (cadadr #1list) #ymin)
      (setq #ymin (cadadr #1list)))
  (if (> (caadr #1list) #xmax)
      (setq #xmax (caadr #1list)))
  (if (> (cadadr #1list) #ymax)
      (setq #ymax (cadadr #1list)))
)
; Set drawing limits
(setq #x (- #xmax #xmin) #y (- #ymax #ymin))
(setvar "limmin" (list
      (- #xmin (/ #x 10.0)) (- #ymin (/ #y 10.0))))
(setvar "limmax" (list
      (+ #xmax (/ #x 2.5)) (+ #ymax (/ #y 10.0))))
(command "zoom" "a")
; Locate center point for use in ADDTEXT function
(setq #cntr
    (list (/ (+ #xmin #xmax) 2)(/ (+ #ymin #ymax) 2)))
)
; -----------------------------------------------------------------
;
;     ** Draw Traverse (DRAWTRAV) Function **
(defun drawtrav (/ #1list #2list #coords)
  (setq #1list (car #clist) #2list (cdr #clist))
  (setq #coords (cadr #1list))
  (command "pline" #coords)
  ;   Loop through coords & draw traverse.
  (repeat #stats
    (setq #1list (car #2list) #2list (cdr #2list)
    #coords (cadr #1list))
    (command #coords)
  ) (command "")
)
; -----------------------------------------------------------------
;
;        ** ADDTEXT function **
(defun addtext (/ #txtht   ; Text height
          #1list   ; List of current station data
          #2list   ; List of remaining station data
          #1coord  ; Coordinates of current station
          #2coord  ; Coordinates of next station
          #1id     ; Identifier of current station
          #2id     ; Identifier of next station
          #0ang    ; Angle of previous station
          #1ang    ; Angle of current station
          #angd    ; Line angle in degrees
          #brg     ; Bearing of a line
          #dist    ; Distance (length) of a line
          #1pt #2pt   ; Points for text
          #1stang  ; Angle if 1'st line
          #per)    ; Traverse perimeter
  (textscr)    ; Switch text screen on.
  ;   Display screen limits - get text height & dimscale.
  (prompt "\n\nThe screen limits are:")
```

```
  (prompt "\n\tLower left corner ")(princ (getvar "limmin"))
  (prompt "\n\tUpper right corner ")(princ (getvar "limmax"))
  (initget (+ 1 2 4))
  (setq #txtht (getreal "\n\nEnter the text height: "))
  (beast)       ; Call BEAring STation function
  (tap)         ; Call Title-Area-Perimeter function
  (net)         ; Call Northing-Easting Table
  (northar)     ; Call NORTHARrow function
  (rat)         ; Call Relative Accuracy raTio function
)
;----------------------------------------------------------------
;
;
;       ** Bearing Station (BEAST) Function **
(defun beast ()
;    Get data for first station
  (setq #1list (car #clist) #2list (cdr #clist))
  (setq #1id (car #1list) #1coord (cadr #1list))
  (setq #0ang 99); Set flag for 1'st station
  ;  Loop through remaining stations
  (repeat (- #stats 1)
    ; Get data for next station
    (setq #1list (car #2list) #2list (cdr #2list))
    (setq #2id (car #1list) #2coord (cadr #1list))
    (brgdst)   ; Call Bearing-Distance function,
    ; IF not equal to 1'st station
    (if (/= 99 #0ang) (sta)); Call Station function
    ; Prepare for repeat
    (setq #1id #2id #1coord #2coord #0ang #1ang)
  )
  ; Last station
  (setq #2coord (cadar #clist))
  (brgdst)      ; Call Bearing-Distance function
  (sta)         ; Call Station function
  ; Add 1'st station identification
  (setq #1id (caar #clist) #1coord (cadar #clist))
  (setq #0ang #1ang #1ang #1stang)
  (sta)         ; Call Station function
)
;----------------------------------------------------------------
;
;
;       ** Bearing Distance (BRGDST) Function **
(defun brgdst ()
  ; Determine angle and distance of line
  (setq #1ang (angle #1coord #2coord)
        #dist (distance #1coord #2coord))
  ; If 1'st station, save #1ang
  (if (= 99 #0ang) (setq #1stang #1ang))
  ; Set Bearing and Distance, and convert to string
  (setq #brg (angtos #1ang 4) #txt (rtos #dist 2 #lprec))
    ; Set bearing text location
  (setq #pt1 (polar (polar #1coord #1ang (/ #dist 2))
           (+ #1ang (/ pi 2))
           (/ #txtht 2)))
  ; Set distance text location
  (setq #pt2 (polar #pt1 (- #1ang (/ pi 2)) (* 2 #txtht)))
    ; Write the text
  ; Check IF text is upside down 90<#1ang<270
  (if (and (> #1ang (/ pi 2)) (< #1ang (* pi 1.5)))
    ; THEN rotate text 180 degrees and move down
    (progn
      ; Add 180 degrees, convert to degrees
      (setq #angd (rtd (+ #1ang pi)))
```

```
      ;  Move text location by #txtht @ 90 degrees
         (setq #pt1 (polar #pt1 (+ #1ang (/ pi 2)) #txtht))
         (setq #pt2 (polar #pt2 (+ #1ang (/ pi 2)) #txtht)))
      ;  ELSE do not rotate
         (setq #angd (rtd #1ang))
   )
   ;    Print bearing and distance text
   (command "text" "c" #pt1 #txtht #angd #brg)
   (command "text" "c" #pt2 #txtht #angd #txt)
)
;-----------------------------------------------------------------
;
;       ** Station (STA) Function **
(defun sta ()
   ;    IF #0ang<90
   (if (<= #0ang (/ pi 2))
      (progn
      ;    THEN IF #1ang<=45 or #1ang>=180
      (if (or (<= #1ang (/ pi 4))(>= #1ang pi))
        ;    THEN print top side
        (progn (setq #pt1 (polar #1coord (/ pi 2) #txtht)))
        ;    ELSE print bottom side
        (setq #pt1 (polar #1coord (* pi 1.5) #txtht)))
        (command "text" "c" #pt1 #txtht 0 #1id))
   )
   ; IF 90<#0ang<=180
   (if (and (> #0ang (/ pi 2))(<= #0ang pi))
      ;    THEN IF #1ang <=90 OR #1ang >=270
      (if (or (<= #1ang (/ pi 2))(>= #1ang (* pi 1.5)))
        ;    THEN print left side
        (progn (setq #pt1 (polar #1coord pi #txtht))
          (command "text" "r" #pt1 #txtht 0 #1id))
        ;    ELSE print right side
        (progn (setq #pt1 (polar #1coord 0 #txtht))
          (command "text" #pt1 #txtht 0 #1id)))
   )
   ,    IF 180<#0ang<=270
   (if (and (> #0ang pi)(<= #0ang (* pi 1.5)))
      ;    THEN IF #1ang<=90 OR #1ang >=270
      (if (or (<= #1ang (/ pi 2))(>= #1ang (* pi 1.5)))
        ;    THEN print left side
        (progn (setq #pt1 (polar #1coord pi #txtht))
          (command "text" "r" #pt1 #txtht 0 #1id))
        ;    ELSE print right side
        (progn (setq #pt1 (polar #1coord 0 #txtht))
          (command "text" #pt1 #txtht 0 #1id)))
   )
   ;    IF #0ang > 270
   (if (> #0ang (* pi 1.5))
      ;    THEN IF 45<=#1ang<=315
      (if (and (>= #1ang (* pi 0.25))(<= #1ang (* pi 1.75)))
        ;    THEN print right side
        (progn (setq #pt1 (polar #1coord 0 #txtht))
          (command "text" #pt1 #txtht 0 #1id))
        ;    ELSE print bottom side
        (progn (setq #pt1 (polar #1coord (* pi 1.5) #txtht))
          (command "text" "r" #pt1 #txtht 0 #1id)))
   )
)
;-----------------------------------------------------------------
;
;       ** Title/Area/Perimeter (TAP) Function **
```

```
(defun tap (/ #title #area #sper #pt1 #1cntr #e)
  (textscr)
  (setq #title (strcat "%%u"
    (getstring t "\nEnter traverse title: ") "%%u"))
  (se)    ; Call SE function to locate polyline
  (command "area" "e" #e)
  (setq #area (getvar "area") #per (getvar "perimeter"))
  (if (= #lunits "ft,")
    ;    THEN units are feet - convert to acres
    (setq #area (strcat
            (rtos (/ #area 4,356e4) 2 #lprec) " acres")
        #sper (strcat (rtos #per 2 #lprec) " feet"))
    ;    ELSE units are metres - convert to ha
    (setq #area (strcat
            (rtos (/ #area 1,0e4) 2 #lprec) " ha")
        #sper (strcat (rtos #per 2 #lprec) " metres")))
  )
  ; Center and print title, area, per, & linear units
  (setq #1cntr (polar #cntr (/ pi 2) #txtht))
  (command "text" "c" #1cntr #txtht 0 #title)
  (command "text" "" #area)(command "text" "" #sper)
)
;------------------------------------------------------------------
;
;       ** Select Entity (SE) Function **
(defun se ()
  (setq #e (entnext))
  (while (/= "POLYLINE" (cdr (assoc 0 (entget #e))))
    (setq #e (entnext))
  )
)
;------------------------------------------------------------------
;
;       ** Northing-Easting Table (NET) Function **
(defun net (/ #1list #2list #id #nrth #east
            #1loc #2loc #3loc)
  (setq #1loc (list (- (car (getvar "limmax")) (* #txtht 20))
              (+ (cadr (getvar "limmin"))
                (* #txtht (+ #stats 20))))
      #2loc (polar #1loc 0 (* #txtht 4))
      #3loc (polar #2loc 0 (* #txtht 6)))
  ; Print headings
  (command "text" #1loc #txtht 0 "%%uSTA,%%u")
  (command "text" #2loc #txtht 0 "%%uNORTH%%u")
  (command "text" #3loc #txtht 0 "%%uEAST%%u")
  ; Print data
  (setq #2list #clist)
  (repeat #stats
    (setq #1list (car #2list) #2list (cdr #2list)
        #1loc (polar #1loc (* pi 1,5) (* 1,5 #txtht))
        #2loc (polar #2loc (* pi 1,5) (* 1,5 #txtht))
        #3loc (polar #3loc (* pi 1,5) (* 1,5 #txtht))
        #id (car #1list); string data
        #nrth (rtos (caadr #1list) 2 #lprec); real-to-string
        #east (rtos (cadadr #1list) 2 #lprec)); real-to-string
    (command "text" #1loc #txtht 0 #id)
    (command "text" #2loc #txtht 0 #nrth)
    (command "text" #3loc #txtht 0 #east)
  )
)
;------------------------------------------------------------------
;
```

```
;       ** NORTH ARrow Function **
(defun northar (/ #pt1 #pt2 #pt3 #pt4 #pt5 #pt6 #ntxtht)
  (setq #pt1 (getpoint "\nLocate tip of NORTH arrow,")
        #pt2 (polar #pt1 (+ (* 1,5 pi) (atan 0,3)) (* #txtht 5))
        #pt3 (polar #pt2 pi (* #txtht 1,5))
        #pt4 (polar #pt3 pi (* #txtht 1,5))
        #pt5 (polar #pt1 (* pi 1,5) (* #txtht 10))
        #pt6 (polar #pt5 (/ pi 2) #txtht))
  (command "pline" #pt1 #pt2 #pt4 #pt1 #pt5)(command "")
  (setvar "fillmode" 1)
  (command "solid" #pt1 #pt2 #pt3)
  (command "")(command "")
  (setq #ntxtht (* 2,5 #txtht))
  (command "text" "c" #pt6 #ntxtht 0 "N")
  (command "text" "0,0" #txtht 0 " ")
  (command "redraw")
)
;------------------------------------------------------------------
;
;       ** Relative Accuracy Ratio (RAT) Function **
(defun rat ()
  (setq #relacc (/ #per #relacc)
        #relacc (strcat "\nRELATIVE ACCURACY of TRAVERSE is 1:"
                (rtos #relacc 1 0)))
  ;       Print the relative accuracy ratio
  (princ #relacc)(princ)
)
;------------------------------------------------------------------
```

G

Plot Script File

One of the biggest problems when plotting is to remember the pen selection settings, scale, etc., for the specific drawing to be plotted. The plot process can be simplified by writing a plot script file immediately upon completion of the drawing.

The following script file, named PLOT-A4, is used to plot an A4-size drawing from within the drawing editor (do not include the comment lines):

PLOT-A4.SCR	Comments
plot	Invoke PLOT command
d	Plot the display
y	Change plot options
y	Change pen options
c1	Go to color 1
1	Select pen #1
c2	
2	
c3	
3	
c4	
4	
c5	
5	
c7	
6	
x	Exit pen options
n	Do not write plot to file
i	Inch size units
0,0	Plot origin (you may use another origin)
10,7.25	Plot sheet binding width, height (Table 3.2)
n	Do not rotate plots
0.010	Pen width

PLOT-A4.SCR	Comments
y	Adjust area fill boundaries for pen width
n	Do not remove hidden lines
F	Fit scale

Do not leave a blank line at the end of the file. The last printer operation is to check the plotter and press Return to continue. A blank line at the end of the file would invoke the Return key without giving you an opportunity to check the plotter.

For specific pens you may wish to set the pen speed also.

The fit option in the last line is based on the fact that the plot sheet width and height in the script is the same size as the plot sheet in the PROTO menu (see Table 3.2). The drawing will be to scale regardless of the scale used to draw it.

The file is invoked from the drawing editor using the SCRIPT command. When specifying the script file name, a path may be included.

The following script file, named PRPLOTA4, is invoked from within the drawing editor to print or plot a drawing:

PRPLOTA4.SCR	Discussion
prplot	Invoke PRPLOT command
d	Plot the display
y	Change default values
n	Do not write the plot to a file
i	Inch-size units
0,0	Plot origin
8.5,11	Sheet width, height
y	Rotate 2-D plots 90 degrees clockwise
n	Do not remove hidden lines
1 = 1	Plot scale

The script file may be invoked from DOS by modifying the beginning of the file as follows:

SCRIPT	Discussion
3	Select task #3—Plot a Drawing
	Blank:Use default name of drawing
d	Plot the last displayed file

The remainder of the file is similar to those listed starting at line 3 of the preceding files.

To invoke the file load AutoCAD using the following:

```
C:\ACAD>acad drawing-name script-name
```

The drawing and script names may be preceded with paths. A batch file named A4.BAT to run the plot script file from the Program Selection Menu (PSM) discussed in Appendix C would be as follows:

```
1: cls
2: path \;\system\acad
3: cd \acad\%1
4: acad %2 plot-a4
5: cd \
6: 0
```

The lines added to the PSM would be:

```
PLOT-A4 . . . . . . . . . . A4 # $

# = Project name $ = Drawing name
```

To plot the drawing \ACAD\101NM89\101SP01C.DWG you would enter:

```
C\>a4 101nm89 101sp01c
```

The A4.BAT file is loaded and the %1 replaceable parameter is replaced by the project name 101NM89 so that in line 3 the directory is changed to C:\ACAD\101NM89>. The %2 replaceable parameter is replaced by the drawing name 101SP01C so that line 5 would be ACAD 101SP01C PLOT-A4. AutoCAD is invoked to load the drawing 101SP01C and the script file PLOT-4. You would have to add a plot option for each size of drawing used in your office.

EDLIN Commands

EDLIN is a simple text editor supplied with MS-DOS. Since it does not place extra characters in the text, it is useful for writing menu files, script files, and AutoLISP programs.

To determine if EDLIN is available, enter **DIR/W** from the DOS prompt. EDLIN.COM should be displayed in the directory listing.

To load EDLIN from DOS, type EDLIN, followed by the file name including any file path. For example:

```
C:\>edlin \acad\lisp\test.txt
```

The procedure for loading EDLIN from the AutoCAD editor is discussed in Section 2.5.

When EDLIN is loaded to start a new file, the following is displayed:

```
New file
*
```

If EDLIN is loaded to edit an existing file, the prompt is:

```
End of input file
*
```

The asterisk (*) is the EDLIN command prompt indicating that you may enter an EDLIN command. It will not be included in the file listing.

H.1   EDLIN Commands

Most EDLIN commands are single letters. The following are a few basic EDLIN commands. For a more thorough listing of the commands refer to your MS-DOS manual. *Insert:* To begin a new file enter i:

```
*i
```

EDLIN responds with:

```
1:*
```

The "1:" is not part of the data and is displayed only to make EDLIN lines easier to read. The "*" is the command prompt and is also not part of the data. You may now begin entering text, for example:

```
1:*** PUNCH <return>
```

Note that although three asterisks are displayed, only two are part of the data.

When Enter is pressed, EDLIN will move to the next line and display:

```
2:*
```

Type in the next line:

```
2:*Nearly all the best men are dead!
```

Add the remaining lines. If you make an error, don't worry about it. Continue to add the remaining entries. The entry errors may be edited after the file is complete. The entries are

```
3:*Carlyle, Tennyson, Browning, George, Elliot!
4:*- I'm not feeling very well myself.
```

Ending entries: To stop adding lines to the file, press Ctrl-C:

```
5: ^c (Ctrl-C)
```

EDLIN will then display the command prompt:

```
*
```

Listing the file: To list the file enter L:

```
*L
   1: **PUNCH
   2: Nearly all the best men are dead!
   3: Carlyle, Tennyson, Browning, George, Elliot!
   4:-I'm not feeling very well myself.
```

To list the file from line 2 enter **2L.**

Inserting lines in a file: Lines may be inserted anywhere in an existing file by preceding the insert command with a line number. To insert two blank lines starting at line 2 enter:

```
*2i
   2:*<Return>
   3:*
   4:*^C
*
```

List the file by entering **1L.**

Deleting lines: Delete a line by typing the line number followed by d. To delete the blank line inserted at line 3:

```
*3d
*
```

List the file and observe that the blank line at 3 is now deleted and that the lines following 3 have moved up to close the gap.

Editing a line: To edit a line, type the line number and press Enter. For example, to change "the" to "our" in line 3:

```
*3
```

EDLIN will list the line and allow editing of the line below it. Move the cursor to "t" in "the" using the right arrow key on the numeric keyboard:

```
3:*Nearly all the best men are dead!
3:*Nearly all t
```

Type our and move the cursor to the end of the line and press Return.

Characters are inserted into an existing line using the Ins key as follows:

```
*3
    3: Nearly all the best men are dead!
    3:*Nearly all t
```

Move the cursor to "t" as illustrated and press Ins to start insertion. Type **of** and press Ins to end insertion. Move the cursor to the end of the line and press Return. Line 3 should appear as follows:

```
    3: Nearly all of the best men are dead!
```

To delete a character in a line, press the Del key. If Punch is to be quoted correctly, the "of" in line 3 should be removed:

```
*3
    3: Nearly all of the best men are dead!
    3:*Nearly all o
```

Press Del three times to delete "of. " Move the cursor to the end of the line and press Return.

Ending EDLIN: To end EDLIN and save the file, respond to the command prompt with e:

```
*e
```

DOS responds with the system prompt:

```
c:\>
```

Aborting an editing session: If you have made changes to an existing file and wish to cancel the changes, end the editing session by responding to the EDLIN command prompt with q:

```
*q
```

EDLIN will ask you to confirm the Quit command.

I

Key Redefinition

Drafters often wish to redefine keys to invoke specific commands. The following procedure outlines a method of redefining keys using the ANSI.SYS driver. For more information on ANSI.SYS refer to your DOS manual or a text on DOS.

Prior to using the ANSI.SYS driver, you must name it in your CONFIG.SYS file. Use EDLIN to add the following line to your CONFIG.SYS file:

```
device=ansi.sys
```

if ANSI.SYS is in your root directory, or

```
device=\system\ansi.sys
```

if ANSI.SYS is in a subdirectory, i.e., \system.

The syntax for ANSI.SYS keyboard commands is as follows:

```
{ESC}[<key code>;<result>p
```

The ANSI.SYS commands begin with the Escape character, {ESC}, and a left bracket [. Text editors differ in their procedure for entering Escape. With EDLIN, press Ctrl-V and then [, which will appear as ^V[. If you use another text editor, refer to your manual for the procedure to enter Escape. Do not confuse the second bracket with the Escape character.

The <key code> is the ASCII code for the key to be pressed to invoke the desired command. Table I.1 lists some codes for ASCII characters (for other codes refer to your DOS manual). For example, to redefine the F2 key to redraw the screen the ANSI.SYS commands are as follows:

TABLE I.1   ASCII Codes

Key	Alt-	Key	Alt-
A	0;30	N	0;49
B	0;48	O	0;24
C	0;46	P	0;25
D	0;32	Q	0;16
E	0;18	R	0;19
F	0;33	S	0;31
G	0;34	T	0;20
H	0;35	U	0;22
I	0;23	V	0;47
J	0;36	W	0;17
K	0;37	X	0;45
L	0;38	Y	0;21
M	0;50	Z	0;44

Key	Alone	Key	Alone
F2	0;60	CTRL-C	3
F3	0;61	RETURN	13
F4	0;62		
F5	0;63		

```
^V[[0;60;'''redraw'';13p
```

where: ^V[is the Escape character from EDLIN, [starts the sequence, 0;60 is the ASCII character for the F2 key, "'redraw" is the transparent REDRAW command, 13 is the ASCII character for RETURN, and p ends the key definition sequence.

The ANSI.SYS codes are "seen" by the screen by loading them into a file and entering the TYPE shell command to list the file to the screen. The following is the screen listing of a file, the key affected, and its new definition:

```
File: \acad\misc\on.key
^V[[0;60;'''redraw'';13p          F2        'REDRAW
^V[[0;61;3;3;3p                   F2        ^C^C^C
^V[[0;31;3;3;3;''save'';13p       Alt-S     ^C^C^CSAVE
^V[[0;20;3;3;3;''dtext'';13p      Alt-T     ^C^C^CDTEXT
^V[[0;17;3;3;3;''zoom w'';13      Alt-W     ^C^C^CZOOM W
^V[[0;32;'''zoom d'';13           Alt-D     'ZOOM D
^V[[0;25;'''zoom p'';13           Alt-P     'ZOOM P
^V[[0;45;''type \acad\misc\off.key'';13p
```

The last line uses Alt-X (ASCII code 0;45) to invoke the TYPE shell command and list a file \ACAD\MISC\OFF.KEY. If Alt-X is pressed, the OFF.KEY file (following) is typed to the screen. This file resets the keys to their original values, i.e., turns them off:

```
File: \acad\misc\off.key
^V[[0;60;0;60p          Resets F2
^V[[0;61;0;61p          Resets F2
```

```
^V[[0;31;0;31p          Resets Alt-S
^V[[0;20;0;20p          Resets Alt-T
^V[[0;17;0;17           Resets Alt-W
^V[[0;32;0;32p          Resets Alt-D
^V[[0;25;0;25p          Resets Alt-P
^V[[0;45;0;45p          Resets Alt-X
^V[[0;45;''type \acad\misc\on.key''
```

The last line uses Alt-X to invoke the TYPE shell command and list the file \ACAD\MISC\ON.KEY. If Alt-X is pressed, the file ON.KEY is typed to the screen. This file sets the keys as indicated earlier, i.e., turns them on.

To initially turn the files on enter:

Command: **type \acad\misc\on.key** **< return >**

Pull-Down Menus

AutoCAD Releases 9 and 10 support 10 pull-down menu devices that overlay the top of the screen when the curser is moved into that area by a mouse or digitizer puck. The menu display disappears as soon as the cursor is moved away from it, and the screen is redrawn.

Ten pull-down menus may be defined with device names POP1 through POP10 as illustrated in Figure J.1. In a menu file, pull-down menus begin with the device name ***POPn. The pull-down menu can access any number of submenus using $P=*name*. The submenu name must be preceded with **.

For the following POP9 device, ***POP9, the title "Functions" is listed in the POP9 position in the menu bar at the top of the screen. The first item in this menu is a submenu named **P9A. Pull-down menus do not have to start with a submenu name. It is used in this menu so that the **P9A submenu can be called by another submenu—see line 16. The title in a pull-down menu is always the first line of the menu unless, as in this case, that line is a submenu name—see line 2.

Each title in a *menu bar* may be up to 14 characters long, but since most screens display a maximum of 80 characters, if you are going to use all 10 pull-down menus, the titles should be limited to 8 characters. Menu item *labels* may be extend the full width of the screen. The file is

```
1: ***POP9
2: **P9A
3: [Functions]
```

POP1	POP2	POP3	POP4	POP5	POP6	POP7	POP8	POP9	POP10	AutoCAD
										* * * *

Figure J.1   Pull-down menu locations.

```
 4: [Traverse]^C^C(if (not traverse) (load ''lisp/traverse''));+
 5: (traverse)
 6: [Entities] ^C^C$P9=ENT;$P9=*
 7: [3D-Functions]^C^C$P9=3DF;$P9=*
 8: **ENT
 9: [Entities]
10: [Entity Data](if (not look) (load ''lisp/look''));(look)
11: [Change Layer](if (not chglay) (load ''lisp/chglay''));+
12: (chglay)
13: [Locate Layers](if (not srchlay) (load ''list/srchlay''));+
14: (srchlay)
15: [--]
16: [Exit]$P9=P9A
17: **3DF
18: [3D-functs]
19: etc.
```

Continue the menu with options to load your 3-D functions from Chapter 10 and an exit to the P9A menu.

J.1   Discussion of POP9 Menu

***POP9 is the device name for the pull-down menu to be displayed in the POP9 position. The heading displayed when this menu is loaded is Functions. If Functions is selected from the pull-down menu, the following is displayed in the POP9 position:

```
Functions
┌─────────────────┐
│ Traverse        │
│                 │
│ Entities        │
│                 │
│ 3D-Functions    │
└─────────────────┘
```

If Traverse is selected, the macro in line 4 is invoked. The two Ctrl-C's are used to cancel any residual commands that may be in effect. The AutoLISP expression checks to see if the function named Traverse is loaded. If it is not loaded, AutoLISP loads the file LISP/TRAVERSE.LSP, which contains the Traverse function. (See Section 5.9 for a discussion of this type of expression.) After the IF function is exited, the Traverse function is invoked. The + at the end of line 4 indicates that the macro continues on line 5.

If Entities is selected, two Ctrl-C's are invoked (see line 6). The next command, $P9=ENT, exchanges the menu in position POP9 for the submenu with the name **ENT (see line 6). The first item in the submenu, Entities, is displayed as the new title in the POP9 position, but the submenu does not appear on the screen. The special command, $P9=*, is used to force the submenu to be displayed in the POP9 position on the screen. The menu displayed is as follows:

```
Entities
┌──────────────────────┐
│ Entity data          │
│                      │
│ Change Layers        │
│                      │
│ Locate Layers        │
│                      │
│ ----------           │
│                      │
│ Exit                 │
└──────────────────────┘
```

If one of the first three items is selected from the Entities menu, the macro in lines 10, 11, or 13 will be invoked. Each contains AutoLISP primitives to check to see if a function is loaded and, if not, to load a .LSP file containing the function. The function is then invoked.

Line 15 has a menu item with two hyphens, [--], which expands to become a separator line filling the entire width of the pull-down menu.

Line 16 loads the submenu **P9A, line 1, into the POP9 position so that the heading changes to Functions. Since the $P9 = * command is not included, the submenu is not displayed.

If you wish to "gray out" an item label that is not a valid selection, you may precede its label with a tilde (˜), for instance [˜Select one of the following].

K

Adding Commands to AutoCAD

ACAD.LSP

AutoLISP functions added to the ACAD.LSP file are evaluated <loaded> automatically each time you begin editing a drawing. You might wish to place functions that you use often into the ACAD.LSP file (which is to be located in the same subdirectory as your ACAD files). Do not place all of your functions there, however, since the files do take up memory space. If the LOCNAME.LSP file (Chapter 9) is placed in the ACAD.LSP file it is invoked as follows:

```
Command: (locname)
```

User-defined functions may be added to AutoCAD's standard commands by preceding the function name with C: and using uppercase text for the function name. The function name must not be the same as an AutoCAD command.

If the Locname function in Chapter 9 is to be an AutoCAD command, the function would be defined as follows:

```
(defun C:LOCNAME (/ T n en flag 1st loc)
```

The remainder of the function would be exactly the same as that illustrated in Section 9.1. The function is invoked from AutoCAD as follows:

```
Command: locname
```

Release 10 allows an AutoLISP file to be loaded from within another function. You can automatically load and run your functions from AutoCAD by including only a small file-loader function in the ACAD.LSP file. For example, to load and invoke the LOCNAME.LSP file (Chapter 9) the following function is placed in the ACAD.LSP file:

```
(defun C:LOCNAME ( )
  (if (not locname) (load ''c:/acad/lisp/locname''))
  (locname))
```

The LOCNAME function is invoked from AutoCAD as follows:

Command: **locname**

The function name is not enclosed with parenthesis when it is called from AutoCAD.

With Release 10, functions whose name begins with S: will be invoked automatically when certain situations arise during an editing session. Currently only one automatic-execution function is available, S::STARTUP, which is invoked automatically (with no arguments) when a new drawing is started or an existing drawing is loaded for editing. A primary use for the S:STARTUP function is to redefine AutoCAD commands. When redefining an AutoCAD command, it must first be undefined using AutoCAD's UNDEFINE command. After being undefined, a command can be returned to normal with AutoCAD's REDEFINE command.

Using EDLIN, add the following program to ACAD.LISP file. The program is useful when you do not want the user to be able to invoke AutoCAD's END command and inadvertently save the drawing to a file with the default drawing name:

```
; This program redefines the END command
(defun S:STARTUP ( )
  (command ''undefine'' ''end'')
)
(defun C:END ( )
  (prompt ''\nEnter a new drawing name.\n'')
  (command ''save'')
  (command ''quit'' ''y'')
)
```

Index

ABOUT THE AUTHOR

John D. Hood is department head of civil, mining, and geology engineering technology at Cambrian College in Sudbury, Ontario, Canada. He has taught AutoCAD for over six years and has conducted AutoCAD seminars both in Canada and the United States. He is the author of *Easy AutoCAD*, second edition, published by McGraw-Hill.

Don't want to type the menus, macros and AutoLISP routines?

Then, order the *Using AutoCAD with AutoLISP* disk which contains *all* the routines in this book on a 5¼-inch floppy disk. The disk will run on any 360K IBM-standard format computer. To order please send a check or money order (no cash please) for $30.00 (U.S.) or $38.00 (Can.) to:

John D. Hood
1337 Orange Grove Dr.
Sudbury, Ontario
P3A 4T9 Canada

Please specify which version of AutoCAD you are using. Add $2.00/disk for UPS "two-day air."